Cambridge Studies in the History and Theory of Politics

EDITORS

MAURICE COWLING   G. R. ELTON   E. KEDOURIE
J. G. A. POCOCK   J. R. POLE
WALTER ULLMANN

Kant's Political Writings

For Michael and Estelle Morgan

Kant's Political Writings

EDITED WITH AN INTRODUCTION
AND NOTES BY

HANS REISS

Professor of German, University of Bristol

TRANSLATED BY

H. B. NISBET

Professor of German, University of St Andrews

CAMBRIDGE UNIVERSITY PRESS

CAMBRIDGE

LONDON   NEW YORK   NEW ROCHELLE
MELBOURNE   SYDNEY

Published by the Press Syndicate of the University of Cambridge
The Pitt Building, Trumpington Street, Cambridge CB2 1RP
32 East 57th Street, New York, NY 10022, USA
296 Beaconsfield Parade, Middle Park, Melbourne 3206, Australia

Library of Congress catalogue card number: 72-93710

ISBN 0 521 07717 6 hard covers
ISBN 0 521 29212 3 paperback

First published 1970
Reprinted 1971
First paperback edition 1977
Reprinted 1979 1980 1983

Printed in Great Britain at the
University Press, Cambridge

Contents

v

CONTENTS

Preface

This volume, to the best of my knowledge, is the first in English to contain all the political writings of Kant which the author himself had published. There have been earlier translations of almost all the pieces which make up this volume; Dr Nisbet has asked me to acknowledge his debt to these, particularly to Professor John Ladd's translation of *The Metaphysical Elements of Right* (*The Metaphysical Elements of Justice*, Indianapolis, New York, Kansas City, 1965). The aim of this volume is to introduce English-speaking readers in general and students of political theory in particular to Kant's political writings. The bibliography in the present volume may serve as a guide for further reading. For a general introduction to Kant, the student can do no better than read Stephan Körner's *Kant* (Penguin Books, Harmondsworth, Middlesex, 1955), easily available in a pocket edition.

Only those writings which deal explicitly with the theory of politics and which were published by him have been included. I have omitted other essays, such as the *Conjectural Beginning of the Human Race* (*Mutmasslicher Anfang des Menschengeschlechts*), *The End of All Things* (*Das Ende aller Dinge*) and Kant's review of J. G. Herder's *Ideen*, which touch only marginally on politics. I have, however, included a brief but essential passage from the *Critique of Pure Reason* (*Kritik der reinen Vernunft*). In accordance with the aims of the series, I have not included any extracts, unless they form self-contained wholes. A few passages in other writings published by Kant are excluded, since they do not add anything of substance to his theory of politics. I decided to include the first part of *Theory and Practice* (*Über den Gemeinspruch : Das mag in der Theorie richtig sein, taugt aber nicht für die Praxis*), which is devoted to ethics. Since this volume does not set out to be a definitive critical edition of Kant's political writings I did not follow this precedent in the case of *The Metaphysics of Morals* (*Die Metaphysik der Sitten*) and *The Contest of Faculties* (*Der Streit der Fakultäten*). To print both works in full would inevitably have distracted attention from the main purpose of this volume. I hope that the brief summaries of what was omitted will give the reader some means of orientation. Except for the appended passage from the *Critique of Pure Reason*, I have also excluded all passages on politics from any other of Kant's larger works, such as the *Critique of Judgement* (*Kritik der Urteilskraft*) and *Religion within the Limits of Reason Alone* (*Religion innerhalb der Grenzen der blossen Vernunft*). I have even excluded a brief appendix attached to *The Metaphysical Elements of Right* (*Die metaphysischen Anfangsgründe des Rechts*). In neither case is anything of substance omitted. Kant is simply repeating points which he has made elsewhere. Those readers who wish to study the omitted parts of *The Metaphysics of Morals* should consult John Ladd's commendable translation in *The Metaphysical Elements of Justice*. For the second part of *The Metaphysics of Morals*, *The Metaphysical Elements of Virtue* (*Die Metaphysischen Anfangsgründe der Tugendlehre*), they should consult the German text, which they will in any case have to do for *The Contest of Faculties*. To consult the original is naturally always the best course, even if it involves learning German; for all translations fail, in some degree or other, to do justice to the original.[1] I also decided not to include either Kant's preliminary studies for his published works on politics as found in volumes XXII and XXIII of the *Akademieausgabe* of his works and in *Kant-Studien* LI, 1959/60, or his notes on politics and law, as found in volumes XIX and XX of the above edition. These writings were published posthumously and Kant did not intend them to be published. They do not offer anything substantially different from what is found in his published writings. They are often repetitive since many of them are rough notes, comments on the textbook which he was using for lectures on the theory of law (Gottfried Achenwall's *Ius naturae*, Göttingen, 1755–6) and notes for lectures or (probably) later publications. It will always be difficult to decide how much weight should be given to material of this kind; for it could easily contain views later rejected by an author on mature consideration. In Kant's case, the notes may occasionally clarify some of his views. Furthermore, they can give us some insight into the origin and development of his political thought. This latter aspect has been exhaustively discussed by Georges Vlachos in his full-length study of Kant's political theory (*La Pensée politique de Kant. Métaphysique de l'ordre et dialectique du progrès*, Paris, 1962, pp. xx and 590). However, the development of Kant's political ideas will always present problems; for although the work of the editors of the *Akademieausgabe* has been dedi-

[1] The translations in this book follow the style and substance of the original texts as closely as possible, except that we have not reproduced the indentation (possibly used for emphasis in the original texts) of some passages on pp. 135, 138–40 and 164.

cated and painstaking, they have found it difficult to date many of the notes exactly.

Finally, I should like to thank all those friends and colleagues who have helped or encouraged me in my work for this volume. I am indebted to my former colleagues and friends at the London School of Economics and Political Science: Ernest Gellner, Morris Ginsberg, the late Harold Laski, William Pickles, Julius Gould, Donald Macrae, Michael Oakeshott, Sir Karl Popper, the late William Rose, K. B. Smellie and J. O. Wisdom. I have profited considerably from the advice of Stephan Körner and Peter Bromhead of the University of Bristol, who were good enough to read the introduction. David Eichholz of the same University kindly translated Kant's Latin quotations for me. I have also greatly benefited from conversations on Kant with Dieter Henrich of the University of Heidelberg. I have to thank Denis Donoghue of University College, Dublin, Irvin Ehrenpreis of the University of Virginia, Raymond Klibansky of McGill University, George Levine and Irving Massey, both of the New York State University at Buffalo, and Philip Harth of the University of Wisconsin for generously helping me to trace some quotations. Above all I must thank Dr H. B. Nisbet, who not only undertook the formidable task of translating Kant, but has also spent much time in checking the notes and bibliography and has offered many valuable suggestions on scrutiny of my introductory essay. He has also helped me in seeing the whole manuscript through the press. I have in turn scrutinised his translation. Mrs M. L. Taylor, Mrs Rosemary White and Miss B. Gertsch have had the unenviable task of typing the manuscript, for which we owe them sincere thanks. Much of my work on Kant was done when I had a year's leave of absence from McGill University in 1962-3 on award of a grant from the Rockefeller Foundation. I am grateful to both institutions for making it possible for me to have leave in Europe for the purpose of study. It is a happy coincidence that, as I conclude my work on this volume, I am once again at McGill, this time as Visiting Professor on leave from the University of Bristol.

For any errors that remain I am alone responsible.

H. S. REISS

Hugessen House
McGill University
Montreal
Autumn 1968

Introduction

I

Immanuel Kant was born on 22 April 1724 in Königsberg (now Kaliningrad) in East Prussia which, except for occasional journeys into the immediate vicinity, he hardly ever left during the whole of his long life of almost eighty years. Königsberg in the eighteenth century was a lively city which, owing to its flourishing trade, was by no means isolated from the world at large. Kant, who was anything but a recluse, enjoyed social life and intelligent conversation. He was friendly with many Königsberg merchants, among whom there were also Englishmen, two of whom, Green and Motherby, were particularly close friends. Although he was meticulous and regular in his habits, punctual to a fault, he was also a man of urbanity and wit.

Kant's parents were not rich. His father was a harness-maker who lived in Königsberg. His family was steeped in Pietism, the Protestant religious movement which stressed emotional religiosity and the development of the inner life. The pietistic atmosphere of his parents' household was a formative influence in his childhood, and he was particularly impressed by his mother's simple piety. After the early death of his parents (his mother died in 1738, his father in 1746), Kant's relations with his family were not very close.

Kant's outstanding intellectual gifts were recognised at school. It was made possible for him to enter the University of Königsberg, where he was a brilliant student. In 1755 he was granted the right to lecture as *Magister legens* or *Privatdozent*, i.e. as an unsalaried lecturer who depended on his lecture fees for his income. Since his lectures were popular and since he gave a large number of them—twenty a week at least—he was able to eke out a meagre living. He lectured on many subjects—logic, metaphysics, ethics, theory of law, geography, anthropology etc. He began to make his name as a scholar and scientist by his writings. In his *General History of Nature and Theory of the Heavens* (1755), he put forward a highly original account of the origin of the universe similar to the one later elaborated by the French scientist Laplace. It is now generally called

I

the 'Kant–Laplace' theory. Kant thus started his academic career by discussing a scientific problem, i.e. he sought to vindicate Newtonian science philosophically—an attempt which later gave rise to his critical philosophy. But it was not until 1770 that he was appointed to the chair of logic and metaphysics and at last found economic security. When his fame spread, his stipend was considerably increased. He was Rector of the University on several occasions.

Kant was a stimulating and powerful lecturer. His students were struck by the originality and liveliness of his observations, which were seasoned with a dry ironic humour.

He was also a prolific writer. His really decisive breakthrough as a philosopher came only in 1781 when he published the *Critique of Pure Reason*. For him, this work initiated a revolution in thought realistically compared by himself to the Copernican revolution in astronomy. In fairly rapid succession, the other important works followed.

The publication of *Religion within the Limits of Reason Alone* (1793, 2nd ed. 1794) offended the then King of Prussia, Frederick William II, who (contrary to Frederick the Great, his predecessor) did not practise tolerance in religious matters. Frederick William II ordered his obscurantist minister Wöllner to write to Kant to extract a promise that he would not write again on religion.[1] Kant reluctantly agreed with their request, which amounted to a Royal command, implicitly qualifying his promise by saying that he would not write again on religious matters as his Majesty's Most Loyal Subject. After the King's death, Kant considered himself to be absolved from this undertaking and explained that his pledge applied only to the life-time of Frederick William II, as this phrase 'Your Majesty's Most Loyal Subject'[2] indicated. He explained his attitude fully in the preface to his *Contest of Faculties*,[3] in which, by implication, he attacked Frederick William II who had died the year before.

Kant was obviously not easy in his mind about this decision. In an unpublished note, he explained his conduct: 'Repudiation and denial of one's inner conviction are evil, but silence in a case like the present one is the duty of a subject; and while all that one says must be true, this does not mean that it is one's duty to speak out the whole truth in public.'[4]

Kant gradually retired from the university. His mind slowly declined,

---

[1] Cabinet order of Frederick William II, King of Prussia, of 1 October 1794; *AA* VII, 6; *AA* XI, 506 f.

[2] Letter to King Frederick William II, 12 October 1794; *AA* VII, 7–10, particularly p. 10; also *AA* XI, 508–11, particularly p. 511; cf. also *AA* XII, 406 f.

[3] *AA* VII, 7–10.

[4] *AA* XII, 406.

his memory gave way, and he had to abandon lecturing. In 1800, his pupil Wasianski had to begin looking after him. Other pupils began to publish his lectures from notes which they had taken down. In 1803, he fell seriously ill for the first time. His mind became more and more clouded. He finally died on 12 February 1804, a few months before the end of his eightieth year.

II

Kant, at least in English speaking countries, is not generally considered to be a political philosopher of note. Indeed histories of political thought do not give him pride of place, but generally mention him only incidentally, if at all. Historians of political thought ignore him, however, at their peril. Only too frequently, he is merely seen as a forerunner of Hegel. The reasons for this neglect and misunderstanding are not hard to discover. Historians of philosophy, even Kant scholars, have neglected his political writings because the philosophy of his three critiques has absorbed attention almost entirely. And historians of political thought have paid little attention to him, because he did not write a masterpiece in that field. *The Metaphysical Elements of Right* has interested legal historians rather than historians of political theory. Furthermore, the very fact that Kant's great works of critical philosophy are so formidable makes his less exacting political writings appear very much less weighty. It also encourages the belief that they are not central to his thought. This assumption, however, is greatly mistaken. While it would be going too far to see in them the ultimate end of his thought, they are not an accidental by-product. Indeed, they grow organically out of his critical philosophy. In fact, Kant has rightly been called the philosopher of the French Revolution.[1] There is, indeed, an analogy between the spirit of Kant's philosophy and the ideas of the French and American revolutions: for Kant asserted the independence of the individual in face of authority, and the problem of human freedom was at the very core of his thought. Similarly, the revolutionaries of 1776 and 1789 believed that they were attempting to realise the rights of man. Besides, the events of the American and of the French Revolution greatly excited and preoccupied him and he sympathised with the aims of the revolutionaries. He did so although he was a man of conservative disposition who refused to countenance revolution in politics as a legitimate principle of action, and certainly did not

[1] Cf. Heine, *Sämtliche Werke*, ed. Ernst Elster, Leipzig and Vienna, n.d., IV, 245; also Karl Marx/Friedrich Engels, *Historisch-Kritische Gesamtausgabe* (Frankfurt/Main, 1927), I, 254.

advocate revolution in his native country, Prussia. But his approach to politics was already shaped well before 1789, as his essays of 1784 reveal. It is possible that the French Revolution may have stimulated him to continue writing on the subject. But the example and influence of Rousseau must not be underrated. Rousseau had taught him to respect the common man;[1] he was for him the Newton of the moral realm.[2] Rousseau's portrait was the only adornment permitted in his house, and when reading *Émile* he even forgot to take his customary afternoon walk, allegedly the only deviation ever to occur from a daily custom followed with clock-like regularity. Kant's views are also, in many ways, close to the aspirations of the French revolutionaries, but in his demand for perpetual peace he goes further. Here he takes up ideas first put forward by Leibniz and the Abbé de St Pierre, but develops them in a novel, original and philosophically rigorous manner.

If it is correct to infer this link between Kant's philosophy and the ideas of the two major eighteenth-century revolutions, the significance of Kant's political thought becomes clear; for the American and French revolutions constituted an open break with the political past. An appeal was made to a secular natural order and to the political rights of individuals for the purpose of initiating large-scale political action. The revolutions, of course, arose from the political, social and economic situation in America and France, but the beliefs of the revolutionaries were not intended as a smoke-screen designed to mislead the public. They depended on a political philosophy in which a belief in the right of the individual would be guaranteed. This attitude was new. In earlier revolutions, even in the English civil war and in 1688, Christian theology had still played an important part in shaping revolutionary thinking in the West. The realities of a revolutionary situation are, of course, always complex. It usually presents a pattern of ideology and political practice which is difficult, if not impossible, to disentangle. Kant did not set out to provide a blueprint for revolutionaries or a theory of revolution. On the contrary, he wanted to arrive at philosophical principles on which a just and lasting internal order and world peace could be based. He wanted to provide a philosophical vindication of representative constitutional government, a vindication which would guarantee respect for the political rights of all individuals.

To understand his political thought, it is necessary to see it in the context of eighteenth-century thought, and against the background of his own general philosophy. The American and French revolutions had,

---

[1] *AA* xx, 44.   [2] *Ibid.* p. 58.

to some extent, been prepared for by the ideas of the Enlightenment, the intellectual movement which dominated so much of eighteenth-century thought.[1] Incontestably, the revolutionaries largely used the vocabulary of the Enlightenment, which had created a climate of opinion in many ways favourable to revolutionary action. In Kant, many of the intellectual strands of the Enlightenment converge. He presents a culmination of this intellectual movement, but he is also one of its most thoroughgoing critics. Kant himself characterised the Enlightenment (*Aufklärung*) as a dynamic process. It was not a static condition, but a continuous process leading to further self-emancipation. The age was not yet enlightened, but still in the process of becoming so. *Aufklärung* meant liberation from prejudice and superstition. It also meant the growing ability to think for oneself. This observation echoes Lessing's famous dictum that what mattered most was not to possess the truth, but to pursue it.[2] In Kant's view, man was to become his own master. In his special function as officer, clergyman, civil-servant etc., he should not reason, but obey the powers that be, but as a man, citizen and scholar, he should have 'the courage to use his own intelligence'.[3] This is the translation which Kant gives to the watchword of the *Aufklärung*, *Sapere Aude*, expanding its meaning for his own purpose. Indeed, this Horatian tag was so popular that it had been inscribed as a motto on a coin struck in 1736 for the society of Alethophiles, or Lovers of Truth, a group of men dedicated to the cause of Enlightenment.[4]

Kant, in his essay *What is Enlightenment?* (*Was ist Aufklärung?*), outlines his view of the major tendencies of his age. The Enlightenment has frequently been called the Age of Reason. One of its most striking characteristics is, indeed, the exaltation of reason, but the term 'Enlightenment' (or *Aufklärung* or *les Lumières*) covers a number of ideas and intellectual tendencies which cannot be adequately summarised. A brief characterisation of this movement, as of any other, must needs remain incomplete. For this movement, like all intellectual movements, is made

[1] For thorough general discussions of the Enlightenment cf. *inter alia* Ernst Cassirer, *Die Philosophie der Aufklärung* (Tübingen, 1932) (*The Philosophy of the Enlightenment*, trs. Fritz A. Koelln and James Pettegrove, Princeton, N.J., 1951); Paul Hazard, *La pensée européenne au XVIIIième siècle. De Montesquieu à Lessing*, 3 vols. (Paris, 1946) (*European Thought in the Eighteenth Century*, trs. J. Lewis May, London, 1953); Jack F. Lively (ed.), *The Enlightenment* (London, 1966); Fritz Valjavec, *Geschichte der abendländischen Aufklärung* (Vienna, 1961).

[2] Gotthold Ephraim Lessing, *Werke* (ed. Julius Petersen and Waldemar von Olshausen), Berlin, Leipzig, Vienna, Stuttgart, n.d. XXIII, 58 f.

[3] *AA* VIII, 35.

[4] Cf. Elizabeth M. Wilkinson and L. A. Willoughby (ed. and trs.), Friedrich Schiller, *On the Aesthetic Education of Man, in a Series of Letters* (Oxford, 1967), LXXIV ff.

up of a number of various, and often conflicting, strains of thought. What binds the thinkers of the Enlightenment together, however, is an attitude of mind, a mood rather than a common body of ideas. A growth of self-consciousness, an increasing awareness of the power of man's mind to subject himself and the world to rational analysis, is perhaps the dominant feature. Reliance on the use of reason was, of course, nothing new, but faith in the power of reason to investigate successfully not only nature, but also man and society, distinguishes the Enlightenment from the period which immediately precedes it. For there is a distinct optimistic streak in the thought of the Enlightenment. It springs from, and promotes, the belief that there is such a thing as intellectual progress. It is also revealed in the increasing and systematic application of scientific method to all areas of life. But there was by no means agreement on what scientific method was. Newton's impressive scientific achievement dominated eighteenth-century thinking on science. One school of thought interpreted his work as a great attempt, in the wake of Descartes, to systematise scientific knowledge, whereas another school was struck rather by his emphasis on observation and experiment.

Voltaire, in his *Lettres Philosophiques* or *Lettres sur les Anglais* (1734) (English translation *Letters concerning the English* 1733), popularised Newton and English science in general. He also praised English political life, not only English constitutional arrangements, but also political theory as represented by Locke. Locke's ideas of government by consent and the toleration of different religious and political views appeared to Voltaire in particular and to the thinkers of the Enlightenment in general as exemplary.

These ideas sounded revolutionary in the atmosphere of French politics. Here Church and State resisted change. On the other hand, they persecuted or suppressed heterodox political and religious thought only intermittently. Many thinkers of the Enlightenment believed not only that politics could be subjected to rational scrutiny, but also that political arrangements and institutions could be reconstructed along rational lines. The sceptical refusal to accept traditional political authority is consonant with scepticism towards authority in general. This critical attitude towards authority led to an incessant questioning of all accepted values, particularly those of religion. Revealed religion was scrutinised; in fact, it was put on trial.

The secularisation of accepted beliefs and doctrines is an important process in the development of the Enlightenment, whether it be in the field of religion, science, morals, politics, history or art. Contrary to

medieval custom, the individual spheres of human experience were isolated from religion. The basic intellectual position, then, was anthropo-
centric. And for the purpose of our enquiry into Kant's politics, it is
particularly important to note that the realms of morality and law,
politics and history were seen in a secular context. Although these
spheres were separated from religion, the view prevailed in the Enlightenment that, for each of them, universal laws could be established.

The tone of the Enlightenment in Germany was somewhat different
from that prevailing in Britain and France. On the whole, considerably
less emphasis was laid on empiricism than in Britain. The German thinkers were more erudite, but also more abstract and professorial than their
English and French counterparts; and they were frequently more heavy-
handed. The absence of a metropolitan culture militated against certainty
of style, while the parochial politics of the many petty principalities and
comparatively small free Imperial cities were not conducive to the rise
of lively political discussion. Unlike Britain, Germany offered virtually
no opportunities for the intellectuals to take part in politics. Frederick
the Great was, of course, an intellectual, but an absolute monarch anyhow
presents a special case.

It is characteristic of this political stagnation that the political event
which most affected eighteenth-century Germany took place in France:
the French Revolution aroused German political thought from its
somnolence.[1] Nonetheless, modern political thought in Germany virtually began with the impact of 1789. Many thinkers, in Germany as
elsewhere, welcomed the revolution at first and believed it to be the dawn
of a new age. But disillusion began to set in with the outbreak of the Terror.
The revolution in practice spread only to those territories occupied by the
French revolutionary armies. Revolutionary sentiment in Germany was a
tender plant capable of blossoming forth only under the stimulus of force.

Kant and Goethe, the two leading German minds of the age, assessed
the political situation correctly. Both recognised that while in France the
revolution had answered a great political need, the political situation in
Germany was not at all ripe for revolutionary activity. In Germany as in
England and France, the rise of the bourgeoisie was noticeable, but the
German bourgeoisie had not become emancipated from the dominance
of the princes and the aristocracy. It did not possess the self-confidence

---

[1] Cf. Jacques Droz, *L'Allemagne et la Révolution Française* (Paris, 1949), pp. 154–71;
G. P. Gooch, *Germany and the French Revolution* (London, 1920), pp. 160–82; Karl
Vorländer, 'Kants Stellung zur französischen Revolution', *Philosophische Abhandlungen
Hermann Cohen gewidmet* (Berlin, 1912); for a full discussion of Kant's attitude to the
French Revolution.

of its French and English counterparts. Germany was a much poorer country than either Britain or France, and a rising self-confident class which is prevented from giving free expression to its political ambitions is much more likely to take revolutionary action than a weak and unsure one. There was little scope for political freedom in Germany. Even in the Prussia of Frederick the Great, freedom of speech, according to Lessing, meant only the ability freely to criticise religion, but not the government.[1] In addition, the small size of most German principalities permitted a much closer supervision of the subjects by rulers than in larger countries. The growth of bureaucratic control also impeded economic development and was another operative factor in sapping the self-confidence of the German bourgeoisie.

Given these political, social and economic conditions, it is not surprising that the Enlightenment in Germany was different from other Western countries. German philosophy, unlike British philosophy for instance, continued in many ways to resist the impact of empirical aspects of science. Rationalism dominated the outlook of German and French universities, but the style of German philosophical writing was, on the whole, much less urbane than that of its French counterpart.

In setting Kant against this background, it must not be forgotten that the Enlightenment was only one body of thought in the eighteenth century, even if it was the dominant one. There were other strands. Criticism of the Enlightenment arose not merely in its decline, but accompanied its rise and predominance. In Germany, and not only in Germany, the eighteenth century saw the spread of scientific ideas through the thinkers of the Enlightenment, but it was also characterised by a religious way of life centred on the emotions and inward experience. In Germany, Pietism stressed the cultivation of the inner life and fostered an emotional approach to religion. (It was not without its counterparts elsewhere—e.g. Methodism and Quietism.) Kant's fervent conviction of man's inward sense of morality may well have been rooted in that particular soil. Furthermore, persistent criticism of the Enlightenment came not only from the orthodoxy of established religion and from privileged or traditional political interests, but also, as the century progressed, from various new irrationalists. It came from those who preferred intuition to reason, the perception of genius to common sense, and spontaneity to calculated reflection. They tended to base their understanding on the individual instance and example rather than on the universal rule, and even on poetry rather than on science. Their attitude to science was, at

[1] Letter from Lessing to Friedrich Nicolai, 25 August 1769.

its very best, ambivalent. One of the ironies of history is that Königsberg harboured at the same time the most potent champion of the Enlightenment, albeit a most critical one, *and* its most original opponent, viz. Johann Georg Hamann. The seminal critic of the Enlightenment, Johann Gottfried Herder, the mentor of the German literary school of the *Sturm und Drang* (Storm and Stress), also spent some time in Königsberg and became a friend of Hamann and a pupil of Kant. Hamann and Herder criticised the claim of the Enlightenment to discover universally valid principles and to see history and society in terms of uniform regularity. For them, the individual instance was more revealing and could not readily be subsumed under general laws. In a particularly incisive and outspoken review of Herder's main work, *Ideen zur Philosophie der Geschichte der Menschheit* (*Ideas for a Philosophy of the History of Mankind*) (1785), Kant took issue with Herder.[1] He apparently sensed that here was not only the decisive issue that separated his approach to knowledge from Herder's, but that it was also the watershed between those who wish to understand the world principally in terms of science and logic and those who do not. Consequently, he mercilessly exposed the logical flaws in Herder's argument. Herder, in turn, reacted with unforgiving bitterness.[2] Indeed, there can be no bridge between Kant's method and an approach to knowledge primarily based on intuitions of poetic truth and emphasis on the individual example.[3]

In the sphere of political thought, the differences between Britain and France on the one hand, and Germany on the other, were as marked as they were in any other area of life. There was no single dominating school of political thinking in Germany prior to Kant. There were many people who wrote about politics, and some of their writings were distinguished. The school of Natural Law forms one strand, the cameralists another. In addition, there were a number of publicists, such as Schlözer and the two Mosers, father and son. The most important, perhaps, and certainly the best known political thinkers, were Leibniz and Frederick the Great. Political theory was not central to the activity of either: general philosophy absorbed Leibniz's interests, and government, war and the administration

---

[1] *AA* VIII, 43–66, *Rezensionen von J. G. Herders Ideen zur Philosophie der Geschichte der Menschheit*, first published in *Allgemeine Literaturzeitung*, IV, No. 271 (Jena, 1785).
[2] *Metakritik zur Kritik der reinen Vernunft* (1799) (Johann Gottfried Herder, *Sämtliche Werke*, ed. B. Suphan, Berlin, 1877–1913, XXI).
[3] For a general account cf. Alexander Gillies, *Herder* (Oxford, 1944); cf. also H. B. Nisbet, *Herder and the Philosophy and History of Science*, 2 vols., unpublished Ph.D. diss. (Edinburgh, 1965) (forthcoming publication by the Modern Humanities Research Association) for a thorough account of Herder's approach to science.

of his country the Prussian king's. The thinkers of the school of Natural Law,[1] indeed, propounded political theories of great importance, and even laid the foundation for revolution, but their style of thinking was not itself revolutionary. Nor was it specifically German. It continued, modified, and even changed a great tradition. The modern representatives of that school—men like Althusius, Grotius and Pufendorf—had continued to uphold an immutable standard of law which was to determine the positive laws enacted by the state and to regulate the conduct of its citizens, but they had liberated the philosophical study of law and politics from its dependence on theology. Its German practitioners dominated the faculties of law in German universities and German jurisprudence in general. Their works were, like many of the philosophical writings of the *Aufklärung*, abstract and dry. It was the accepted doctrine; it is therefore not surprising that Wolff, the leading philosopher of the *Aufklärung*, wrote a treatise on this subject. Not even Leibniz or Frederick the Great brought about a revolution in political thinking in Germany. It needed perhaps both the events of the French Revolution and the radical reorientation of thought promoted by Kant's philosophy to set in train a new mode of political thinking.

Kant assimilated or criticised the political ideas of many great thinkers, such as Machiavelli, the theorists of the school of Natural Law, Hobbes, Locke, Hume and Rousseau. Of these, only Hobbes was singled out for attack (in *Theory and Practice*), a fact which calls perhaps for comment. The political theories of the two philosophers, of course, differed greatly. Kant rejected Hobbes' authoritarian view of sovereignty, his rationalism, his attempt to apply the methods of geometry to human and social affairs and his explanation of society based on a psychological assumption, that of the fear of sudden death. Yet the basic political problem is the same for both: to turn a state of war into a state of order and peace. Law is a command and has necessarily to be enforced. Sovereignty is indivisible; the individual's status as an independent rational being can be safeguarded only in a civil state. Finally, despite all radical differences in method and conclusions, both thinkers are exemplary in their attempt to develop a rigorous, consistent and coherent argument based on an appeal to reason, unhampered by tradition or any other form of tutelage. In contrast to Hobbes, Kant is indebted to the school of Natural Law and believes in an immutable standard of right. He was, however, much more radical than

[1] See A. P. D'Entrèves, *Natural Law* (London and New York, 1951); cf. also Otto von Gierke, *Natural Law and The Theory of Society* (ed. and trs. Ernest Barker), 2 vols. (Cambridge, 1934).

the traditional proponents of that school; for he mapped out a theory of politics independent of experience. Another patent influence was Rousseau,[1] but Kant differed from Rousseau in his interpretation of nature and of the general will. Above all, whereas Rousseau is frequently ambiguous, he is clear.

As a thinker, Kant was adventurous and differed courageously, though tacitly rather than explicitly, from his king. He differed from Frederick the Great's view that the king was the first servant of the state and that the state should be run on the patriarchic lines of benevolent despotism. Not only did he oppose Frederick's doctrine of enlightened autocracy (admittedly not always followed by the Prussian king in practice), but he also rejected cameralism, the doctrine that politics is a mere exercise in statecraft. And he also argued against the Machiavellian view that political actions arise solely from egotism. To emphasise the need to obey the law, as Kant did, could imply a bias in favour of authoritarianism.[2] In Germany his theory has, indeed, been invoked to strengthen the executive prerogative in carrying out the law, the *Obrigkeitsstaat*, the state in which obedience to political authority is writ large. In fact, his outlook was liberal. The citizens of Königsberg, his native city, knew it well; when he died they followed his coffin because they saw in him a great champion of human freedom in an age in which benevolent dynastic despotism was the prevailing mode of government. But Kant's influence has been greatest in shaping the doctrine of the *Rechtsstaat*, the state governed according to the rule of law. It has been the ideal to which at least lipservice has been paid during most of the nineteenth and twentieth centuries in Germany, though there have, of course, been significant and disastrous deviations from this ideal in practice.

Kant is in fact the fountain-head of modern German political thought. Political thinkers who followed him differed from him in profound respects, but his political thought was for many either the starting-point of their own enquiries or he was an opponent against whom they pitted their strength. Kant's political writings appeared when his reputation was established. His views rapidly commanded attention. They were challenged by men like Justus Möser,[3] who, from a conservative standpoint,

---

[1] Cf. Ernst Cassirer, *Rousseau, Kant, Goethe* (History of Ideas Series, No. 1), Princeton, N.J., 1945, for a penetrating study of Rousseau's influence on Kant.

[2] G. Vlachos, *La Pensée politique de Kant. Métaphysique de l'ordre et dialectique du progrès* (Paris, 1962), *passim*, argues that Kant's political theory favours the state against the individual. He calls it *étatiste*. I cannot accept this interpretation.

[3] Cf. Hans Reiss, 'Justus Möser und Wilhelm von Humboldt. Konservative und liberale politische Ideen im Deutschland des 18. Jahrhunderts', *Politische Vierteljahresschrift*, VIII (1967).

rejected Kant's approach. Möser believed it was wrong to theorise from lofty presuppositions, and political practice and experience mattered considerably more than abstract liberal ideas. On the other hand, many German thinkers disagreed with Kant's conservatism; to respect law and to reject the right of rebellion was, in their view, mistaken. Among them Rehberg and Gentz sought to defend the prerogative of the individual confronted by tyranny.[1]

On a more profound level, two thinkers sought to follow and improve on Kant's liberal approach to politics; Friedrich Schiller[2] and Wilhelm von Humboldt.[3] For Schiller, the Kantian approach to politics was inadequate, because Kant did not pay any attention to the psychological basis of our political decisions. Schiller wanted to show that it is not enough to obey the dictates of duty; that men are able to live a harmonious moral life only if they act in accordance with nature. In order to bridge the gulf between instinct and reason, between will and knowledge, a third mode of experience, the aesthetic mode, is necessary. In his major work on the relationship between aesthetics and politics, *On the Aesthetic Education of Man, in a Series of Letters* (*Über die aesthetische Erziehung des Menschen in einer Reihe von Briefen*) (1795), Schiller delineated an approach which, while respecting the tenor of Kant's political thinking, would be capable of taking account of the whole complexity of man's involvement in the political process. It should, so to speak, map out the interrelations between the aesthetic response to life and political practice. Schiller's political writings, profound and interesting as they are, have not attracted much attention. The first truly exciting and subtle attempt to put across his message and to spell out its cogency and significance in terms of our own age is very recent indeed.[4] Schiller has been influential as a political thinker only indirectly, through his dramas, whose political import has only too frequently been misunderstood.

Schiller's friend, Wilhelm von Humboldt, also felt that Kant's political theory needed to be supplemented by an awareness of man's character. His theory of politics, as expressed in his treatise *The Limits of the State*

---

[1] Cf. Dieter Henrich, Introduction to *Kant. Gentz. Rehberg. Über Theorie und Praxis* (Frankfurt/Main, 1967).
[2] Cf. Wilkinson—Willoughby's edition of Schiller's *Aesthetic Letters*; cf. also H. S. Reiss, 'The Concept of the Aesthetic State in the Work of Schiller and Novalis', *Publications of the English Goethe Society*, XXVI (1957).
[3] For an account of Humboldt's political thought, and references to further secondary literature, see Reiss, 'Justus Möser und Wilhelm von Humboldt', *Politische Vierteljahresschrift*, VIII (1967).
[4] Elizabeth M. Wilkinson's and L. A. Willoughby's profound analysis of Schiller's *Aesthetic Letters* appeared only last year (1967); cf. above, p. 12, n. 2.

(1793),[1] sought to safeguard the creative power and cultural development of man.

Kant's impact on German legal history was profound, but the rise of nationalism prevented his work from being the dominant force in German political thought during the nineteenth and early twentieth centuries which it might easily have been. For the Romantic mode of thought introduced into German political thought a note of irrationalism which permeated almost all areas of German thinking for a century and a half between the Napoleonic wars and the end of the Second World War.[2] The Romantics' rejection of Kant's cosmopolitanism in politics meant that, with his death—followed a year later by that of Schiller—(most of von Humboldt's political writings were only published many decades later)—the climate of opinion changed drastically. It no longer mattered much whether the individual was politically free. The organic theory of the state, which subordinated the individual to the community, prevailed.

For the German Romantics, Kant was an arch-enemy; for he embodied for them the characteristics of the *Aufklärung* which they fought so vehemently. Fichte, who started as a self-professed disciple of Kant and who even, in a private letter to Kant, claimed to be his successor, developed a theory of politics diametrically opposed to Kant's.[3] Fichte paid lip-service to Kant's method, but his political theory can be interpreted as an attempt to supersede Kant's political thought. In Fichte's view, freedom is no longer to be seen in negative terms, but becomes a positive force to be utilised by the initiated, who alone can interpret the collective will. Whilst Schiller, in contrast to Kant, had sought to explore the relationship between art and politics, seeking to preserve a careful balance between the two realms, Romantics such as Fichte, Novalis, Schelling and Adam Müller sought to see life and politics from an aesthetic point of view. This method of reasoning is, on the whole, anti-Kantian, but they discernibly write in the shadow of his work. Only too frequently they are, one feels, either seeking to escape from his dominance or implicitly repudiating his method and thought. They base their principles of politics on feeling and intuition, a mode of thought rejected by Kant as a 'lawless use of reason'.[4] The historical approach to politics and law, too,

---

[1] The exact title is *Ideas towards an Attempt to Delineate the Limits of the Activity of the State* (*Ideen zu einem Versuch, die Grenzen der Wirksamkeit des Staates zu bestimmen*).
[2] Cf. Reiss, *The Political Thought of the German Romantics* (Oxford, 1955), and *Politisches Denken in der Deutschen Romantik* (Munich and Berne, 1966), for further literature on German Romantic political thinkers.
[3] Cf. *ibid.*
[4] *What does it mean : to orientate one's thinking?* (*Was heißt : sich im Denken orientieren?*) (1786); *AA* VIII, 145.

is fundamentally different from Kant's own mode of thinking. It culminated in the thought of Hegel, which, like that of early adherents of the historical approach such as Herder[1] and Savigny,[2] becomes fully intelligible only if set against Kant's philosophy. (Hegel's approach to political philosophy is, of course, profoundly different from that of Kant.) Through Hegel, Kant affected Marx, and the impact of Marx on modern political thinking has been powerful, to say the least. Much of modern political thinking thus continues the revolution begun by Kant, just as the American and French revolutions, whose ideas Kant vindicated, set a movement afoot which has shaped much of modern European political history.

Kant's influence on Hegel and his successors is frequently more general than specific. There were, of course, many thinkers who specifically sought to elaborate and apply his political ideas. Jakob Friedrich Fries[3] is the most prominent among them, and his ideas were taken up again a century later by Leonard Nelson[4] who founded the so-called Neo-Friesian school. Or we might mention Sir Karl Popper,[5] on whose conception of the open society the imprint of Kant's political thought can be discerned. But to single out any specific instances is perhaps less worthwhile than to note the impact of his general philosophy on Western thought through which modern political thought has been affected more profoundly than is sometimes realised. It is the touchstone of a great thinker that he not only makes us view the thought of those who have gone before him in a different light, but that subsequent philosophy, too, is affected by him.

Kant's ideas have thus been a significant political force. But they have also been attacked and modified, sometimes beyond recognition. In any case, they are ideas that look ahead into the future. But more than that: Kant's theory of politics philosophically justifies man's right to political freedom, the view that he should no longer be considered to be under tutelage. Man's growing political and intellectual maturity must be recognised. According to Kant, man is in the process of becoming enlightened.

---

[1] Cf. F. M. Barnard, *Herder's Social and Political Thought: From Enlightenment to Nationalism* (Oxford, 1965).
[2] *Of the Vocation of our Age for Legislation and Jurisprudence (Vom Beruf unserer Zeit für Gesetzgebung und Rechtswissenschaft)* (Heidelberg, 1814).
[3] Cf. Jakob Friedrich Fries, *Vom deutschen Bund und deutscher Staatsverfassung. Allgemeine staatsrechtliche Ansichten* (Heidelberg, 1816); *Politik oder philosophische Staatslehre* (ed. E. F. Apelt) (Jena, 1846).
[4] Cf. Leonard Nelson, *System der philosophischen Rechtslehre* (Leipzig, 1920), for example.
[5] Cf. Karl R. Popper, *The Open Society and its Enemies*, 2 vols. (London, 1952).

Man has both the opportunity and the responsibility to make use of his mind in the spirit of criticism. Such is the temper and the message of the Enlightenment as understood by Kant.

III

Kant had been thinking about political theory for many years before he first published any of his views on this subject. His notes, published posthumously and never intended for publication, reveal his continued preoccupation with and interest in political ideas. The first extant notes probably date from the 1760s when he was studying Rousseau and Natural Law.[1] Kant gave his first lecture-course on the Theory of Right in the summer term of 1767, a course which he repeated twelve times. The kernel of his political philosophy, however, is summed up in a passage from the *Critique of Pure Reason* of 1781 in the section entitled 'Transcendental Dialectic I'.[2] It is the first substantial account of his political thought, but the first writings published by Kant which explicitly deal with politics, the two essays *What is Enlightenment?* and *Idea for a Universal History with a Cosmopolitan Purpose* of 1784, were written after the publication of the *Critique of Pure Reason* (1781), while the later writings, *Theory and Practice* (1792), *Perpetual Peace* (1795), *The Metaphysical Elements of Right* (1797) and *The Contest of Faculties* (1798) follow the publication of the *Critique of Judgement* (1790). But we do not know whether he ever planned a comprehensive treatise on politics. Whether he did or not, his intellectual vigour gradually began to wane in the last decade of his life, and he never produced a work in which he summarised his philosophical discussion of politics. But the political events which really stirred him occurred relatively late in his life. He was over fifty at the outbreak of the American Revolution and in his mid-sixties at the beginning of the French Revolution. He was sixty when he published his first political essays, and he was in his seventy-fifth year when he published his last piece on this subject. We thus have to turn to these scattered political writings for his views.

Kant's standing and influence as a political philosopher would indubitably have been greater if he had left a more highly organised comprehensive work on politics. His style did not increase his popularity. The reader should not, however, be put off by his relatively unattractive

---

[1] Cf. *AA* XIX, 334; 445 ff. These entries date from approximately 1766–8. Cf. also Georges Vlachos, *La Pensée politique de Kant*, pp. 20 ff., who argues that we can date Kant's reflections on politics only from 1763 onwards.

[2] *AA* III, 247 f.; *AA* IV, 201 f.; cf. p. 191 below.

manner of writing. His political essays do not in fact require the same extreme intellectual effort as the *Critique of Pure Reason*, although this does not mean that they do not tax the mind. Except for *The Metaphysical Elements of Right*, they are not written solely for the technical philosopher, but also for the educated general public. The essays belong to his so-called popular writings. He did not, however, claim to be able to master so 'subtle and at the same time so attractive'[1] a manner of writing as Hume. Indeed, he wrote when German was still emerging as a literary language.[2] Heine, a brilliant stylist himself, called Kant's mode of writing 'a grey wrapping-paper style'.[3] He accused him of 'being afraid to speak in an easy, pleasant and gay manner'[4] and of thus being 'a philistine'.[5] According to Heine, the effect of Kant's manner of writing was highly detrimental to the development of a clear and elegant philosophical language in Germany. He writes in the *History of Religion and Philosophy in Germany* (*Geschichte der Religion und Philosophie in Deutschland*): 'by his awkward, heavy style...he [Kant] did much damage. For the unintelligent imitators aped him in this externality and the superstition arose that one could not be a philosopher if one wrote well.'[6] Nonetheless, Kant's political writings, though far from elegant, are not always cumbersome, and are at times vigorous and characterised by a dry irony. Although the structure of his sentences is frequently complicated, memorable key-sentences occur. And there are impressive passages.[7]

IV

To understand Kant's political thought it is necessary to see it in the context of his general philosophy. His writings on politics correspond with the period of his critical philosophy. They were all written after the completion of the first critique, the *Critique of Pure Reason*, in 1781. Ideally, I should first give a summary of his critical philosophy but it is virtually impossible to summarise! It must here suffice to indicate the trend of his critical thinking, though this will necessarily be somewhat misleading.[8]

Both rationalism and empiricism appeared to him inadequate modes of

[1] *AA* IV, 262 (preface to *Prolegomena for any Future Metaphysics that may be given the Status of a Science*).
[2] Cf. Eric A. Blackall, *The Emergence of German as a Literary Language, 1700–1775* (Cambridge, 1959).
[3] Heine, *Sämtliche Werke*, ed. Ernst Elster, IV, 251.
[4] *Ibid.*   [5] *Ibid.*   [6] *Ibid.* p. 252.
[7] Cf. S. Morris Engel, 'On the Composition of the *Critique*. A Brief Comment', *Ratio*, VI (1964) for a discussion of Kant's style.
[8] For the following account I owe much to Stephan Körner's fine analysis in his *Kant* (Harmondsworth, Middlesex, 1955).

explanation to account for mathematics and science, particularly Newtonian science. Hume had convincingly refuted the possibility of philosophically justifying induction, the method of establishing necessary
universal laws proceeding from individual instances; for him causality
was only the result of a habitual association of the mind. Hume's writings
roused Kant from his 'dogmatic slumber'.[1] In order to refute Hume and
to vindicate science philosophically, he found it necessary to start his
enquiry not from objects of experience, but from the mind. For him, the
laws of nature were not inherent in nature, but constructions of the mind
used for the purpose of understanding nature. We can never explain the
world as it appears to us merely by reference to experience; to do so we
need necessary principles logically prior to and independent of experience.
Only then can we see any order in nature. In fact, uniformity, coherence
and order are imposed on nature by our minds. In other words, we cannot
know the world other than as it appears to us, for we must see it within
the framework of our mind. The world of appearance is thus conditioned
by being located in the particulars of space and time and ordered by
a priori concepts of our understanding or categories such as causality. The
world as it really is, the noumenal world or the world of things-in-
themselves, is unknowable. We can apprehend only the world of appearances. This does not mean that the external world is a world of mere
appearances or illusions—on the contrary, Kant had the greatest respect
for empirical fact and had been a scientist of note—but rather that the
world of appearances or the phenomenal world is not self-sufficient for
the purpose of explanation. For this purpose it is necessary to have
a priori principles and ideas of reason. Kant expresses this problem, which
is for him *the* philosophical problem of epistemology, in the question:
How are synthetic *a priori* judgements possible?—i.e. how can we formulate propositions which are necessary, universal, logically independent of
sense experience and capable of being contradicted? Kant's critical
method thus seeks to establish a system of synthetic *a priori* principles
for the purpose of understanding the external world. This emphasis on
the function of the mind in ordering scientific experience Kant called,
with just pride, the Copernican revolution in philosophy, and his achievement, argued and elaborated in the *Critique of Pure Reason*, has always
been hailed as a landmark in philosophy.

The *Critique of Pure Reason* deals with the problem of how we can
understand science, but there are other realms of human experience
which are not scientific—moral experience, for example. In order to

[1] *AA* IV, 260.

understand its character we must follow a method similar to that delineated in Kant's account of theoretical scientific enquiry; that is to say,
we can understand moral conduct only if we discover rules or principles
which are logically independent of experience and which are capable of
contradiction. Kant calls such rules 'practical synthetic *a priori* judgements'. He believes that they underlie all moral decisions and are inherent
in all arguments about moral issues. To justify these rules we must
suppose that man is not only a phenomenal being, subject to strict causal
laws, but also a noumenal being who is free. For moral decisions are
possible only if the will is assumed to be free to act. Each man has a will.
This will alone can make a moral choice. To will is to decide on action. An
action, however, is moral only if it is done for the sake of duty. In a case
of a conflict of interest this criterion allows us to distinguish between
actions which are right and those which are not. It allows us to distinguish
between duty and desire. Kant calls the general moral law the 'categorical
imperative'. It categorically enjoins us to act in accordance with morality.
A hypothetical injunction, on the other hand, cannot carry this universal
and necessary force, for it merely commands us to follow a course of action
if we wish to attain a particular end. The categorical imperative in its
basic formulation tells us to act according to that maxim which we can
at the same time will should become a universal law.[1] A maxim is a subjective principle of action. It is, in fact, a general rule which we choose to
follow. 'To choose maxims is to choose a policy.'[2] The test of the morality
of a maxim is whether or not it agrees with the moral principle of the
maxim becoming a universal law.

For Kant, the categorical imperative is the objective principle of
morality. The statement that the will of the rational being is subject to the
categorical imperative is an *a priori* synthetic proposition. It is also practically necessary. This is so because man is not only a means for the
arbitrary use of this will or that, but as Kant says in the *Groundwork of
the Metaphysics of Morals* 'he must in all his actions...be regarded at
the same time as an end'.[3] From this postulate follows the second formulation of the categorical imperative which says: 'Act always so that you
treat humanity whether in your person or in that of another always as an
end, but never as a means only.'[4] Although this formulation is 'at bottom
one and the same thing' as the first one,[5] it is, in another sense, already
an application of the supreme moral principle; for it indicates to us what
kind of maxims could be willed as universal laws. We thus learn what

---

[1] *Ibid.* pp. 437 f. [2] Körner, *Kant*, p. 134.
[3] *AA* IV, 428. [4] *Ibid.* p. 429. [5] *Ibid.* p. 438.

right actions are, whether in morality or politics; for they involve our not using ourselves or others as means to our subjective ends. Man should not merely be subject to another will, but he should be his own law-giver. This view leads to another formulation of the categorical imperative: 'Act always in such a way as if you were through your maxims a law-making member of a universal kingdom of ends.'[1] To act for the sake of duty is thus to act in order to conform to some self-imposed law. This last formulation of the categorical imperative also implies an affinity between morals and politics, for man's actions, it suggests, do not take place in a vacuum, but always in relation to other men—thus implicitly suggesting a theory of politics, a system of principles governing organised human relations.

Kant's principles of morality are formal. Their very generality means that they do not say anything about the content of an action, but they supply rules to which we can appeal if we wish to judge actions and if we wish to decide what action is moral in the case of a conflict of interest. They rule out reference to, or regard for, the consequences of our actions, such as concern for the attainment of happiness. If the pursuit of happiness is made the maxim of our actions, the will is not autonomous. It does not then live under self-imposed laws, but follows heteronomous principles on which, in Kant's view, a sound moral theory cannot be founded. 'A practical law of reason', on the contrary, is 'the principle which makes certain actions a duty'.[2]

Such is Kant's view of the character of morality. Because of his approach to knowledge, be it in science or morality, Kant did not work out a system of nature nor did he set out to provide a complete system of morality which would take account of 'empirical diversity'.[3] A complete account of moral practice in all particular instances where the concept of morality can be applied is impossible. What Kant wishes to provide is an approximation to such a system, elaborating the relevant *a priori* principles. An attempt of this kind Kant calls a metaphysics, which, for him, is a set of the fundamental *a priori* principles of a particular discipline. According to him, all propositions of right are *a priori* propositions; for they are laws of reason. It can often be a matter for discussion whether some sentences stating such principles are to be interpreted as synthetic *a priori* propositions, or as analytic *a priori* (i.e. where the meaning of the sentence is contained in the term and does not permit contradiction) or synthetic *a posteriori* propositions (which are logically dependent on experience).

[1] *Ibid.*   [2] *AA* VI, 225.
[3] *Ibid.* p. 205.

The line between one and the other is not always easy to draw,[1] but the case for a Kantian approach to morality—and thus also to politics—is not refuted if any one sentence (or indeed any number of sentences) can be interpreted as not being a synthetic *a priori* proposition.[2] It suffices if some of them are of that type—and clearly the categorical imperative and its various formulations and immediate derivations are. This presupposes Kant's view that a metaphysics of morality is at least possible. For Kant, a theory of politics (which, for him, amounts in the main to a metaphysics of law) is inevitably a part of a metaphysics of morality. This is so because politics deals with the question of what we ought to do in our social and political context, or in other words, it is concerned with establishing criteria by which we can settle public conflicts of interests. The principle of universality demands that our social and political relations should be governed and our public conflicts settled in a universal manner. This requires the existence of law. The principles of morality would, in one way, go beyond purely legal questions; for they affect private inner decisions by men which can neither be regulated nor enforced publicly. Law deals only with what remains once such inner decisions have been subtracted. It is the outer shell, so to speak, of the moral realm. And a theory of law is that which can be necessary and universal in the realm of politics. A metaphysics of law is thus all that a metaphysics of politics can ever amount to. Such a metaphysics will set out the *a priori* principles of reason according to which we can judge the lawfulness of any given positive laws and thus of any form which political action may take. Kant's political theory is thus closely bound up with his ethics, though this is not its only affinity; for it is also closely connected with his philosophy of history. On the one hand, ethics and politics overlap. On the other hand, moral and political duties are clearly different. Political duties are not perfect duties towards oneself, but only what Kant calls perfect duties towards others, whose non-performance is wrong and whose performance may therefore be enforced. Kant here rules out from consideration all actions which merely concern oneself. He also does not consider those actions which are imperfect duties to others, i.e. actions involving the choice of one person and the mere aims and wishes of another. For instance, he does not prescribe acts of benevolence as legal duties. Perfect duties to others are therefore an object of law and thus of

---

[1] According to Mary J. Gregor, *Laws of Freedom* (Oxford, 1963), pp. 4 ff., Kant does not distinguish very clearly between pure knowledge and *a priori* knowledge. The former does not contain any empirical elements, the latter presupposes concepts of sensuous origin.

[2] I owe this observation to Stephan Körner.

politics; for law is *the* universalised expression of politics. In other words, an action is a moral action only if the maxim on which it is based agrees with the idea of duty; morality is therefore concerned only with subjective motives. Law, on the other hand, is concerned with the actions themselves, i.e. with objective facts. Moral actions can thus only be commanded; legal actions, however, can be enforced.

V

If politics results in law, what then, are Kant's principles of politics? They are substantially the principles of right (*Recht*). The philosophical enquiry into politics must establish which political actions are just or unjust. It must show by what principles we can establish the demands of justice in a given situation. Justice must, however, be universal, but only law can bring it about. A coherent political order must then be a legal order. Just as in Kant's ethics actions ought to be based on maxims capable of being formulated as universal laws, so in politics political arrangements ought to be organised according to universally valid laws. Political action and legislation ought thus to be based on such rules as will allow of no exception. Kant's principles of politics are normative. They are applications of principles of right to experience.[1] Right, in a succinct phrase of Kant's, 'ought never to be adapted to politics, but politics ought always to be adapted to right'.[2]

There is, of course, no reason whatsoever to believe that Kant was not aware that the details of the political situation always vary. His aim, however, was to discover the philosophical foundations on which political actions could, and ought to, be based. Right is to be found only in external relations which are the proper business of politics. External relations are relations which arise because we have possessions, 'an external mine and thine' as Kant calls it. He here uses the terminology of Roman Law for the concept of 'mine and thine' (*meum et tuum*).[3] These relations have to be placed under rules. Politics, as Hobbes had argued, belongs to that sphere of human experience in which man's will can be coerced by another will; for like Hobbes, Kant reduces all action to the will. If coercion is exercised according to a universal principle, it is law. Thus, law is conceived as 'a coercive order'.[4] Legality is therefore the decisive

---

[1] *On an Alleged Right to Lie for the Sake of Philanthropy (Über ein vermeintes Recht aus Menschenliebe zu lügen)* (1797), *AA* VIII, 429.
[2] *Ibid.*   [3] *AA* VI, 245 ff.
[4] John Ladd, introduction to *Immanuel Kant. The Metaphysical Elements of Justice* (Indianapolis, New York and Kansas City, 1965), p. xviii.

principle in the sphere of politics. The moral decision of the inner man finds outward expression in legality, i.e. in an action conforming with law. But man's inner life must not be subject to coercion. Because we cannot know for certain anything about another person's inner life, it ought not to be the task of political action or legislation to change or in any way to condition another person's thought. As men we are free. Our freedom implies that we have a hypothetical right to acquire anything in the world of a nature which we are potentially capable of acquiring.

Not only any one particular individual, but all individuals have this right of acquiring possessions. It is the expression of their freedom. Collision between the freedom of one individual and that of others must, however, be avoided. Otherwise there would be chaos and constant strife. The freedom of each individual has consequently to be regulated in a universally binding manner. Thus, external freedom is freedom from any constraint except coercion by law, a freedom which allows each individual to pursue his own ends, whatever they may be, provided that this pursuit leaves the same kind of freedom to all others.

Acquired rights do not, however, belong to us merely by virtue of our humanity. They can be regulated or even curtailed by law. The act of acquisition establishes the right to property. It does not necessarily mean physical possession, but rather an intelligible or noumenal possession independent of time. In order to distinguish my possession from that of others, it is necessary that the choice of others should agree with my own. This condition is only possible under a law regulating possessions. But such a law is not possible in a state of nature, only in a civil society. From the principle that everyone has a right to acquire external possessions, therefore, there arises the command that everyone ought to act in such a way that everyone is able to acquire the external 'His' (or his external possessions). This in turn amounts to a command to enter civil society, to become a member of the state. Or, in other words, when a conflict about external possessions arises, as it inevitably does, a right exists to compel the other person to enter civil society.

In establishing this view of right, Kant is again not concerned with delineating the content of relations between individuals (i.e. the ends which they desire or ought to desire), but only with the form. What matters is the arrangement which establishes that the free actions of one individual 'can be reconciled with the freedom of the other in accordance with a universal law'.[1]

From this conclusion, the universal principle of right can be deduced.

[1] *AA* VI, 230.

It runs: 'Every action which by itself or by its maxim enables the freedom of each individual's will to coexist with the freedom of everyone else in accordance with a universal law is *right*.'[1] This universal principle of right imposes an obligation upon us, but it does not expect, let alone require, us to act in accordance with it. It tells us merely that if freedom is to be restricted in accordance with right and if justice is to prevail it must do so in accordance with this universal principle of right. To restrict freedom in this manner does not entail interfering with the freedom of an individual, but merely establishes the condition of his external freedom.

The universal principle of right is basically only an application of the universal principle of morality, as laid down in the Categorical Imperative, to the sphere of law, and thus also to the sphere of politics.[2] But since it is morally necessary to realise external freedom, we can be compelled by others to carry out our duty of entering civil society. But we do not have to become morally better to enter it; for the political problem must be capable of solution not only by good men, but even by 'a nation of devils (so long as they possess understanding)'.[3]

To restrict freedom except on the basis of the universal principle of right is wrong. It is not only wrong, but will also lead to strife, and thus is self-defeating. He who restricts freedom otherwise, i.e. arbitrarily, violates the freedom of another and abuses his own. To use constraint against anyone who violates the freedom of another is, however, right. The principle of right implies analytically the authorisation to use coercion by means of or on the basis of law against anyone who violates freedom illegitimately.

If this principle is applied to politics it is necessary that there should be established: 'A constitution allowing the *greatest possible human freedom* in accordance with laws which ensure *that the freedom of each can coexist with the freedom of all the others*'.[4] Kant elaborates this principle by saying that it is 'a necessary idea which must be made the basis not only of the first outline of a political constitution but of all laws as well'.[5] This fundamental principle could, by way of analogy, be called the universal principle of political right, although Kant himself does not use this term in the *Critique of Pure Reason* where he discusses it.

From these elementary principles, all other Kantian principles of politics follow—Kant's approach also makes it clear that, for him, the philosophical problem of politics is virtually that of Hobbes, viz. the

[1] *Ibid.*; cf. p. 133 below.
[2] Gregor, *Laws of Freedom*, p. 13.
[3] *AA* VIII, 366; cf. p. 112 below.
[4] *AA* III, 247; *AA* IV, 201.
[5] *AA* III, 247 f.; *AA* IV, 201.

transition from a state of war to a state of peace and security.[1] But Kant's solution is different.

What further principles did Kant then formulate which ought to govern external relations among men? A state is a union of a group of men under laws.[2] Since laws must then be based on the principle that we ought to be treated as ends and not as means, and since we must be considered as our own law-givers, we should be asked to consider as right only those laws to which we could agree or ought to have agreed if we had been asked to do so. 'For so long as it is not self-contradictory to say that an entire people could agree to such a law, however painful it might seem, then the law is in harmony with right.'[3] An important corollary of this principle is the necessity that all laws be public laws. Any legislation based on a maxim that needs publicity to achieve its end is just.

The sovereign has not only rights, but also duties. He thus has not only the right but also the duty to coerce his subjects by the giving of laws; it is, however, his (moral) duty to treat his subjects as ends and not as means. Kant here is not entirely clear. It is not at all certain whether he refers to the sovereign (legislature) or to the ruler (executive). The sovereign (according to him) can never do wrong;[4] whatever the laws given by him are, they have to be obeyed. But the positive law which is given has still to be judged by the standard found in the principles of right. The ruler cannot be judged by the sovereign since if this were done the legislature would usurp the power of the executive or judiciary which is self-contradictory and thus not right.

The problem of sovereignty, in fact, greatly occupied Kant; for he reverts to it again and again in his unpublished notes.[5] His discussion is not without occasional contradiction, as might be expected from a philosopher wrestling with a problem which he had not solved entirely to his satisfaction. The whole trend of Kant's thinking as revealed in these notes, makes it, however, abundantly plain that, according to him, sovereignty resides or originates in the people[6] which ought to possess legislative

[1] Cf. Pierre Hassner, 'Situation de la philosophie politique chez Kant', *Annales de philosophie politique*, IV (Paris, 1962), 77 ff.

[2] *AA* VI, 313; cf. p. 138 below.

[3] *AA* VIII, 299; cf. p. 80 f. below.

[4] Cf. for example *AA* XIX, 515 No. 7782; 566 No. 7965; 572 No. 7982.

[5] Cf. for instance *AA* XIX, 414 No. 7494; 480 No. 7660; 498 No. 7713; 499 No. 7719; 515 No. 7781; 549 No. 7905; 555 No. 7921; 555 No. 7922; 561 No. 7941; 563 No. 7952; 567 No. 7971; 572 No. 7982; 575 No. 7991; 582 No. 8016; 582 No. 8018; 584 No. 8020; 593 No. 8049; to mention only some of the more important reflections on this question of sovereignty and its implications.

[6] Cf. *AA* XIX, 503 No. 7734.

power.[1] However, a monarch could possess it as a representative of the people in a derivative form. Yet Kant appears convinced that if the monarch is to exercise this power together with executive powers, his rule is despotic.

It is also the sovereign's (moral) duty to give just laws and to introduce constitutional reforms so that a republican constitution can be established. (The term 'republican' in Kant's writings could be interpreted to represent what nowadays is generally called parliamentary democracy, though it does not necessarily have this connotation.) But the subject cannot coerce the ruler (or sovereign) to exercise these duties. They are therefore not legal, but moral duties for the ruler.

All this also implies that men have inalienable rights. In a state of nature, the war of all against all may prevail, but in a state where men live under law it is different. Men are free, equal and self-dependent. This statement is derived from the idea of freedom. For if all individuals are free, they must necessarily be equally so; for the freedom of all individuals is absolute and can only be universally and equally restricted by law. Each free person must also be self-dependent. The idea of freedom entails the individual's autonomy, for it postulates the individual's power of exercising his will independently, uninhibited by improper constraint.

Kant thus starts his enquiry into politics from the standpoint of the individual. This view reflects his emphasis on the need of the free individual to make decisions, a view which he had propounded in his writings on ethics. The political freedom of the individual can, as we have seen, be understood only in terms of legal arrangements guaranteeing the freedom of all individuals.

But Kant states the political problem in a negative manner. He does not consider it to be the purpose of politics to make people happy. Happiness is subjective. He thus strongly condemns utilitarianism in politics, just as he objects to utilitarianism in pure ethics. This argument, of course, does not mean that he does not wish people to be happy. It only means that political arrangements should not be organised in such a way as to aim at promoting happiness, but that they should permit men to attain happiness in their own way. He thus rules out benevolent despotism as practised, and defended in his writings on politics, by Frederick the Great.

Kant realises, indeed, that it is necessary for the ruler to give such laws and act in such a manner that the subject will not seek to destroy the state

---

[1] Cf. Gierke, *Natural Law and the Theory of Society*, p. 153, who maintains that the principle of popular sovereignty is for practical purposes 'a mere idea of reason'. Gierke, in my view, overstates his case.

and to overthrow the system of laws. For this purpose, men must be treated as ends and not as means. A genuine paradox, the paradox of political freedom, appears to arise. Man's freedom can be safeguarded only by his submitting to coercion; for law presupposes coercion, and thus an infringement of the individual's freedom. Rousseau saw this paradox clearly when he stated at the very beginning of the *Contrat Social* 'Man is born free, and everywhere he is in chains'.[1] He blamed society for this state of affairs. Kant agrees with him in considering this act of coercion to be a result of man's membership of civil society, of his citizenship of the state, but he solves the paradox by seeing it as a necessary condition of civilisation. He resorts to the following explanation. We are free only in so far as, in the case of a conflict of interests, we obey the law to which we would have agreed, i.e. we submit only to coercion which is legally exercised, on the basis of public law given by the sovereign authority. The sovereign ought thus to be obliged to respect the laws which he has given. Kant here differs from Hobbes for whom the sovereign is above the law; law is the sovereign's command to the people. Man, according to Kant, preserves his freedom by remaining his own law-giver. In principle, every subject thus participates in all legislation as a fellow-legislator, and the ruler when legislating ought to respect this right of his subjects. This solution ensures freedom and security for all. Political freedom, then, is independence from coercion by another will.

If freedom is the first principal right of a citizen in a state, equality is the second. Men must be equal before the law; legislation must not make an exception nor must the law be administered so as to allow for exceptions. Kant attacks the entire heritage of feudal privilege, a foremost contemporary issue. He also rules out in principle slavery or any inferior political status for a citizen. But he thinks of political equality only, and does not at all consider the question of economic equality. He does not, however, ignore economic issues entirely. He asserts the right of man to own property. He even goes further; for he makes economic independence a criterion for active participation in political affairs.

The third principal right, independence (or *Selbständigkeit* as Kant calls it), requires that each citizen must have a right to participate in the government. He ought to do this not directly, but indirectly by the exercise of the vote. Each citizen must have one vote, however large his estate may be. No one must, by statute, have more legislative power than has been agreed to by a law concerning the delegation of legislative power.

---

[1] Jean Jacques Rousseau, *The Political Writings*, II, ed. C. E. Vaughan (Cambridge, 1915), II, 23: 'L'homme est né libre, et partout il est dans les fers'.

But while every one is free and equal and ought to enjoy the protection of law in these respects, not every one has a right to participate in the making of laws. Kant, if judged by modern criteria, here appears to depart from his own enlightened standpoint. Although in many ways he was ahead of his time, he was not so in all respects. He is still, not surprisingly perhaps, profoundly steeped in eighteenth-century traditions. He may be the philosopher of the American and French revolutions, but it should not be forgotten that the former was essentially a revolution of landowners and the latter a revolution of the bourgeoisie. So Kant, perhaps understandably, differentiates between men of independence and those who have none. He classes those who are independent as *active* citizens and those who are dependent as *passive* citizens. Only active citizens have a right to vote and to legislate. Women are, on principle, disqualified. But any legislation should always be enacted and carried out as if the passive citizens too were participating, for, inherently, they have the same political right as active citizens. The requirements for independence are, for him, partly economic. A man must not be dependent on any one else economically, as a servant or as an employee, for otherwise he cannot freely and independently take part in politics. No self-dependent citizen untainted by crime or insanity can abdicate the duty of participating in legislating. He cannot relinquish this duty even if he were mistakenly to find the spectacle of politics abhorrent and beneath his dignity. For while no one has a right to coerce others except by a public law executed by the sovereign, no one can divest himself of this right either.

These three rights of freedom, equality and self-dependence show that, in a properly organised state, men can find security and justice. Kant differs from Rousseau, since he believes that the state of nature is not a state of innocence. Thus, man is not corrupted by society. On the contrary, society has civilised him. Kant rather agrees with Hobbes that the state of nature is the state of a war of all against all.

What is therefore needed is a will that binds every one equally, i.e. a collectively universal will that alone can give security to each and all. Consequently, everyone has to restrict his freedom so as to make possible the establishment of such a supreme power and to avoid collision with the freedom of others. Kant, following the tradition of his age, uses the analogy of the social contract to explain this existence of the state governing a people by a system of civil law. For Kant, however, the social contract must not be considered a historical fact. On this point, he is quite unambiguous. Any such conception would be fraught with peril; for it is likely to encourage disobedience of, or even active rebellion against, the prevailing law. The social contract must therefore be seen as a practical Idea of reason. (An Idea, for Kant, is not found in experience and can thus be neither proved nor disproved by scientific enquiry, but is a regulative principle of Reason in the light of which experience can be given order and unity, which it would otherwise lack.) It is a practical Idea of reason in so far as it can be applied to the world of practical affairs or to experience, i.e. the phenomenal world; for it allows us to say something about the kind of state which ought to exist, i.e. the state which ought to be established in accordance with the principles of right. The social contract is thus a criterion of political judgement, but it should not lead us to go into historical reasons for the purpose of drawing practical conclusions. The Idea that men have made a contract to establish the state means rather that they have been prepared to submit their own personal will in matters external to them to a universal will. This universal or general will is, of course, the will of reason. It is not the united will of all, even if this were to be found so in fact, nor is it the will of the majority. Kant is again close to Rousseau, but again, where Rousseau is ambiguous, he is decisively clear. He transfers the conception of the general will, which might be embodied in the government, to an Idea of reason which entitles the government to exercise the power of political action, to coerce others according to universal law. He differs cardinally from Hobbes, who ruled out the question as to whether the sovereign could make just or unjust laws as illegitimate; for in Hobbes' view, there can be no such moral yardstick to measure existing laws.

For Kant, the Idea of the social contract also implies the necessity of a civil constitution. While it is necessary and obligatory, as he believes, to establish a civil constitution, it is also the greatest practical problem for mankind to attain this end; for only in a civil society, universally administering right according to law, can freedom exist. Only then does the freedom of one co-exist with the freedom of others. But to find a just government ruling according to a just constitution is not easy. For who is to safeguard the rights of the individual in face of authority? Who will see to it that a just constitution is established and that the government will act in accordance with the principles of right?

There is no perfect solution to the old problem *quis custodiet ipsos custodes?* This means that 'only an approximation to the idea'[1] of a just constitution and a just government is given to us by nature.

According to what principles, then, should a rightful government be organised, even if completely just political arrangements can never be

---

[1] *AA* VIII, 23: cf. p. 46 below.

attained? Kant differentiates between the republican form of government, where the executive is separated from the legislature, and the despotic, where it is not.[1] Republican government is impossible in a democracy; for a 'democracy' is necessarily despotic. A power is established where all rule. It means that all take decisions about all and also against any one who decides to differ from the prevailing majority view. It would in fact be a contradiction of the universal will with itself and with freedom.

Republican government, however, is rightful government. A republican constitution is established in accordance with the principles of right if powers independent from one another are set up. First, there is the sovereign, in the person of the legislator who represents the united (or general) will of the people, which, in theory, is the will of reason. The ruler (or regent), i.e. the government or the executive, cannot be the legislator. Finally, neither the legislator nor the ruler can be the judiciary. For interpreting the law and for making individual judgements, an individual justice is required. For this function, a special representative of the people—a court of law or a jury—has to be appointed.

The legislative sovereign power, according to Kant, ought to be vested in the people. He also states that, in practice, the idea can only be approximated to. The most that we can hope for is that this power will be exercised indirectly by representatives of the people.[2] It cannot be expected that all should give laws and agree on legislation. All that can be attained is apparently a representative assembly which will legislate for all. The people as a whole must be expected to agree to this procedure and accept the legislation. They are, of course, bound by it.

Kant does not specify in detail how the representatives of the people ought to exercise their power, nor does he say according to what principle they should be chosen. He does not advocate the rule of the majority, and certainly not its unfettered power to legislate, which would have appeared to him only another form of the arbitrary will in action. He does, however, state explicitly that all should combine to give laws[3] and that legislation is to spring from the united will of all.[4] But he criticises the constitutional practice prevailing in eighteenth-century Britain.[5] For British constitutional monarchy appeared to him merely as a device designed to cloak an autocratic rule. He warns that the danger of a monarch becoming a

---

[1] Unfortunately he does not always appear to use his terms consistently. Indeed, he makes the distinction only in later writings, such as *Perpetual Peace* and *The Theory of Public Right*. Even then, when he speaks of the ruler, he sometimes appears to mean the sovereign legislative assembly, but at other times he appears to mean the executive of the government, which on other occasions again is described merely as an organ of the legislative.

[2] Cf. *AA* VI, 341. [3] *AA* VII, 90 f.

[4] *AA* VI, 313. [5] Cf. *AA* VII, 90; *AA* XIX, 606.

despot is particularly great, because one man is more easily tempted to become a tyrant. But he also states that where the government is in the hands of the smallest number of people and the representation is at its widest, republican rule will be most easily assured. He even appears to prefer a monarchy to an aristocracy. Yet he appears to be somewhat obscure on this point. The general drift of his argument is clear, however; his use of the term 'republican' shows us that he is basically anti-monarchic. And because he knew of the dangers of one man abusing his power, he, like Rousseau, did not believe that the united will of all could well be represented by one man. There can also be no doubt as to his basic plea for separation of powers and his conviction that the sovereign authority should rest in the people or its representatives. And he is equally clear in his demand that the sovereign must not own any private property so that he may be unable either to exercise private power or to be affected by private interest.

The fundamental element of any republican constitution, however, is respect for law. The subjects as well as the ruler and the sovereign must possess this respect. In the last resort, the subject can be expected to respect those laws in the giving of which he has participated as fellow-legislator. But the subject or citizen must neither rebel against the laws which the sovereign has made nor against the regent who carries them out, whether he likes the laws or approves of the regent or does neither. This attitude is perhaps surprising, especially if we consider Kant's attitude to the French Revolution.[1] It follows, however, from Kant's general conception of the supremacy of law, for to rebel against the supreme power would amount to disregarding, or even overturning the law. This is evil. Kant is most outspoken on this point.

His favourable view of the French Revolution, however, complicated his argument.[2] He tries to give legal status to the revolution by saying that it was not in fact a revolution at all in the legal sense; for the king had surrendered his sovereign power to the Third Estate. This is a dubious contention, though admittedly Louis XVI had abandoned absolute monarchy when he called the States-General.[3] It is, however, doubtful

---

[1] See the titles listed under p. 7 above, n. 1, for discussions of Kant's attitude.

[2] Cf. H. S. Reiss, 'Kant and the Right of Rebellion', *Journal of the History of Ideas*, XVII (1956), 179–92 for a discussion of these difficulties.

[3] Cf. Alfred Cobban, in his *History of Modern France* (London, 1962), I, 138 for instance, who writes: 'The calling of the States-General was undoubtedly the critical step, for it meant the abdication of absolute monarchy': cf. Kant's comments on this very theme in one of his notes (*AA* XIX, 595 No. 8055) where he expands his contention that by asking the States-General for assistance to solve the financial problems of France, he did in fact surrender his sovereignty.

whether he relinquished sovereign power. Kant's argument on this point remains controversial, to say the least, and does not carry much conviction.

According to Kant, the case against rebellion is unambiguous. The people cannot possess a right to rebel. There can be no power to determine what constitutes the right to rebel. Rebellion would upset the whole system of laws. It would create anarchy and violence. It would also destroy the civil constitution which the idea of the social contract demands. For if a constitution contained an article permitting a people to rebel or to depose a sovereign, a second sovereign would thereby be established. This event would be a contradiction. It would, in fact, require a further, third sovereign to decide between the two, which is absurd. There cannot therefore be in a constitution a clause giving any one a right to resist or to rebel against supreme authority.[1] The idea of the civil constitution must be sacred and irresistible. To overthrow the sovereign or the ruler is not only wrong but will also fail to achieve its end; for it does not produce a true reform of thought.

But once a revolution has taken place, attempts to undo it and re-establish the old order are just as wrong, for it is men's duty to obey as citizens. If a government is newly established, as in England in 1688, it has to be accepted and obeyed. On the other hand, there exists no right to punish the ruler for deeds committed as ruler, for the ruler's deeds, in principle, are not subject to punishment. The sovereign cannot be punished for issuing unjust laws or for committing unrightful political actions; for such an endeavour would amount to rebellion while he is in power, and would violate the same principle after he had been deposed.

The sovereign has the right to dismiss the ruler, but he has no right to punish the dismissed ruler for actions committed as ruler. Judicial action against, and punishment of, the ruler are worse than the assassination of a tyrant. In fact, the judicial punishment of a (sovereign) ruler, such as the regicide of Charles I or Louis XVI, is the worst crime imaginable. It is a perversion of the Idea of the law itself.

[1] There is, of course, the possibility of passive resistance or disobedience to a government. While Kant unambiguously rules out active rebellion and states that we should not reason about the origins of the supreme power with a view to action, he suggests in his treatise *Religion within the Limits of Reason Alone* that passive resistance or passive disobedience by not carrying out the decrees of a government may be legitimate. He argues there that the verse 'we ought to obey God rather than men' (Acts v. 29) means that when men command what is evil-in-itself, i.e. what runs directly counter to the moral law, we ought not to obey (*AA* vi, 99). But it should also not be forgotten in this context that this passage, as well as a similar one from the same treatise (*AA* vi, 154), cannot nullify Kant's general hostility to the right of rebellion which necessarily rules out civil disobedience.

Kant, however, demands from the sovereign that he should promote a spirit of liberty. Only if it prevails is it likely that the coercive ends of the ruler will not be defeated. The rulers are, in fact, aware of the desire for liberty; for no ruler dares to say that he does not recognize any rights whatsoever in the people, that they owe their happiness exclusively to the government, and that any claims of the subjects to have rights against him are a punishable offence. Rulers dare not say this because a declaration of this kind would make the citizens band together in protest. Yet even if citizens conclude that their happiness could be taken away, they have no right to rebel. Obedience, however, does not mean silence. What must and does remain for the people is the right of public criticism, i.e. not only freedom of the press, but the right of open criticism of the powers that be. Following Voltaire, Kant believed that '*Freedom of the pen* is the only safeguard of the rights of the people'.[1] This is tantamount to demanding an open society, a society which seeks to carry on government and to give laws by a process of free rational discussion.

The right to criticise in public ought, therefore, to be guaranteed by the republican constitution. This right is restricted only by 'respect and devotion towards the existing constitution'[2] of the state in which it is exercised.

To qualify the right of public criticism by the proviso that it should be resorted to only if respect for the republican constitution is not infringed implicitly establishes the principle of the limits of tolerance. This principle amounts to saying that all views must be tolerated provided that they are views which involve the toleration of the views of others. Or, in other words, only those views ought to be tolerated which do not advocate the overthrow of the constitution established according to the principles of right. For anyone publicly to advocate views calculated to overthrow the republican constitution amounts to a demand for violating the principles of right and thus the freedom of others. It is, therefore, legitimate to frame laws which restrict the freedom of the pen in this respect, but in this respect only. Such a law can be made universally applicable. If, on the other hand, violation of a republican constitution and of the principles of right and thus of the freedom of others is advocated, a demand of this kind cannot be given the form of a universal law. For if such a violation were to prevail, chaos, and with it the erosion of all laws, would ensue. A law permitting violation of the constitution and thus of the system of laws itself would amount to a law contradicting itself, which is absurd. It must, however, be made equally clear that this restriction is the only

---

[1] *AA* VIII, 304; cf. p. 85 below.　　　　　　　　[2] *Ibid.*

possible one. To restrict public criticism in any other way would amount to violating the principles of right and thus of freedom. And this limitation of public criticism must not be construed to mean that the government has a right to suppress public criticism as such, but only public criticism which has no respect for the constitution (i.e. criticism which amounts to advocating, or involves violation of, a republican constitution). Kant does not lay down the exact limits beyond which it is not legitimate to criticise a constitution publicly. The phrase 'respect' should not be taken to mean that it could be illegitimate to discuss the principles of right and their application in practice in a philosophical manner. But it does suggest that an unreasoned or forcible attack upon a republican constitution and any attempt to establish a rule which does not permit public criticism can, in principle, be legislated against. For such attacks do not carry respect, while a philosophical enquiry into the constitution and the principles underlying it does.

Unfortunately, Kant does not elaborate on this point. He was much more concerned with the problem of his age, with establishing the right of public criticism in face of a paternalistic ruler, and much less with problems of modern liberal democracy, the need to limit this right and to define the limits of tolerance so as to avoid destruction of public freedom by excessive liberality in tolerating views hostile to free public criticism and thus to freedom itself. The limits of public criticism are thus the defences which must needs be erected against those who wish to destroy it, from whatever quarter they may come; but this is the only frontier which requires protection.

VI

Right, however, cannot possibly prevail among men within a state if their freedom is threatened by the action of other states. The law can prevail only if the rule of law prevails in all states and in international relations. Only then are all individuals free; only then does right prevail everywhere. Clearly, the very universality of the demand that right should prevail makes it imperative that it should apply to all men and provide legal protection against all kinds of violence. This is possible only if war is abolished as a means of politics and peace is established and safeguarded on earth according to the principles of right. This is the ultimate problem of politics. Kant had predecessors in this view of international politics, but once again the rigour of his argument and the relentless search for philosophical vindication are unprecedented.

In Kant's view, right can be jeopardised by war or by preparations for war. As he writes in his essay *Conjectural Beginning of the Human Race* (1786): 'It must be admitted that the greatest evils which afflict civilised nations are brought about by war, and not so much by actual wars in the past or the present as by never ending and indeed continually increasing preparations for war.'[1] Neither a republican state (however just its legal arrangements are) nor its citizens are safe unless they avoid conflicts with other states. The only way to do so is by establishing peaceful relations between independent states according to the principles of right. Kant realises, as his ironic preamble to his treatise *Perpetual Peace* indicates, that the ultimate alternative to this view is the graveyard, the death of all, a possibility which has become only too real in this nuclear age of ours.

It is a duty to work towards the establishment of a cosmopolitan society. A world state would be the ideal solution, but states are not likely to agree to a complete surrender of their sovereignty, nor is the territory of the world compact enough to permit control by one supreme authority. (Modern technology has, so to speak, made the world shrink since 1795, but there are still almost insuperable barriers to effective control of the globe by a world government, owing to the diversity of nations.) This positive solution is therefore unrealistic; a negative solution must suffice. As war becomes more and more expensive and as the peoples (not the sovereigns) will have to bear the burden, they will not desire war any more. Necessity will bring about this state of right; for the balance of power is too precarious. Indeed, Kant harshly attacks the concept of the balance of power because it cannot lead to perpetual peace. This state of affairs can be brought about only gradually. It needs a nucleus of republican states. To have a world republic is impossible unless all nations agree to it, which is not very likely. Kant admits that, on the analogy of individuals uniting to form a state, all states might be compelled to unite into a world state governed by law. He points out that states would not wish to abandon their sovereignty. In his view, so it would seem, they are intrinsically incapable of doing so.[2] This is surprising, since for him, as distinct from Fichte or the Romantics, states do not have an unalterable traditional, natural or linguistic basis. Since the states persist, a world state would create only the semblance of public international law; it would, in fact, be likely to result in a particularly oppressive despotism.

What could be brought about is a federation of states which are opposed to war. Again the *a priori* principles of right decide the issue. War is not the right way of settling disputes between nations. Nor is war invigorating

[1] *AA* VIII, 121.   [2] Cf. *ibid.* p. 357; *AA* XXIII, 169.

or noble. Kant's principles of right demand that the nations agree to laws capable of settling disputes between them and that they be prepared to submit to arbitration according to law. The respect for law which prevails in a republican state makes it incumbent upon its citizens and its government to establish a similar system of law in international affairs.

Kant was thus well aware of the role of power in politics. He was certainly not so naïve as to believe that it would be sufficient to proclaim such rules in order to bring about perpetual peace. But in Kant's view, the sense of right is all-pervasive; for even the mighty tend to appeal to right when they violate law. It is an observation which Machiavelli, though from a completely different standpoint, had also made. Kant therefore thinks it imperative to make men aware of the principles of right and accept the rule of justice.

Kant expressly rejects the rule of expediency in international politics. Men who espouse expediency, however, also have principles, principles which are derived from the view that might is right. Kant shrewdly analyses them. He was indeed aware of customary political practice and he acutely discerned the arguments usually put forward to deceive political opponents.

Kant considers it essential to demonstrate that perpetual peace cannot be established by following the doctrines of expediency which are: *fac et excusa, si fecisti nega* and *divide et impera*.[1] These principles are not objective *a priori* principles of right on which men can agree and act. They involve considering the consequences of one's action and not the maxims of one's action. They are therefore heteronomous, i.e. uncertain and imprecise. It is impossible to agree on them by the use of reason. They do not allow of a philosophical enquiry into politics, nor do they afford points of orientation for rightful political action.

VII

Just as Kant did not write a single masterpiece on political philosophy, he did not write a single comprehensive work on the philosophy of history. We have to turn to the essays *What is Enlightenment?* and *Idea for a Universal History with a Cosmopolitan Purpose* of 1784 and to a section of *The Contest of Faculties* of 1798. What then is his view of history?

First of all, Kant asks whether we can formulate laws in history, just as we can formulate laws in nature, so that we can understand history in the

---

[1] Cf. p. 120 below.

way in which we understand nature. In his view, it is difficult to detect these laws, but perhaps biography—and Kant here takes up a point frequently raised in eighteenth-century German discussions by Mendelssohn, Hamann, and Herder, for instance—may serve as a suitable analogy. Perhaps the general course of history shows a development in mankind similar to that which biography discerns in the individual. If there is progress, this is certainly not due to human wisdom; for even the philosophers, Kant ironically remarks, are not wise enough to plan their lives.

Kant nevertheless sets high standards. He intends to discover the natural laws of history, just as Kepler had discovered the natural laws of the planets. When Kant talks of plans of nature in history, he does not mean that there is an actual legislator or mind called nature which has consciously made a plan to be carried out in history, but merely that if we wish to understand history as (according to him) we have to, we must resort to an Idea, such as the one that nature has a purpose in history. This Idea cannot be proved or disproved by a scientific enquiry, but without it, we cannot understand history at all. Nor must this Idea be considered to have equal status to a scientific law. Kant adopts a point of view, admittedly a subjective one, from which it is not only 'possible, but profitable, and not only profitable, but necessary'[1] to look at the facts of history. Since his main concern is with human freedom, the development of human freedom provides him with the necessary clue. He therefore assumes that a plan of nature must intend the education of mankind to a state of freedom. Or (to put it differently) since nature has endowed man with reason, and since the purpose of nature is to realise man's essence, nature has made man in order that he should become rational. Kant's view that man's essence must be realised follows an argument later developed in the *Critique of Judgement* where Kant had maintained that the teleology of nature is internal, not external. It is also a peculiarity of reason that it cannot be completely realised in the lifetime of an individual, but only in the entire species. This view represents a pivotal point in Kant's philosophy of history. His anthropological studies, to which he devoted much time and energy, had confirmed him in his conception of the unity of mankind.[2] Culture was not the result of individual effort, but was produced by mankind as a whole. Man as a rational being therefore needs to live in a historical process. History is a progress towards rationality, but it must not be thought that this process involves a con-

---

[1] R. G. Collingwood, *The Idea of History* (Oxford, 1946), p. 95.
[2] Cf. Vlachos, *La Pensée politique de Kant*, pp. 19-26.

tinuous advance in rationality all the time. In *The Contest of Faculties*, Kant explicitly rejects the suggestion that the question of progress can be solved by appealing to experience. None of the possibilities which he can envisage supplies an answer. The first possibility is that everything is getting worse and worse. He calls it 'terrorism'. This hypothesis does not work, because after a certain stage, things would have become so bad that everything would disintegrate. The second possibility, which is called 'chiliasm',[1] implies that everything is getting better and better, but it is equally mistaken. It is false, because there is evil in any individual which cannot be diminished and because there is good which cannot be increased. To increase the good, man would need to possess more good than he has, which is untenable. The third possibility he calls 'abderitism':[2] this implies that everything gets neither better nor worse, but is simply stagnating. Good and evil seem to neutralise one another. But this is a farcical situation which must be considered unworthy of man.

We must therefore look for a principle outside experience. We can find it in the moral character of man. Outwardly, this moral character is realised in legal arrangements, i.e. by instituting a republican constitution. The French Revolution seems to him to represent this kind of event; for its aims are precisely the establishment of a republican state. To advance the spread of rationality is a moral obligation, for this advance is the only way in which our moral nature can be fully realised. It is our duty to further the establishing of a republican constitution, but it is also our duty to maintain the existing system of laws, whatever its character may be. We may, indeed we ought to improve the existing system of laws by criticism, so that it may approach the system of laws which ought to prevail in accordance with the principles of right. These aims are not chimerical; for the goal towards which history is moving is the establishment of a republican civil constitution. Since it is an ideal, it is not possible to realise it completely, but it can be approached. If it were merely to depend on man's moral decision whether a republican constitution be established, the outlook would indeed be bleak; for we must not expect too much of men. But nature is on our side. History can be interpreted only if we fully understand the conflict among men. Man is not only social, but anti-social too. The unsocial sociability, the mutual antagonism which prevails in

[1] Originally the belief that the millennium will be established on earth before the Day of Judgement.

[2] Abdera was a city in ancient Greece whose inhabitants were alleged to be extremely foolish. The name was popular in eighteenth-century Germany because of Christian Martin Wieland's novel *Geschichte der Abderiten* (*The Story of the Abderites*) (1774–81), in which human follies are satirised.

society, is thus the means which nature employs to bring about the development of all capacities implanted in men, but only in so far as the antagonism will eventually bring about an order regulated by law: 'Man wishes concord, but nature, knowing better what is good for his species, wishes discord.'[1]

Kant then certainly does not ignore the role which might and strife play in life. Like Hobbes, he sees in the antagonism among men, in the war of all against all, the mainspring for the establishment of a civil society. Logically, this view is in keeping with his assumption that, if history is the process by which man becomes rational, he cannot be rational at the beginning. Consequently, the force which serves as the mainspring of the process cannot be reason. It must be something radically different from it, such as mutual anti-rational antagonism among men.

Kant's philosophy of history is of considerable consequence for his political theory. Rebellion is condemned not only because it runs counter to the principle of law, but also because it is unnecessary in the light of historical development. Progress towards rationality, i.e. the establishment of a republican constitution, cannot be held up for long. To rebel against the powers that be would not hasten this process. It would even be likely to retard it; for rebellion would create a bad example. If a ruler sets men free there will usually at first be difficulties, even dangers, but 'men must be free in order to be able to use their power wisely in freedom'.[2] Sooner or later, reason will assert itself and the principles of right will be respected.

VIII

Such are the aims and principles of Kant's theory of politics. It is an impressive picture of a world that ought to be governed entirely by the principles of right. It would be easy to be sceptical and to dismiss the attempt as unrealistic. Kant anticipated this objection, and explicitly based his principles not on a high-minded view of man, but on a conviction, doubtless inherited from the Christian dogma of original sin, of the radical evil in human nature. Kant's principles of politics are laid down neither by tradition nor by the sovereign power. They are found neither in experience nor in nature. Like Hobbes, he believes in the power of reason to judge politics. But unlike the principles of Hobbes, they are not the logical consequences of definitions derived from a detached observation of life. They are independent of experience. Kant's principles

---

[1] *AA* VIII, 21; cf. p. 45 below.
[2] *Religion within the Limits of Reason Alone, AA* VI, 188.

are not part of an elaborate system of politics, but elementary principles which can help us to guide our actions. They can help us to orientate ourselves in politics if we wish to safeguard our freedom and that of others. They are analogous to the categorical imperative and require universal application. Kant, however, was not concerned with elaborating political programmes. For his conception of political freedom is not positive, but negative. It is concerned with those restraints which the individual must accept in order to avoid conflict with others so that he may enjoy the freedom of moral action.

For Kant, what is true in theory also applies in practice. By practice, he means the activities of practical life in a wide sense.[1] His theory of politics is capable of explaining political life; a theory based on heteronomous elements, i.e. a theory seeking to explain political life by reference to might, is unable to do so; for political life is only superficially concerned with political power. Power cannot be ignored, but the real problem of politics is to ensure right, i.e. law and justice. If we take the dignity of man, his freedom as a rational being, as the starting-point of our enquiry into political practice, only a theory of right based on principles of pure reason is capable of explaining political life. Other theories are false and thus mislead not only in their understanding of political practice, but also in their political repercussions.

The right theory does afford points of orientation for political practice, though it is never by itself enough. Prudence and practical skill are also needed in the conduct of political affairs. Kant was not a blinkered visionary, nor was he even an unpractical utopian dreamer. As a scientist, he had learnt to respect fact. His own philosophical polemics and his attitude to the government of the day reveal a keen awareness of the needs of the actual situation, and he did not resort to lying or to a flagrant compromise with his own principles.[2] He sought to follow the maxim accepted in *Perpetual Peace*: 'Be ye therefore wise as serpents, and harmless as doves.'[3]

Kant should be accorded a prominent place in the history of Western political thought, a place which has far too long been denied to him. He ought to be ranked among the leading political thinkers of all times. Plato, Aristotle, Hobbes are his peers. He is second to none in the acuteness of his thinking. His attempt to formulate rational principles of

---

[1] Dieter Henrich, Introduction to *Kant. Gentz. Rehberg. Über Theorie und Praxis*, pp. 14 ff.
[2] Hans Saner, *Kants Weg vom Krieg zum Frieden*, I: *Widerstreit und Einheit, Wege zu Kants politischem Denken* (Munich, 1967).
[3] *AA* VIII, 370; cf. p. 116 below (Matt. x. 16).

politics on which all men can, and even ought to, agree of their own accord is as important for the modern world as Hobbes' endeavour to free political thought from the quagmire of tradition and superstition. To read Kant's political writings is to scale the heights of philosophical reflection on politics. His political thought should be of interest to all those who value the use of reason in public life.

Idea for a Universal History with a Cosmopolitan Purpose[*][1]

Whatever conception of the freedom of the will one may form in terms of metaphysics, the will's manifestations in the world of phenomena, i.e. human actions, are determined in accordance with natural laws, as is every other natural event. History is concerned with giving an account of these phenomena, no matter how deeply concealed their causes may be, and it allows us to hope that, if it examines the free exercise of the human will *on a large scale*, it will be able to discover a regular progression among freely willed actions. In the same way, we may hope that what strikes us in the actions of individuals as confused and fortuitous may be recognised, in the history of the entire species, as a steadily advancing but slow development of man's original capacities. Thus marriages, births, and deaths do not seem to be subject to any rule by which their numbers could be calculated in advance, since the free human will has such a great influence upon them; and yet the annual statistics for them in large countries prove that they are just as subject to constant natural laws as are the changes in the weather, which in themselves are so inconsistent that their individual occurrence cannot be determined in advance, but which nevertheless do not fail as a whole to sustain the growth of plants, the flow of rivers, and other natural functions in a uniform and uninterrupted course. Individual men and even entire nations little imagine that, while they are pursuing their own ends, each in his own way and often in opposition to others, they are unwittingly guided in their advance along a course intended by nature. They are unconsciously promoting an end which, even if they knew what it was, would scarcely arouse their interest.

Since men neither pursue their aims purely by instinct, as the animals do, nor act in accordance with any integral, prearranged plan like rational cosmopolitans, it would appear that no law-governed history of mankind

---

* A passage printed this year among other brief notices in the twelfth issue of the *Gothaische Gelehrte Zeitungen*, based, no doubt, on a conversation of mine with a passing scholar, calls for the present elucidation, without which the passage referred to would be unintelligible.

is possible (as it would be, for example, with bees or beavers). We can scarcely help feeling a certain distaste on observing their activities as enacted in the great world-drama, for we find that, despite the apparent wisdom of individual actions here and there, everything as a whole is made up of folly and childish vanity, and often of childish malice and destructiveness. The result is that we do not know what sort of opinion we should form of our species, which is so proud of its supposed superiority. The only way out for the philosopher, since he cannot assume that mankind follows any rational *purpose of its own* in its collective actions, is for him to attempt to discover a *purpose in nature* behind this senseless course of human events, and decide whether it is after all possible to formulate in terms of a definite plan of nature a history of creatures who act without a plan of their own.—Let us now see if we can succeed in finding a guiding principle for such a history, and then leave it to nature to produce someone capable of writing it along the lines suggested. Thus nature produced a Kepler who found an unexpected means of reducing the eccentric orbits of the planets to definite laws, and a Newton who explained these laws in terms of a universal natural cause.

First Proposition

All the natural capacities of a creature are destined sooner or later to be developed completely and in conformity with their end. This can be verified in all animals by external and internal or anatomical examination. An organ which is not meant for use or an arrangement which does not fulfil its purpose is a contradiction in the teleological theory of nature. For if we abandon this basic principle, we are faced not with a law-governed nature, but with an aimless, random process, and the dismal reign of chance replaces the guiding principle of reason.

Second Proposition

In man (as the only rational creature on earth), *those natural capacities which are directed towards the use of his reason are such that they could be fully developed only in the species, but not in the individual.* Reason, in a creature, is a faculty which enables that creature to extend far beyond the limits of natural instinct the rules and intentions it follows in using its various powers, and the range of its projects is unbounded. But reason does not itself work instinctively, for it requires trial, practice and instruction to enable it to progress gradually from one stage of insight to the next. Accordingly, every individual man would have to live for a vast length of time if he were to learn how to make complete use of all his natural capacities; or if nature has fixed only a short term for each man's life (as is in fact the case), then it will require a long, perhaps incalculable series of generations, each passing on its enlightenment to the next, before the germs implanted by nature in our species can be developed to that degree which corresponds to nature's original intention. And the point of time at which this degree of development is reached must be the goal of man's aspirations (at least as an idea in his mind), or else his natural capacities would necessarily appear by and large to be purposeless and wasted. In the latter case, all practical principles would have to be abandoned, and nature, whose wisdom we must take as axiomatic in judging all other situations, would incur the suspicion of indulging in childish play in the case of man alone.

Third Proposition

Nature has willed that man should produce entirely by his own initiative everything which goes beyond the mechanical ordering of his animal existence, and that he should not partake of any other happiness or perfection than that which he has procured for himself without instinct and by his own reason. For nature does nothing unnecessarily and is not extravagant in the means employed to reach its ends. Nature gave man reason, and freedom of will based upon reason, and this in itself was a clear indication of nature's intention as regards his endowments. For it showed that man was not meant to be guided by instinct or equipped and instructed by innate knowledge; on the contrary, he was meant to produce everything out of himself. Everything had to be entirely of his own making—the discovery of a suitable diet, of clothing, of external security and defence (for which nature gave him neither the bull's horns, the lion's claws, nor the dog's teeth, but only his hands), as well as all the pleasures that can make life agreeable, and even his insight and circumspection and the goodness of his will. Nature seems here to have taken pleasure in exercising the strictest economy and to have measured out the basic animal equipment so sparingly as to be just enough for the most pressing needs of the beginnings of existence. It seems as if nature had intended that man, once he had finally worked his way up from the uttermost barbarism to the highest degree of skill, to inner perfection in his manner of thought and thence (as far as is possible on earth) to happiness, should be able to take for himself the entire credit for doing so and have only himself to thank for it. It seems that nature has worked more with a view to man's rational *self-esteem* than to his mere well-being. For in the actual course of human affairs, a whole host of hardships awaits him. Yet nature does not seem to have been concerned with seeing that man should live agreeably, but with seeing that he should work his way onwards to make himself by his own conduct worthy of life and well-being. What remains disconcerting about all this is firstly, that the earlier generations seem to perform their laborious tasks only for the sake of the later ones, so as to prepare for them a further stage from which they can raise still higher the structure intended by nature; and secondly, that only the later generations will in fact have the good fortune to inhabit the building on which a whole series of their forefathers (admittedly, without any conscious intention) had worked without themselves being able to share in the happiness they were preparing. But no matter how puzzling this may be, it will appear as necessary as it is puzzling if we simply assume that one animal species was intended to have reason, and that, as a class of rational beings who are mortal as individuals but immortal as a species, it was still meant to develop its capacities completely.

Fourth Proposition

The means which nature employs to bring about the development of innate capacities is that of antagonism within society, in so far as this antagonism becomes in the long run the cause of a law-governed social order. By antagonism, I mean in this context the *unsocial sociability* of men, that is, their tendency to come together in society, coupled, however, with a continual resistance which constantly threatens to break this society up. This propensity is obviously rooted in human nature. Man has an inclination to *live in society*, since he feels in this state more like a man, that is, he feels able to develop his natural capacities. But he also has a great tendency to *live as an individual*, to isolate himself, since he also encounters in himself the unsocial characteristic of wanting to direct everything in accordance with his own ideas. He therefore expects resistance all around, just as he knows of himself that he is in turn inclined to offer resistance to others. It is this very resistance which awakens all man's powers and induces him to overcome his tendency to laziness. Through the desire for honour, power or property, it drives him to seek status among his fellows, whom he cannot *bear* yet cannot *bear to leave*. Then the first true steps are taken from barbarism to culture, which in fact consists in the social worthiness of man. All man's talents are now gradually developed, his taste cultivated, and by a continued process of enlightenment, a beginning is made towards establishing a way of thinking which can with time transform the primitive natural capacity for moral discrimination into definite practical principles; and thus a *pathologically* enforced social union is transformed into a *moral* whole. Without these asocial qualities (far from admirable in themselves) which cause the resistance inevitably encountered by each individual as he furthers his self-seeking pretensions, man would live an Arcadian, pastoral existence of perfect concord, self-sufficiency and mutual love. But all human talents would remain hidden for ever in a dormant state, and men, as good-natured as the sheep they tended, would scarcely render their existence more valuable than that of their animals. The end for which they were created, their rational nature, would be an unfilled void. Nature should thus be thanked for fostering social incompatibility, enviously competitive vanity, and insatiable desires for possession or even power. Without these desires, all man's excellent natural capacities would never be roused to develop. Man wishes concord, but nature, knowing better what is good for his species, wishes discord. Man wishes to live comfortably and pleasantly, but nature intends that he should abandon idleness and inactive self-sufficiency and plunge instead into labour and hardships, so that he may by his own adroitness find means of liberating himself from them in turn. The natural impulses which make this possible, the sources of the very unsociableness and continual resistance which cause so many evils, at the same time encourage man towards new exertions of his powers and thus towards further development of his natural capacities. They would thus seem to indicate the design of a wise creator—not, as it might seem, the hand of a malicious spirit who had meddled in the creator's glorious work or spoiled it out of envy.

Fifth Proposition

The greatest problem for the human species, the solution of which nature compels him to seek, is that of attaining a civil society which can administer justice universally.

The highest purpose of nature—i.e. the development of all natural capacities—can be fulfilled for mankind only in society, and nature intends that man should accomplish this, and indeed all his appointed ends, by his own efforts. This purpose can be fulfilled only in a society which has not only the greatest freedom, and therefore a continual antagonism among its members, but also the most precise specification and preservation of the limits of this freedom in order that it can co-exist with the freedom of others. The highest task which nature has set for mankind must therefore be that of establishing a society in which *freedom under external laws* would be combined to the greatest possible extent with irresistible force, in other words of establishing a perfectly *just civil constitution*. For only through the solution and fulfilment of this task can nature accomplish its other intentions with our species. Man, who is otherwise so enamoured with unrestrained freedom, is forced to enter this state of restriction by sheer necessity. And this is indeed the most stringent of all forms of necessity, for it is imposed by men upon themselves, in that their inclinations make it impossible for them to exist side by side for long in a state of wild freedom. But once enclosed within a precinct like that of civil union, the same inclinations have the most beneficial effect. In the same way, trees in a forest, by seeking to deprive each other of air and sunlight, compel each other to find these by upward growth, so that they grow beautiful and straight—whereas those which put out branches at will, in freedom and in isolation from others, grow stunted, bent and twisted. All the culture and art which adorn mankind and the finest social order man creates are fruits of his unsociability. For it is compelled by its own nature to discipline itself, and thus, by enforced art, to develop completely the germs which nature implanted.

Sixth Proposition

This problem is both the most difficult and the last to be solved by the human race. The difficulty (which the very idea of this problem clearly presents) is this: if he lives among others of his own species, man is *an animal who needs a master*. For he certainly abuses his freedom in relation to others of his own kind. And even although, as a rational creature, he desires a law to impose limits on the freedom of all, he is still misled by his self-seeking animal inclinations into exempting himself from the law where he can. He thus requires a *master* to break his self-will and force him to obey a universally valid will under which everyone can be free. But where is he to find such a master? Nowhere else but in the human species. But this master will also be an animal who needs a master. Thus while man may try as he will, it is hard to see how he can obtain for public justice a supreme authority which would itself be just, whether he seeks this authority in a single person or in a group of many persons selected for this purpose. For each one of them will always misuse his freedom if he does not have anyone above him to apply force to him as the laws should require it. Yet the highest authority has to be just *in itself* and yet also a *man*. This is therefore the most difficult of all tasks, and a perfect solution is impossible. Nothing straight can be constructed from such warped wood as that which man is made of. Nature only requires of us that we should approximate to this idea.* A further reason why this task must be the last to be accomplished is that man needs for it a correct conception of the nature of a possible constitution, great experience tested in many affairs of the world, and above all else a good will prepared to accept the findings of this experience. But three factors such as these will not easily be found in conjunction, and if they are, it will happen only at a late stage and after many unsuccessful attempts.

Seventh Proposition

*The problem of establishing a perfect civil constitution is subordinate to the problem of a law-governed **external relationship** with other states, and cannot be solved unless the latter is also solved.* What is the use of working for a law-governed civil constitution among individual men, i.e. of planning a *commonwealth*? The same unsociability which forced men to do so gives rise in turn to a situation whereby each commonwealth, in its external relations (i.e. as a state in relation to other states), is in a position of unrestricted freedom. Each must accordingly expect from any other precisely the same evils which formerly oppressed individual men and forced them into a law-governed civil state. Nature has thus again employed the unsociableness of men, and even of the large societies and states which human beings construct, as a means of arriving at a condition of calm and security through their inevitable *antagonism*. Wars, tense and unremitting military preparations, and the resultant distress which every state must eventually feel within itself, even in the midst of peace—these are the means by which nature drives nations to make initially imperfect attempts, but finally, after many devastations, upheavals and even complete inner exhaustion of their powers, to take the step which reason could have suggested to them even without so many sad experiences—that of abandoning a lawless state of savagery and entering a federation of peoples in which every state, even the smallest, could expect to derive its security and rights not from its own power or its own legal judgement, but solely from this great federation (*Foedus Amphictyonum*), from a united power and the law-governed decisions of a united will. However wild and fanciful this idea may appear—and it has been ridiculed as such when put forward by the Abbé St Pierre[2] and Rousseau[3] (perhaps because they

* Man's role is thus a highly artificial one. We do not know how it is with the inhabitants of other planets and with their nature, but if we ourselves execute this commission of nature well, we may surely flatter ourselves that we occupy no mean status among our neighbours in the cosmos. Perhaps their position is such that each individual can fulfil his destiny completely within his own lifetime. With us it is otherwise; only the species as a whole can hope for this.

thought that its realisation was so imminent)—it is nonetheless the inevitable outcome of the distress in which men involve one another. For this distress must force the states to make exactly the same decision (however difficult it may be for them) as that which man was forced to make, equally unwillingly, in his savage state—the decision to renounce his brutish freedom and seek calm and security within a law-governed constitution. All wars are accordingly so many attempts (not indeed by the intention of men, but by the intention of nature) to bring about new relations between states, and, by the destruction or at least the dismemberment of old entities, to create new ones. But these new bodies, either in themselves or alongside one another, will in turn be unable to survive, and will thus necessarily undergo further revolutions of a similar sort, till finally, partly by an optimal internal arrangement of the civil constitution, and partly by common external agreement and legislation, a state of affairs is created which, like a civil commonwealth, can maintain itself *automatically*.

Whether we should firstly expect that the states, by an Epicurean concourse[4] of efficient causes, should enter by random collisions (like those of small material particles) into all kinds of formations which are again destroyed by new collisions, until they arrive *by chance* at a formation which can survive in its existing form (a lucky accident which is hardly likely ever to occur); or whether we should assume as a second possibility that nature in this case follows a regular course in leading our species gradually upwards from the lower level of animality to the highest level of humanity through forcing man to employ an art which is nonetheless his own, and hence that nature develops man's original capacities by a perfectly regular process within this apparently disorderly arrangement; or whether we should rather accept the third possibility that nothing at all, or at least nothing rational, will anywhere emerge from all these actions and counter-actions among men as a whole, that things will remain as they have always been, and that it would thus be impossible to predict whether the discord which is so natural to our species is not preparing the way for a hell of evils to overtake us, however civilised our condition, in that nature, by barbaric devastation, might perhaps again destroy this civilised state and all the cultural progress hitherto achieved (a fate against which it would be impossible to guard under a rule of blind chance, with which the state of lawless freedom is in fact identical, unless we assume that the latter is secretly guided by the wisdom of nature)—these three possibilities boil down to the question of whether it is rational to assume that the order of nature is *purposive* in its parts but *purposeless* as a whole.

While the purposeless state of savagery did hold up the development of all the natural capacities of human beings, it nonetheless finally forced them, through the evils in which it involved them, to leave this state and enter into a civil constitution in which all their dormant capacities could be developed. The same applies to the barbarous freedom of established states. For while the full development of natural capacities is here likewise held up by the expenditure of each commonwealth's whole resources on armaments against the others, and by the depredations caused by war (but most of all by the necessity of constantly remaining in readiness for war), the resultant evils still have a beneficial effect. For they compel our species to discover a law of equilibrium to regulate the essentially healthy hostility which prevails among the states and is produced by their freedom. Men are compelled to reinforce this law by introducing a system of united power, hence a cosmopolitan system of general political security. This state of affairs is not completely free from *danger*, lest human energies should lapse into inactivity, but it is also not without a principle of *equality* governing the *actions and counter-actions* of these energies, lest they should destroy one another. When it is little beyond the half-way mark in its development, human nature has to endure the hardest of evils under the guise of outward prosperity before this final step (i.e. the union of states) is taken; and Rousseau's preference for the state of savagery does not appear so very mistaken if only we leave out of consideration this last stage which our species still has to surmount. We are *cultivated* to a high degree by art and science. We are *civilised* to the point of excess in all kinds of social courtesies and proprieties. But we are still a long way from the point where we could consider ourselves *morally* mature. For while the idea of morality is indeed present in culture, an application of this idea which only extends to the semblances of morality, as in love of honour and outward propriety, amounts merely to civilisation. But as long as states apply all their resources to their vain and violent schemes of expansion, thus incessantly obstructing the slow and laborious efforts of their citizens to cultivate their minds, and even deprive them of all support in these efforts, no progress in this direction can be expected. For a long internal process of careful work on the part of each commonwealth is necessary for the education of its citizens. But all good enterprises which are not grafted on to a morally good attitude of mind are nothing but illusion and outwardly glittering misery. The human race will no doubt remain in this condition until it has worked itself out of the chaotic state of its political relations in the way I have described.

Eighth Proposition

The history of the human race as a whole can be regarded as the realisation of a hidden plan of nature to bring about an internally—and for this purpose also externally—perfect political constitution as the only possible state within which all natural capacities of mankind can be developed completely. This proposition follows from the previous one. We can see that philosophy too may have its *chiliastic*[5] expectations; but they are of such a kind that their fulfilment can be hastened, if only indirectly, by a knowledge of the idea they are based on, so that they are anything but over-fanciful. The real test is whether experience can discover anything to indicate a purposeful natural process of this kind. In my opinion, it can discover *a little*; for this cycle of events seems to take so long a time to complete, that the small part of it traversed by mankind up till now does not allow us to determine with certainty the shape of the whole cycle, and the relation of its parts to the whole. It is no easier than it is to determine, from all hitherto available astronomical observations, the path which our sun with its whole swarm of satellites is following within the vast system of the fixed stars; although from the general premise that the universe is constituted as a system and from the little which has been learnt by observation, we can conclude with sufficient certainty that a movement of this kind does exist in reality. Nevertheless, human nature is such that it cannot be indifferent even to the most remote epoch which may eventually affect our species, so long as this epoch can be expected with certainty. And in the present case, it is especially hard to be indifferent, for it appears that we might by our own rational projects accelerate the coming of this period which will be so welcome to our descendants. For this reason, even the faintest signs of its approach will be extremely important to us. The mutual relationships between states are already so sophisticated that none of them can neglect its internal culture without losing power and influence in relation to the others. Thus the purpose of nature is at least fairly well safeguarded (if not actually furthered) even by the ambitious schemes of the various states. Furthermore, civil freedom can no longer be so easily infringed without disadvantage to all trades and industries, and especially to commerce, in the event of which the state's power in its external relations will also decline. But this freedom is gradually increasing. If the citizen is deterred from seeking his personal welfare in any way he chooses which is consistent with the freedom of others, the vitality of business in general and hence also the strength of the whole are held in check. For this reason, restrictions placed upon personal activities are increasingly relaxed, and general freedom of religion is granted. And thus, although folly and caprice creep in at times, *enlightenment* gradually arises. It is a great benefit which the human race must reap even from its rulers' self-seeking schemes of expansion, if only they realise what is to their own advantage. But this enlightenment, and with it a certain sympathetic interest which the enlightened man inevitably feels for anything good which he comprehends fully, must gradually spread upwards towards the thrones and even influence their principles of government. But while, for example, the world's present rulers have no money to spare for public educational institutions or indeed for anything which concerns the world's best interests (for everything has already been calculated out in advance for the next war), they will nonetheless find that it is to their own advantage at least not to hinder their citizens' private efforts in this direction, however weak and slow they may be. But eventually, war itself gradually becomes not only a highly artificial undertaking, extremely uncertain in its outcome for both parties, but also a very dubious risk to take, since its aftermath is felt by the state in the shape of a constantly increasing national debt (a modern invention) whose repayment becomes interminable. And in addition, the effects which an upheaval in any state produces upon all the others in our continent, where all are so closely linked by trade, are so perceptible that these other states are forced by their own insecurity to offer themselves as arbiters, albeit without legal authority, so that they indirectly prepare the way for a great political body of the future, without precedent in the past. Although this political body exists for the present only in the roughest of outlines, it nonetheless seems as if a feeling is beginning to stir in all its members, each of which has an interest in maintaining the whole. And this encourages the hope that, after many revolutions, with all their transforming effects, the highest purpose of nature, a universal *cosmopolitan existence*, will at last be realised as the matrix within which all the original capacities of the human race may develop.

Ninth Proposition

A philosophical attempt to work out a universal history of the world in accordance with a plan of nature aimed at a perfect civil union of mankind, must be regarded as possible and even as capable of furthering the purpose of nature itself. It is admittedly a strange and at first sight absurd proposition to write a *history* according to an idea of how world events must develop if they are to conform to certain rational ends; it would seem that only a *novel* could result from such premises. Yet if it may be assumed that nature does not work without a plan and purposeful end, even amidst the arbitrary play of human freedom, this idea might nevertheless prove useful. And although we are too short-sighted to perceive the hidden mechanism of nature's scheme, this idea may yet serve as a guide to us in representing an otherwise planless *aggregate* of human actions as conforming, at least when considered as a whole, to a *system*. For if we start out from *Greek* history as that in which all other earlier or contemporary histories are preserved or at least authenticated,* if we next trace the influence of the Greeks upon the shaping and mis-shaping of the body politic of *Rome*, which engulfed the Greek state, and follow down to our own times the influence of Rome upon the *Barbarians* who in turn destroyed it, and if we finally add the political history of other peoples *episodically*, in so far as knowledge of them has gradually come down to us through these enlightened nations, we shall discover a regular process of improvement in the political constitutions of our continent (which will probably legislate eventually for all other continents). Furthermore, we must always concentrate our attention on civil constitutions, their laws, and the mutual relations among states, and notice how these factors, by virtue of the good they contained, served for a time to elevate and glorify nations (and with them the arts and sciences). Conversely, we should observe how their inherent defects led to their overthrow, but in such a way that a germ of enlightenment always survived, developing further with each revolution, and prepared the way for a subsequent higher level of improvement.

All this, I believe, should give us some guidance in explaining the thoroughly confused interplay of human affairs and in prophesying future political changes. Yet the same use has already been made of human history even when it was regarded as the disjointed product of unregulated freedom. But if we assume a plan of nature, we have grounds for greater hopes. For such a plan opens up the comforting prospect of a future in which we are shown from afar how the human race eventually works its way upward to a situation in which all the germs implanted by nature can be developed fully, and in which man's destiny can be fulfilled

---

* Only an *educated public* which has existed uninterruptedly from its origin to our times can authenticate ancient history. Beyond that, all is *terra incognita*;[6] and the history of peoples who lived outside this public can begin only from the time at which they entered it. This occurred with the *Jewish* people at the time of the Ptolemies through the Greek translation of the Bible,[7] without which their *isolated* reports would meet with little belief. From this point, once it has been properly ascertained, their narratives can be followed backwards. And it is the same with all other peoples. The first page of Thucydides, as Hume[8] puts it, is the only beginning of all true history.

here on earth. Such a *justification* of nature—or rather perhaps of *providence*—is no mean motive for adopting a particular point of view in considering the world. For what is the use of lauding and holding up for contemplation the glory and wisdom of creation in the non-rational sphere of nature, if the history of mankind, the very part of this great display of supreme wisdom which contains the purpose of all the rest, is to remain a constant reproach to everything else? Such a spectacle would force us to turn away in revulsion, and, by making us despair of ever finding any completed rational aim behind it, would reduce us to hoping for it only in some other world.

It would be a misinterpretation of my intention to contend that I meant this idea of a universal history, which to some extent follows an *a priori* rule, to supersede the task of history proper, that of *empirical* composition. My idea is only a notion of what a philosophical mind, well acquainted with history, might be able to attempt from a different angle. Besides, the otherwise praiseworthy detail in which each age now composes its history must naturally cause everyone concern as to how our remote descendants will manage to cope with the burden of history which we shall bequeath to them a few centuries from now. No doubt they will value the history of the oldest times, of which the original documents would long since have vanished, only from the point of view of what interests *them*, i.e. the positive and negative achievements of nations and governments in relation to the cosmopolitan goal. We should bear this in mind, and we should likewise observe the ambitions of rulers and their servants, in order to indicate to them the only means by which they can be honourably remembered in the most distant ages. And this may provide us with another *small* motive for attempting a philosophical history of this kind.

An Answer to the Question: 'What is Enlightenment?'[1]

Enlightenment is man's emergence from his self-incurred immaturity.
Immaturity is the inability to use one's own understanding without the
guidance of another. This immaturity is *self-incurred* if its cause is not
lack of understanding, but lack of resolution and courage to use it without
the guidance of another. The motto of enlightenment is therefore: *Sapere
aude!*[2] Have courage to use your *own* understanding!

Laziness and cowardice are the reasons why such a large proportion of
men, even when nature has long emancipated them from alien guidance
(*naturaliter maiorennes*),[3] nevertheless gladly remain immature for life.
For the same reasons, it is all too easy for others to set themselves up as
their guardians. It is so convenient to be immature! If I have a book to
have understanding in place of me, a spiritual adviser to have a conscience
for me, a doctor to judge my diet for me, and so on, I need not make any
efforts at all. I need not think, so long as I can pay; others will soon enough
take the tiresome job over for me. The guardians who have kindly taken
upon themselves the work of supervision will soon see to it that by far
the largest part of mankind (including the entire fair sex) should consider
the step forward to maturity not only as difficult but also as highly
dangerous. Having first infatuated their domesticated animals, and carefully prevented the docile creatures from daring to take a single step without the leading-strings to which they are tied, they next show them the
danger which threatens them if they try to walk unaided. Now this danger
is not in fact so very great, for they would certainly learn to walk eventually after a few falls. But an example of this kind is intimidating, and
usually frightens them off from further attempts.

Thus it is difficult for each separate individual to work his way out of
the immaturity which has become almost second nature to him. He has
even grown fond of it and is really incapable for the time being of using
his own understanding, because he was never allowed to make the attempt.
Dogmas and formulas, those mechanical instruments for rational use (or

rather misuse) of his natural endowments, are the ball and chain of his permanent immaturity. And if anyone did throw them off, he would still be uncertain about jumping over even the narrowest of trenches, for he would be unaccustomed to free movement of this kind. Thus only a few, by cultivating their own minds, have succeeded in freeing themselves from immaturity and in continuing boldly on their way.

There is more chance of an entire public enlightening itself. This is indeed almost inevitable, if only the public concerned is left in freedom. For there will always be a few who think for themselves, even among those appointed as guardians of the common mass. Such guardians, once they have themselves thrown off the yoke of immaturity, will disseminate the spirit of rational respect for personal value and for the duty of all men to think for themselves. The remarkable thing about this is that if the public, which was previously put under this yoke by the guardians, is suitably stirred up by some of the latter who are incapable of enlightenment, it may subsequently compel the guardians themselves to remain under the yoke. For it is very harmful to propagate prejudices, because they finally avenge themselves on the very people who first encouraged them (or whose predecessors did so). Thus a public can only achieve enlightenment slowly. A revolution may well put an end to autocratic despotism and to rapacious or power-seeking oppression, but it will never produce a true reform in ways of thinking. Instead, new prejudices, like the ones they replaced, will serve as a leash to control the great unthinking mass.

For enlightenment of this kind, all that is needed is *freedom*. And the freedom in question is the most innocuous form of all—freedom to make *public use* of one's reason in all matters. But I hear on all sides the cry: *Don't argue!* The officer says: Don't argue, get on parade! The tax-official: Don't argue, pay! The clergyman: Don't argue, believe! (Only one ruler in the world says: *Argue* as much as you like and about whatever you like, *but obey!*)[4] All this means restrictions on freedom everywhere. But which sort of restriction prevents enlightenment, and which, instead of hindering it, can actually promote it? I reply: The *public* use of man's reason must always be free, and it alone can bring about enlightenment among men; the *private use* of reason may quite often be very narrowly restricted, however, without undue hindrance to the progress of enlightenment. But by the public use of one's own reason I mean that use which anyone may make of it *as a man of learning* addressing the entire *reading public*. What I term the private use of reason is that which a person may make of it in a particular *civil* post or office with which he is entrusted.

Now in some affairs which affect the interests of the commonwealth, we require a certain mechanism whereby some members of the commonwealth must behave purely passively, so that they may, by an artificial common agreement, be employed by the government for public ends (or at least deterred from vitiating them). It is, of course, impermissible to argue in such cases; obedience is imperative. But in so far as this or that individual who acts as part of the machine also considers himself as a member of a complete commonwealth or even of cosmopolitan society, and thence as a man of learning who may through his writings address a public in the truest sense of the word, he may indeed argue without harming the affairs in which he is employed for some of the time in a passive capacity. Thus it would be very harmful if an officer receiving an order from his superiors were to quibble openly, while on duty, about the appropriateness or usefulness of the order in question. He must simply obey. But he cannot reasonably be banned from making observations as a man of learning on the errors in the military service, and from submitting these to his public for judgement. The citizen cannot refuse to pay the taxes imposed upon him; presumptuous criticisms of such taxes, where someone is called upon to pay them, may be punished as an outrage which could lead to general insubordination. Nonetheless, the same citizen does not contravene his civil obligations if, as a learned individual, he publicly voices his thoughts on the impropriety or even injustice of such fiscal measures. In the same way, a clergyman is bound to instruct his pupils and his congregation in accordance with the doctrines of the church he serves, for he was employed by it on that condition. But as a scholar, he is completely free as well as obliged to impart to the public all his carefully considered, well-intentioned thoughts on the mistaken aspects of those doctrines, and to offer suggestions for a better arrangement of religious and ecclesiastical affairs. And there is nothing in this which need trouble the conscience. For what he teaches in pursuit of his duties as an active servant of the church is presented by him as something which he is not empowered to teach at his own discretion, but which he is employed to expound in a prescribed manner and in someone else's name. He will say: Our church teaches this or that, and these are the arguments it uses. He then extracts as much practical value as possible for his congregation from precepts to which he would not himself subscribe with full conviction, but which he can nevertheless undertake to expound, since it is not in fact wholly impossible that they may contain truth. At all events, nothing opposed to the essence of religion is present in such doctrines. For if the clergyman thought he could find anything of this sort in them, he would not be able to carry out his official duties in good conscience, and would have to resign. Thus the use which someone employed as a teacher makes of his reason in the presence of his congregation is purely *private*, since a congregation, however large it is, is never any more than a domestic gathering. In view of this, he is not and cannot be free as a priest, since he is acting on a commission imposed from outside. Conversely, as a scholar addressing the real public (i.e. the world at large) through his writings, the clergyman making *public use* of his reason enjoys unlimited freedom to use his own reason and to speak in his own person. For to maintain that the guardians of the people in spiritual matters should themselves be immature, is an absurdity which amounts to making absurdities permanent.

But should not a society of clergymen, for example an ecclesiastical synod or a venerable presbytery (as the Dutch call it), be entitled to commit itself by oath to a certain unalterable set of doctrines, in order to secure for all time a constant guardianship over each of its members, and through them over the people? I reply that this is quite impossible. A contract of this kind, concluded with a view to preventing all further enlightenment of mankind for ever, is absolutely null and void, even if it is ratified by the supreme power, by Imperial Diets and the most solemn peace treaties. One age cannot enter into an alliance on oath to put the next age in a position where it would be impossible for it to extend and correct its knowledge, particularly on such important matters, or to make any progress whatsoever in enlightenment. This would be a crime against human nature, whose original destiny lies precisely in such progress. Later generations are thus perfectly entitled to dismiss these agreements as unauthorised and criminal. To test whether any particular measure can be agreed upon as a law for a people, we need only ask whether a people could well impose such a law upon itself. This might well be possible for a specified short period as a means of introducing a certain order, pending, as it were, a better solution. This would also mean that each citizen, particularly the clergyman, would be given a free hand as a scholar to comment publicly, i.e. in his writings, on the inadequacies of current institutions. Meanwhile, the newly established order would continue to exist, until public insight into the nature of such matters had progressed and proved itself to the point where, by general consent (if not unanimously), a proposal could be submitted to the crown. This would seek to protect the congregations who had, for instance, agreed to alter their religious establishment in accordance with their own notions of what higher insight is, but it would not try to obstruct those who wanted to let things remain as before. But it is absolutely impermissible to agree, even for a single lifetime, to a permanent religious constitution which no-one might publicly question. For this would virtually nullify a phase in man's upward progress, thus making it fruitless and even detrimental to subsequent generations. A man may for his own person, and even then only for a limited period, postpone enlightening himself in matters he ought to know about. But to renounce such enlightenment completely, whether for his own person or even more so for later generations, means violating and trampling underfoot the sacred rights of mankind. But something which a people may not even impose upon itself can still less be imposed on it by a monarch; for his legislative authority depends precisely upon his uniting the collective will of the people in his own. So long as he sees to it that all true or imagined improvements are compatible with the civil order, he can otherwise leave his subjects to do whatever they find necessary for their salvation, which is none of his business. But it is his business to stop anyone forcibly hindering others from working as best they can to define and promote their salvation. It indeed detracts from his majesty if he interferes in these affairs by subjecting the writings in which his subjects attempt to clarify their religious ideas to governmental supervision. This applies if he does so acting upon his own exalted opinions—in which case he exposes himself to the reproach: *Caesar non est supra Grammaticos*[5]—but much more so if he demeans his high authority so far as to support the spiritual despotism of a few tyrants within his state against the rest of his subjects.

If it is now asked whether we at present live in an *enlightened* age, the answer is: No, but we do live in an age of *enlightenment*. As things are at present, we still have a long way to go before men as a whole can be in a position (or can even be put into a position) of using their own understanding confidently and well in religious matters, without outside guidance. But we do have distinct indications that the way is now being cleared for them to work freely in this direction, and that the obstacles to universal enlightenment, to man's emergence from his self-incurred immaturity, are gradually becoming fewer. In this respect our age is the age of enlightenment, the century of *Frederick*.[6]

A prince who does not regard it as beneath him to say that he considers it his duty, in religious matters, not to prescribe anything to his people, but to allow them complete freedom, a prince who thus even declines to accept the presumptuous title of *tolerant*, is himself enlightened. He deserves to be praised by a grateful present and posterity as the man who first liberated mankind from immaturity (as far as government is concerned), and who left all men free to use their own reason in all matters of conscience. Under his rule, ecclesiastical dignitaries, notwithstanding their official duties, may in their capacity as scholars freely and publicly submit to the judgement of the world their verdicts and opinions, even if these deviate here and there from orthodox doctrine. This applies even more to all others who are not restricted by any official duties. This spirit of freedom is also spreading abroad, even where it has to struggle with outward obstacles imposed by governments which misunderstand their own function. For such governments can now witness a shining example of how freedom may exist without in the least jeopardising public concord and the unity of the commonwealth. Men will of their own accord gradually work their way out of barbarism so long as artificial measures are not deliberately adopted to keep them in it.

I have portrayed *matters of religion* as the focal point of enlightenment, i.e. of man's emergence from his self-incurred immaturity. This is firstly because our rulers have no interest in assuming the role of guardians over their subjects so far as the arts and sciences are concerned, and secondly, because religious immaturity is the most pernicious and dishonourable variety of all. But the attitude of mind of a head of state who favours freedom in the arts and sciences extends even further, for he realises that there is no danger even to his *legislation* if he allows his subjects to make *public* use of their own reason and to put before the public their thoughts on better ways of drawing up laws, even if this entails forthright criticism of the current legislation. We have before us a brilliant example of this kind, in which no monarch has yet surpassed the one to whom we now pay tribute.

But only a ruler who is himself enlightened and has no fear of phantoms, yet who likewise has at hand a well-disciplined and numerous army to guarantee public security, may say what no republic would dare to say: *Argue as much as you like and about whatever you like, but obey!* This reveals to us a strange and unexpected pattern in human affairs (such as we shall always find if we consider them in the widest sense, in which nearly everything is paradoxical). A high degree of civil freedom seems advantageous to a people's *intellectual* freedom, yet it also sets up insuperable barriers to it. Conversely, a lesser degree of civil freedom gives intellectual freedom enough room to expand to its fullest extent. Thus once the germ on which nature has lavished most care—man's inclination and vocation to *think freely*—has developed within this hard shell, it gradually reacts upon the mentality of the people, who thus gradually become increasingly able to *act freely*. Eventually, it even influences the principles of governments, which find that they can themselves profit by treating man, who is *more than a machine*,[7] in a manner appropriate to his dignity.*

Königsberg in Prussia, 30th September, 1784.

* I read today on the 30th September in Büsching's[8] *Wöchentliche Nachrichten* of 13th September a notice concerning this month's *Berlinische Monatsschrift*. The notice mentions Mendelssohn's[9] answer to the same question as that which I have answered. I have not yet seen this journal, otherwise I should have held back the above reflections. I let them stand only as a means of finding out by comparison how far the thoughts of two individuals may coincide by chance.

On the Common Saying: 'This May be True in Theory, but it does not Apply in Practice'[1]

A collection of rules, even of practical rules, is termed a *theory* if the rules concerned are envisaged as principles of a fairly general nature, and if they are abstracted from numerous conditions which, nonetheless, necessarily influence their practical application. Conversely, not all activities are called *practice*, but only those realisations of a particular purpose which are considered to comply with certain generally conceived principles of procedure.

It is obvious that no matter how complete the theory may be, a middle term is required between theory and practice, providing a link and a transition from one to the other. For a concept of the understanding, which contains the general rule, must be supplemented by an act of judgement whereby the practitioner distinguishes instances where the rule applies from those where it does not. And since rules cannot in turn be provided on every occasion to direct the judgement in subsuming each instance under the previous rule (for this would involve an infinite regress), theoreticians will be found who can never in all their lives become practical, since they lack judgement. There are, for example, doctors or lawyers who did well during their schooling but who do not know how to act when asked to give advice. But even where a natural talent for judgement is present, there may still be a lack of premises. In other words, the theory may be incomplete, and can perhaps be perfected only by future experiments and experiences from which the newly qualified doctor, agriculturalist or economist can and ought to abstract new rules for himself to complete his theory. It is therefore not the fault of the theory if it is of little practical use in such cases. The fault is that there is *not enough* theory; the person concerned ought to have learnt from experience. What he learnt from experience might well be true theory, even if he were unable to impart it to others and to expound it as a teacher in systematic general propositions, and were consequently unable to claim the title of a theoretical physician, agriculturalist or the like. Thus no-one can pretend to be practically versed in a branch of knowledge and yet treat theory with scorn, without exposing the fact that he is an ignoramus in his subject. He no doubt imagines that he can get further than he could through theory if he gropes around in experiments and experiences, without collecting certain principles (which in fact amount to what we term theory) and without relating his activities to an integral whole (which, if treated methodically, is what we call a system).

Yet it is easier to excuse an ignoramus who claims that theory is unnecessary and superfluous in his supposed practice than a would-be expert who admits the value of theory for teaching purposes, for example as a mental exercise, but at the same time maintains that it is quite different in practice, and that anyone leaving his studies to go out into the world will realise he has been pursuing empty ideals and philosopher's dreams—in short, that whatever sounds good in theory has no practical validity. (This doctrine is often expressed as: 'this or that proposition is valid *in thesi*, but not *in hypothesi*'.) Now all of us would merely ridicule the empirical engineer who criticised general mechanics or the artilleryman who criticised the mathematical theory of ballistics by declaring that, while the theory is ingeniously conceived, it is not valid in practice, since experience in applying it gives results quite different from those predicted theoretically. For if mechanics were supplemented by the theory of friction and ballistics by the theory of air resistance, in other words if only more theory were added, these theoretical disciplines would harmonise very well with practice. But a theory which concerns objects of perception[2] is quite different from one in which such objects are represented only through concepts, as with objects of mathematics and of philosophy. The latter objects can perhaps quite legitimately be *thought* of by reason, yet it may be impossible for them to be *given*. They may merely exist as empty ideas which either cannot be used at all in practice or only with some practical disadvantages. This would mean that the aforesaid common saying might well be correct in such cases.

But in a theory founded on the *concept of duty*, any worries about the empty ideality of the concept completely disappear. For it would not be a duty to strive after a certain effect of our will if this effect were impossible in experience (whether we envisage the experience as complete or as progressively approximating to completion). And it is with theory of this kind that the present essay is exclusively concerned. For to the shame of philosophy, it is not uncommonly alleged of such theory that whatever may be correct in it is in fact invalid in practice. We usually hear this said in an arrogant, disdainful tone, which comes of presuming to use experience to reform reason itself in the very attributes which do it most credit. Such illusory wisdom imagines it can see further and more clearly with its mole-like gaze fixed on experience than with the eyes which were bestowed on a being designed to stand upright and to scan the heavens.

This maxim, so very common in our sententious, inactive times, does very great harm if applied to matters of morality, i.e. to moral or legal duty. For in such cases, the canon of reason is related to practice in such a way that the value of the practice depends entirely upon its appropriateness to the theory it is based on; all is lost if the empirical (hence contingent) conditions governing the execution of the law are made into conditions of the law itself, so that a practice calculated to produce a result which *previous* experience makes probable is given the right to dominate a theory which is in fact self-sufficient.

I shall divide up this essay in terms of three points of view which the worthy gentleman[3] who so boldly criticises theories and systems adopts in judging his objects. The three attitudes are those of the private individual or *man of affairs*, the *statesman*, and the *man of the world* or cosmopolitan. These three individuals are united in attacking the *academic*, who works for them all, for their own good, on matters of theory. Since they fancy that they understand this better than he does, they seek to relegate him to his classroom (*illa se iactet in aula!*)[4] as a pedant who, unfitted for practical affairs, merely stands in the way of their experienced wisdom.

We shall therefore deal with the relationship of theory to practice in three separate areas: firstly in *morality* in general, with regard to the welfare of each *individual man*, secondly in *politics*, with regard to the welfare of *states*, and thirdly in the *cosmopolitical* sphere, with regard to the welfare of the *human race* as a whole, in so far as the welfare of mankind is increasing within a series of developments extending into all future ages. The titles of the sections, for reasons arising out of the essay itself, will express the relationship of theory to practice in *morality*, in *political right* [*Staatsrecht*], and in *international right* [*Völkerrecht*].[5]

I

ON THE RELATIONSHIP OF THEORY TO PRACTICE IN MORALITY IN GENERAL

(In Reply to some Objections by Professor Garve*)[6]

Before I proceed to the actual controversy over what is valid in theory and practice in the application of one and the same concept, I must compare my theory, as I have myself presented it elsewhere, with the picture which Professor Garve presents of it. We may thus see in advance whether we have understood one another.

A. I had provisionally designated the study of morals as the introduction to a discipline which would teach us not how to be happy, but how we should become worthy of happiness.† Nor had I omitted to point out at the same time that man is not thereby expected to *renounce* his natural aim of attaining happiness as soon as the question of following his duty arises; for like any finite rational being, he simply cannot do so. Instead, he must completely *abstract* from such considerations as soon as the imperative of duty supervenes, and must on no account make them a *condition* of his obeying the law prescribed to him by reason. He must indeed make every possible conscious effort to ensure that no *motive* derived from the desire for happiness imperceptibly infiltrates his conceptions of duty. To do this, he should think rather of the sacrifices which obedience to duty (i.e. virtue) entails than of the benefits he might reap from it, so that he will comprehend the imperative of duty in its full authority as a self-sufficient law, independent of all other influences, which requires unconditional obedience.

a. This proposition of mine is expressed by Garve as follows: I had asserted 'that adherence to the moral law, regardless of happiness, is *the*

---

* Cf. *Versuche über verschiedne Gegenstände aus der Moral und Literatur* (*Essays on Various Topics from Morality and Literature*), by C. Garve, Pt. I, pp. 111–16. I call this estimable writer's disagreements with my propositions *objections*, for they concern matters in which (as I hope) he wishes to reach agreement with me. They are not attacks, which are disparaging statements designed to provoke defence, for which I here find neither the space nor the inclination.

† Being worthy of happiness is that quality of a person which depends upon the subject's own individual free will and in accordance with which a universal reason, legislating both to nature and to the free will, would agree with all the aims of that person. It is thus entirely different from any aptitude for attaining happiness itself. For if a person's will does not harmonise with the only form of will which is fit to legislate universally to the reason, and thus cannot be contained within the latter (in other words, if his will conflicts with morality), he is not worthy of happiness and of that gift of attaining happiness with which nature endowed him.

one and only ultimate end for man, and that it must be considered as the creator's unique intention'. (My theory is that the creator's unique inten tion is neither human morality in itself nor happiness in itself, but the highest good possible on earth, the union and harmony of them both.)

B. I had further noted that this concept of duty does not need to be based on any particular end, but rather itself *occasions* a new end for the human will, that of striving with all one's power towards the highest good possible on earth, towards the universal happiness of the whole world, combined with and in keeping with the purest morality. Since the attain- ment of this good lies within our power in one of its two aspects, but not in both taken together, it elicits from our reason a faith, *for practical purposes*, in a moral being who governs the world, and in a future existence. This does not mean that faith in both of these is a necessary condition lending 'support and stability' (i.e. a solid foundation and enough strength to constitute a *motive*) to the general concept of duty. It merely ensures that this concept acquires an *object* in the shape of an ideal of pure reason.* For in itself, duty is nothing more than a *limitation* of the will within a universal legislation which was made possible by an initially

---

* The necessity of assuming as the ultimate end of all things a *highest good* on earth, which it is possible to achieve with our collaboration, is not a necessity created by a lack of moral incentives, but by a lack of external circumstances within which an object appropriate to these incentives can alone be produced as an end in itself, as an *ultimate moral end*. For there can be no *will* without an end in view, although we must abstract from this end whenever the question of straightforward legal compulsion of our deeds arises, in which case the law alone becomes its determinant. But not every end is moral (that of personal happiness, for example, is not); the end must be an unselfish one. And the necessity of an ultimate end posited by pure reason and comprehending the totality of all ends within a single principle (i.e. a world in which the highest possible good can be realised with our collaboration) is a necessity experienced by the unselfish will as it *rises beyond* mere obedience to formal laws and creates as its own object the highest good. This idea of the totality of all ends is a peculiar kind of determinant for the will. For it basically implies that *if* we stand in a moral relationship to things in the world around us, we must everywhere obey the moral law; and to this is added the further duty of working with all our power to *ensure* that the state of affairs described (i.e. a world conforming to the highest moral ends) will actually exist. In all this, man may see himself as analogous to the divinity. For while the divinity has no subjective need of any external object, it cannot be conceived of as closed up within itself, but only as compelled by the very awareness of its own all-sufficiency to produce the highest good outside itself. In the case of the supreme being, this necessity (which corresponds to duty in man) can be envisaged *by us* only as a moral need. With man likewise, the motive provided by the idea of the highest possible earthly good, attainable through his collaboration, is there- fore not that of his own intended happiness, but only that of the idea as an end in itself and of obedience to it as a duty. For it does not hold out any prospect of happiness in the absolute sense, but only of a constant ratio between happiness and the worthiness of the subject, whatever the latter may be. But a determinant of the will which imposes this restriction both on itself and on its intention of becoming part of a whole such as we have described is *not selfish*.

accepted maxim. The object or aim of the will can be of any kind what-soever (even including happiness). But in this case, we completely abstract from whatever particular end is adopted. Thus so far as the *principle* of morality is concerned, the doctrine of the *highest good* as the ultimate end of a will which is determined by this doctrine and which conforms to its laws can be by-passed and set aside as incidental. And it will emerge from what follows that the actual controversy is not in fact concerned with this at all, but only with morality in general.

b. Garve expresses the above propositions as follows: 'The virtuous man cannot and may not ever lose sight of this consideration (i.e. that of his own happiness), since he would otherwise be completely without access to the invisible world and to belief in the existence of God and of immortality. Such belief, according to this theory, is absolutely neces-sary *to lend support and stability to the moral system.*' He concludes by briefly summing up as follows the statements he ascribes to me: 'The virtuous man, according to these principles, constantly strives to be worthy of happiness, but never, *in so far as* he is truly virtuous, to be actually happy.' (The words *in so far as* create an ambiguity which must be eliminated before we go any further. They can signify *in the act* of submit-ting, as a virtuous man, to one's duty—in which case the sentence is perfectly compatible with my theory—or they could imply that if he is never anything but virtuous, the virtuous man should not take happiness into consideration at all, even where the question of duty does not arise and where there is no conflict with duty—in which case the sentence is totally at variance with my statements.)

These objections are therefore nothing but misunderstandings (for I have no wish to see them as misrepresentations). Their very possibility would astonish us, if it were not that such phenomena can be adequately explained by the human tendency to follow a habitual train of thought, even in judging the thoughts of others, and thus to carry the former over into the latter.

Garve follows up this polemical account of the above moral principle with a dogmatic exposition of its direct opposite. By analytical methods, he comes to the following conclusion: 'In the ordering of *concepts*, the states which entitle us to give *preference* to one rather than others must first be recognised and distinguished before we choose any one of them and thus decide in advance what aim we shall pursue. But a state which a being who is aware of himself and of his own state would *prefer* to other ways of existence as soon as he saw it before him, is a *good* state; and a series of good states is the most general notion expressed by the word *happiness.*' He continues: 'A law presupposes motives, but motives presuppose that a difference has already been recognised between a worse state and a better one. This recognised difference is the element of the concept of happiness', and so on. And again: '*Happiness*, in the most general sense of the word, *is the source of the motives behind every effort*, including obedience to the moral law. I must first of all know whether something is good before I can ask whether the fulfilment of moral duties belongs to the category of good things. Man must have an *incentive* to set him in motion *before* he can be given a *goal** towards which this motion should be directed.'

This argument is nothing more than a play upon the ambiguity of the word *good*. For it can be taken to mean something absolutely good in itself, as opposed to that which is evil in itself, or something only relatively good, as opposed to something more or less good than itself. In the latter case, the preferred state may be only comparatively better, yet nonetheless evil in itself. The maxim of absolute obedience to a categorically binding law of the free will (i.e. of duty), without reference to any ulterior end, is essentially different (i.e. different *in kind*) from the maxim of pursuing, as a motive for a certain way of acting, the end which nature itself has imposed upon us and which is generally known as happiness. For the first maxim is good in itself, but the second is not. The second may, if it conflicts with duty, be thoroughly evil. But if a certain end is made basic, so that no law is absolutely binding but always relative to the end adopted, two opposing actions might both be relatively good, with one better than the other, which would then count as comparatively evil. For they would differ only in *degree*, not in *kind*. And it is the same with all actions whose motive is not the absolute law of reason (duty), but an end which we have arbitrarily taken as a basis. For this end will be a part of the total of ends whose attainment we call happiness, and one action may contribute more, and another less to my happiness, so that one will be better or worse than the other. But to *give preference* to one state rather than another as a determinant of the will is merely an act of freedom (*res merae facultatis*,[7] as the lawyers say) which takes no account of whether the particular determinant is good or evil in itself, and is thus neutral in both respects.

A state of being bound by a certain *given end* which I have preferred to all others *of the same kind*, is a comparatively better state in terms of

---

* This is exactly what I myself insist upon. The incentive which men can have before they are given a specific goal (or end) can obviously be none other than the law itself, through the esteem which it inspires (irrespective of what ends one may have and seek to attain through obedience to the law). For the law, as the formal aspect of will, is all that remains if we discount the will's particular content (i.e. the goal, as Garve calls it).

happiness (which *reason* never recognises as more than *relatively good*, according to the extent to which a person is worthy of it). But that state of consciously preferring the moral law of duty in cases where it conflicts with certain of my ends is not just a better state, but the only state which is good in itself. It is good in a completely different sense, in that it takes no account whatsoever of any ends that may present themselves (including their sum total, which is happiness). The determinant in this case is not the content of the will (i.e. a particular basic object) but the pure form of universal lawfulness embodied in its maxim.—Thus it can by no means be said that I class as happiness every state which I *prefer* to all other modes of existence. For I must first be certain that I am not acting against my duty. Only then am I entitled to look round for happiness, in so far as I can reconcile it with the state I know to be morally (not physically) good.*

The will, however, must have *motives*. But these are not objects of *physical feeling* as predetermined ends in themselves. They are none other than the absolute *law* itself, and the will's receptivity to it as an absolute compulsion is known as *moral feeling*. This feeling is therefore not the cause but the effect of the will's determinant, and we should not have the least awareness of it within ourselves if such compulsion were not already present in us. Thus the old refrain that this feeling, i.e. a desire which we take as our end, is the first cause determining the will, so that happiness (of which that desire is an element) is the basis of all objective necessity of action and thus of all moral obligations, is a piece of *trivial sophistry*. For if we go on asking even after we know the cause of a given event, we end up by making an effect the cause of itself.

I have now reached the point which really concerns us here, the task of testing and illustrating with examples the supposedly conflicting interest of theory and practice in philosophy. Garve's above-quoted essay furnishes the best possible illustration. He first says (with reference to the distinction I make between a doctrine of how to be *happy* and one of how to be *worthy* of happiness): 'For my own part, I admit that while I well understand this distinction among ideas in my *mind*, I do not find any such distinction among the desires and aspirations in my *heart*, so that I fail

* Happiness embodies everything that nature has given us and nothing else. But virtue embodies that which no-one but man can give or take away from himself. If it were replied that by deviating from the latter, man could at least incur blame and moral self-reproach, hence dissatisfaction and unhappiness, we might by all means agree. But only the virtuous man or one who is on the way to virtue is capable of this pure moral dissatisfaction, which comes not from any disadvantage resulting from his actions, but from their unlawfulness itself. His dissatisfaction is consequently not the cause but the effect of his being virtuous; and this unhappiness (if we choose to describe regrets over a crime as such) could not furnish a motive for being virtuous.

even to comprehend how anyone can be aware of having neatly set apart his actual desire for happiness and thus of having fulfilled his duty completely unselfishly.'

I shall answer the last point first. I willingly concede that no-one can have certain awareness of *having fulfilled* his duty completely unselfishly. For this is part of inward experience, and such awareness of one's psychological state would involve an absolutely clear conception of all the secondary notions and considerations which, through imagination, habit and inclination, accompany the concept of duty. And this is too much to ask for. Besides, the non-existence of something (including that of an unconsciously intended advantage) can never be an object of experience. But man is aware with the utmost clarity that he *ought to fulfil* his duty completely unselfishly, and *must* totally separate his desire for happiness from the concept of duty, in order to preserve the latter's purity. For if anyone thought he did not have this clear awareness, he could reasonably be asked to acquire it, so far as his powers might permit. And he must be able to do so, for the true value of morality consists precisely in the purity of its concept. Perhaps no recognised and respected duty has ever been carried out by anyone without some selfishness or interference from other motives; perhaps no-one will ever succeed in doing so, however hard he tries. But by careful self-examination, we can perceive a certain amount. We can be aware not so much of any accompanying motives, but rather of our own self-denial with respect to many motives which conflict with the idea of duty. In other words, we can be aware of the maxim of striving towards moral purity. And this is sufficient for us to observe our duty. On the other hand, it is the death of all morality if we make it our maxim to foster such motives, on the pretext that human nature does not permit moral purity (which no-one can say with certainty in any case).

As for Garve's above confession that he cannot find such a distinction (more correctly a separation) in his *heart*, I have no hesitation in contradicting his self-accusation outright and in championing his heart against his mind. For as an honest man, he has in fact always found this separation in his heart, i.e. in the determinants of his will. But even for the purposes of speculative thinking and of comprehending that which is incomprehensible or inexplicable (i.e. the possibility of categorical imperatives such as those of duty), he was unable in his own mind to reconcile this separation with the usual principles of psychological explanation, which are all based on the mechanism of natural necessity.*

* Garve, in his notes to Cicero's *De Officiis*, 1783 edition, p. 69, makes the following admission, which does credit to his own acuteness: 'It is my innermost conviction that

But I must loudly and resolutely disagree with Garve when he concludes by saying: 'Such subtle distinctions between ideas become *obscure* even when we *think* about particular objects; but they *vanish completely* when it comes to *action*, when they are supposed to apply to desires and intentions. The more simple, rapid and *devoid of clear ideas* the step from consideration of motives to actual action is, the less possible it is to determine exactly and unerringly the precise momentum which each motive has contributed in guiding the step in this and in no other direction.'

The concept of duty in its complete purity is incomparably simpler, clearer and more natural and easily comprehensible to everyone than any motive derived from, combined with, or influenced by happiness, for motives involving happiness always require a great deal of resourcefulness and deliberation. Besides, the concept of duty, if it is presented to the exclusive judgement of even the most ordinary human reason, and confronts the human will separately and in actual opposition to other motives, is far *more powerful*, incisive and likely to promote success than all incentives borrowed from the latter selfish principle. Let us take, for example, the case of someone who has under his trust an endowment (*depositum*), the owner of which is deceased, while the heirs are ignorant of and could never discover its existence. Let us also suppose that the trustee of this deposit, through no fault of his own, has at this very time suffered a complete collapse in his financial circumstances, and has around him a miserable family of wife and children, oppressed by want, and knows that he could at once relieve this distress if he appropriated the pledge entrusted to him. He is also benevolent and philanthropic, while the heirs are rich, uncharitable, thoroughly extravagant and luxurious, so that it would make little difference if the aforesaid addition to their property were thrown into the sea. Now if this case is explained even to a child of around eight or nine years old, and it is asked whether it might be permissible under the circumstances to devote the deposit to one's own use, the reply will undoubtedly be negative. Whoever we ask will merely answer, without further ado, that *it is wrong*, i.e. that it conflicts with duty. Nothing can be clearer than this, while it is genuinely not the case that the trustee would

freedom will always remain unresolved and will never be explained.' It is absolutely impossible to find a proof of its reality either in direct or indirect experience, and it cannot be accepted without any proof. Such a proof cannot be derived from purely theoretical considerations (for these would have to be sought in experience), nor therefore from purely practical propositions of reason, nor alternatively from practical propositions in the technical sense (for these too would have to be based on experience), but accordingly only from moral-practical ones. One must therefore wonder why Garve did not take refuge in the concept of freedom, at least in order to salvage the possibility of such imperatives.

be furthering his own *happiness* if he surrendered the deposit. For if he expected his decision to be dictated by such considerations, he might for instance reason as follows: 'If I give up unasked to the real owners the property I have here, they will presumably reward me for my honesty. Or if they do not, I will still acquire a good reputation at large, and this could prove very remunerative. But all this is most uncertain. Yet various doubts can also be raised in support of this argument. For if I were to embezzle the deposit to relieve my depressed circumstances at one stroke, I should incur suspicion, if I made quick use of it, as to how and by what means I had so soon bettered my circumstances. But if I used it slowly, my poverty would meanwhile increase so greatly that it would become impossible to alleviate it at all.' Thus a will which follows the maxim of happiness vacillates between various motives in trying to reach a decision. For it considers the possible results of its decision, and these are highly uncertain; and it takes a good head to find a way out of the host of arguments and counter-arguments without miscalculating the total effect. On the other hand, if we ask what duty requires, there is no confusion whatsoever about the answer, and we are at once certain what action to take. We even feel, if the concept of duty means anything to us, a revulsion at the very idea of calculating the advantages we might gain through violating our duty, just as if the choice were still a real one.

When Garve says that these distinctions (which, as we have shown, are not so subtle as he thinks, but are inscribed in the soul of man in the plainest and most legible characters) *vanish completely when it comes to action*, this contradicts even his own experience. Admittedly, it does not contradict the experience which the *history* of maxims derived from various principles provides. Such experience, alas, proves that most of them are based on selfishness. But it does contradict our (necessarily inward) experience that no idea can so greatly elevate the human mind and inspire it with such enthusiasm as that of a pure moral conviction, respecting duty above all else, struggling with countless evils of existence and even with their most seductive temptations, and yet overcoming them—for we may rightly assume that man can do so. The fact that man is aware that he can do this just because he ought to discloses within him an ample store of divine capabilities and inspires him, so to speak, with a holy awe at the greatness and sublimity of his true vocation. And if man were frequently enough reminded so that it became a habit for him to purge virtue of all the superfluous wealth of advantages which could be amassed through obeying his duty, and if he always conceived of virtue in its complete purity and made it a principle of private and public instruction always to use this insight (a method of inculcating duties which has almost invariably been neglected), human morality would soon be improved. Historical experience has not proved the success of our ethical doctrines. The fault lies in the erroneous assumption that a motive derived from the idea of duty in itself is far too subtle for the common understanding, whereas a cruder motive based on advantages which can be expected either in this or in a future world from obedience to duty (without consideration of the latter itself as a motive) would act more forcibly upon the mind. Another fault is that it has hitherto been a principle of education and homiletics to place more stress on the quest for happiness than on worthiness of happiness, which is the highest postulate of reason. For *precepts* on how to be happy or at least how to avoid one's own disadvantage are not the same as *commandments*. They are never absolutely binding, for having first warned us, they leave us free to choose what we think best, provided that we are prepared to face the consequences. And any evils which might result from our failure to follow the advice we were given could not justifiably be regarded as penalties. For penalties apply only to a free will which violates the law. But nature and inclination cannot give laws to the free will. It is quite different with the idea of duty, for if we violate it, even without considering the disadvantages which might result, we feel the consequences directly, and appear despicable and culpable in our own eyes.

Here, then, is a clear proof that everything in morals which is true in theory must also be valid in practice. As a human being, a being subjected by his own reason to certain duties, each of us is therefore a *man of affairs*; and since, as human beings, we never grow out of the school of wisdom, we cannot arrogantly and scornfully relegate the adherent of theory to the classroom and set ourselves up as better trained by experience in all that a man is and all that can be required of him. For all this experience will not in any way help us to escape the precepts of theory, but at most to learn how to apply it in better and more universal ways after we have assimilated it into our principles. But we are here concerned only with the latter, and not with any pragmatic abilities.

II

ON THE RELATIONSHIP OF THEORY TO PRACTICE IN POLITICAL RIGHT

(*Against Hobbes*)[8]

Among all the contracts by which a large group of men unites to form a society (*pactum sociale*), the contract establishing a *civil constitution* (*pactum unionis civilis*) is of an exceptional nature. For while, so far as its execution is concerned, it has much in common with all others that are likewise directed towards a chosen end to be pursued by joint effort, it is essentially different from all others in the principle of its constitution (*constitutionis civilis*). In all social contracts, we find a union of many individuals for some common end which they all *share*. But a union as an end in itself which they all *ought to share* and which is thus an absolute and primary duty in all external relationships whatsoever among human beings (who cannot avoid mutually influencing one another), is only found in a society in so far as it constitutes a civil state, i.e. a commonwealth. And the end which is a duty in itself in such external relationships, and which is indeed the highest formal condition (*conditio sine qua non*) of all other external duties, is the *right* of men *under coercive public laws* by which each can be given what is due to him and secured against attack from any others. But the whole concept of an external right is derived entirely from the concept of *freedom* in the mutual external relationships of human beings, and has nothing to do with the end which all men have by nature (i.e. the aim of achieving happiness) or with the recognised means of attaining this end. And thus the latter end must on no account interfere as a determinant with the laws governing external right. *Right* is the restriction of each individual's freedom so that it harmonises with the freedom of everyone else (in so far as this is possible within the terms of a general law). And *public right* is the distinctive quality of the *external laws* which make this constant harmony possible. Since every restriction of freedom through the arbitrary will of another party is termed *coercion*, it follows that a civil constitution is a relationship among *free* men who are subject to coercive laws, while they retain their freedom within the general union with their fellows. Such is the requirement of pure reason, which legislates *a priori*, regardless of all empirical ends (which can all be summed up under the general heading of happiness). Men have different views on the empirical end of happiness and what it consists of, so that as far as happiness is concerned, their will cannot be brought under any

73

common principle nor thus under any external law harmonising with the freedom of everyone.

The civil state, regarded purely as a lawful state, is based on the following *a priori* principles:

1. The *freedom* of every member of society as a *human being*.
2. The *equality* of each with all the others as a *subject*.
3. The *independence* of each member of a commonwealth as a *citizen*.

These principles are not so much laws given by an already established state, as laws by which a state can alone be established in accordance with pure rational principles of external human right. Thus:

1. Man's *freedom* as a human being, as a principle for the constitution of a commonwealth, can be expressed in the following formula. No-one can compel me to be happy in accordance with his conception of the welfare of others, for each may seek his happiness in whatever way he sees fit, so long as he does not infringe upon the freedom of others to pursue a similar end which can be reconciled with the freedom of everyone else within a workable general law—i.e. he must accord to others the same right as he enjoys himself. A government might be established on the principle of benevolence towards the people, like that of a father towards his children. Under such a *paternal government* (*imperium paternale*), the subjects, as immature children who cannot distinguish what is truly useful or harmful to themselves, would be obliged to behave purely passively and to rely upon the judgement of the head of state as to how they *ought* to be happy, and upon his kindness in willing their happiness at all. Such a government is the greatest conceivable *despotism*, i.e. a constitution which suspends the entire freedom of its subjects, who thenceforth have no rights whatsoever. The only conceivable government for men who are capable of possessing rights, even if the ruler is benevolent, is not a *paternal* but a *patriotic* government (*imperium non paternale, sed patrioticum*). A *patriotic* attitude is one where everyone in the state, not excepting its head, regards the commonwealth as a maternal womb, or the land as the paternal ground from which he himself sprang and which he must leave to his descendants as a treasured pledge. Each regards himself as authorised to protect the rights of the commonwealth by laws of the general will, but not to submit it to his personal use at his own absolute pleasure. This right of freedom belongs to each member of the commonwealth as a human being, in so far as each is a being capable of possessing rights.

2. Man's *equality* as a subject might be formulated as follows. Each member of the commonwealth has rights of coercion in relation to all the

others, except in relation to the head of state. For he alone is not a member of the commonwealth, but its creator or preserver, and he alone is authorised to coerce others without being subject to any coercive law himself. But all who are subject to laws are the subjects of a state, and are thus subject to the right of coercion along with all other members of the commonwealth; the only exception is a single person (in either the physical or the moral sense of the word), the head of state, through whom alone the rightful coercion of all others can be exercised. For if he too could be coerced, he would not be the head of state, and the hierarchy of subordination would ascend infinitely. But if there were two persons exempt from coercion, neither would be subject to coercive laws, and neither could do to the other anything contrary to right, which is impossible.

This uniform equality of human beings as subjects of a state is, however, perfectly consistent with the utmost inequality of the mass in the degree of its possessions, whether these take the form of physical or mental superiority over others, or of fortuitous external property and of particular rights (of which there may be many) with respect to others. Thus the welfare of the one depends very much on the will of the other (the poor depending on the rich), the one must obey the other (as the child its parents or the wife her husband), the one serves (the labourer) while the other pays, etc. Nevertheless, they are all equal as subjects *before the law*, which, as the pronouncement of the general will, can only be single in form, and which concerns the form of right and not the material or object in relation to which I possess rights. For no-one can coerce anyone else other than through the public law and its executor, the head of state, while everyone else can resist the others in the same way and to the same degree. No-one, however, can lose this authority to coerce others and to have rights towards them except through committing a crime. And no-one can voluntarily renounce his rights by a contract or legal transaction to the effect that he has no rights but only duties, for such a contract would deprive him of the right to make a contract, and would thus invalidate the one he had already made.

From this idea of the equality of men as subjects in a commonwealth, there emerges this further formula: every member of the commonwealth must be entitled to reach any degree of rank which a subject can earn through his talent, his industry and his good fortune. And his fellow-subjects may not stand in his way by *hereditary* prerogatives or privileges of rank and thereby hold him and his descendants back indefinitely.

All right consists solely in the restriction of the freedom of others, with the qualification that their freedom can co-exist with my freedom within the terms of a general law; and public right in a commonwealth is simply a state of affairs regulated by a real legislation which conforms to this principle and is backed up by power, and under which a whole people live as subjects in a lawful state (*status iuridicus*). This is what we call a civil state, and it is characterised by equality in the effects and counter-effects of freely willed actions which limit one another in accordance with the general law of freedom. Thus the *birthright* of each individual in such a state (i.e. before he has performed any acts which can be judged in relation to right) is absolutely *equal* as regards his authority to coerce others to use their freedom in a way which harmonises with his freedom. Since birth is not an act on the part of the one who is born, it cannot create any inequality in his legal position and cannot make him submit to any coercive laws except in so far as he is a subject, along with all the others, of the one supreme legislative power. Thus no member of the commonwealth can have a hereditary privilege as against his fellow-subjects; and no-one can hand down to his descendants the privileges attached to the rank he occupies in the commonwealth, nor act as if he were qualified as a ruler by birth and forcibly prevent others from reaching the higher levels of the hierarchy (which are *superior* and *inferior*, but never *imperans* and *subiectus*) through their own merit. He may hand down everything else, so long as it is material and not pertaining to his person, for it may be acquired and disposed of as property and may over a series of generations create considerable inequalities in wealth among the members of the commonwealth (the employee and the employer, the landowner and the agricultural servants, etc.). But he may not prevent his subordinates from raising themselves to his own level if they are able and entitled to do so by their talent, industry and good fortune. If this were not so, he would be allowed to practise coercion without himself being subject to coercive counter-measures from others, and would thus be more than their fellow-subject. No-one who lives within the lawful state of a commonwealth can forfeit this equality other than through some crime of his own, but never by contract or through military force (*occupatio bellica*). For no legal transaction on his part or on that of anyone else can make him cease to be his own master. He cannot become like a domestic animal to be employed in any chosen capacity and retained therein without consent for any desired period, even with the reservation (which is at times sanctioned by religion, as among the Indians) that he may not be maimed or killed. He can be considered happy in any condition so long as he is aware that, if he does not reach the same level as others, the fault lies either with himself (i.e. lack of ability or serious endeavour) or with circumstances for which he cannot blame others, and not with the irresistible will of any outside party. For as far as right is concerned, his fellow-subjects have no advantage over him.*

3. The *independence* (*sibisufficientia*) of a member of the commonwealth as a *citizen*, i.e. as a co-legislator, may be defined as follows. In the question of actual legislation, all who are free and equal under existing public laws may be considered equal, but not as regards the right to make these laws. Those who are not entitled to this right are nonetheless obliged, as members of the commonwealth, to comply with these laws, and they thus likewise enjoy their protection (not as *citizens* but as co-beneficiaries of this protection). For all right depends on laws. But a public law which defines for everyone that which is permitted and prohibited by right, is the act of a public will, from which all right proceeds and which must not therefore itself be able to do an injustice to any one. And this requires no less than the will of the entire people (since all men decide for all men and each decides for himself). For only towards oneself can one never act unjustly. But on the other hand, the will of another person cannot decide anything for someone without injustice, so that the law made by this other person would require a further law to limit his legislation. Thus an individual will cannot legislate for a commonwealth. For this requires freedom, equality and *unity* of the will of *all* the members. And the prerequisite for unity, since it necessitates a general vote (if freedom and equality are both present), is independence. The basic law, which can come only from the general, united will of the people, is called the *original contract*.

Anyone who has the right to vote on this legislation is a *citizen* (*citoyen*,

* If we try to find a definite meaning for the word *gracious*, as distinct from kind, beneficent, protective etc., we see that it can be attributed only to a person to whom no *coercive rights* apply. Thus only the head of the *state's government*, who enacts and distributes all benefits that are possible within the public laws (for the *sovereign* who provides them is, as it were, invisible, and is not an agent but the personified law itself), can be given the title of *gracious lord*, for he is the only individual to whom coercive rights do not apply. And even in an aristocratic government, as for example in Venice, the *senate* is the only 'gracious lord'. The nobles who belong to it, even including the *Doge* (for only the *plenary council* is the sovereign), are all subjects and equal to the others so far as the exercise of rights is concerned, for each subject has coercive rights towards every one of them. Princes (i.e. persons with a hereditary right to become rulers) are themselves called gracious lords only with future reference, an account of their claims to become rulers (i.e. by courtly etiquette, *par courtoisie*). But as owners of property, they are nonetheless fellow-subjects of the others, and even the humblest of their servants must possess a right of coercion against them through the head of state. Thus there can be no more than one gracious lord in a state. And as for gracious (more correctly *distinguished*) ladies, they can be considered entitled to this appellation by their *rank* and their *sex* (thus only as opposed to the *male* sex), and this only by virtue of a refinement of manners (known as gallantry) whereby the male sex imagines that it does itself greater honour by giving the fair sex precedence over itself.

i.e. citizen of a state, not *bourgeois* or citizen of a town). The only qualification required by a citizen (apart, of course, from being an adult male)
is that he must be his *own master* (*sui iuris*), and must have some *property*
(which can include any skill, trade, fine art or science) to support himself.
In cases where he must earn his living from others, he must earn it only
by *selling* that which is his,* and not by allowing others to make use of
him; for he must in the true sense of the word *serve* no-one but the
commonwealth. In this respect, artisans and large or small landowners are
all equal, and each is entitled to one vote only. As for landowners, we leave
aside the question of how anyone can have rightfully acquired more land
than he can cultivate with his own hands (for acquisition by military
seizure is not primary acquisition), and how it came about that numerous
people who might otherwise have acquired permanent property were
thereby reduced to serving someone else in order to live at all. It would
certainly conflict with the above principle of equality if a law were to
grant them a privileged status so that their descendants would always
remain feudal landowners, without their land being sold or divided by
inheritance and thus made useful to more people; it would also be unjust
if only those belonging to an arbitrarily selected class were allowed to
acquire land, should the estates in fact be divided. The owner of a large
estate keeps out as many smaller property owners (and their votes) as
could otherwise occupy his territories. He does not vote on their behalf,
and himself has only *one* vote. It should be left exclusively to the ability,
industry and good fortune of each member of the commonwealth to enable
each to acquire a part and all to acquire the whole, although this distinction cannot be observed within the general legislation itself. The number
of those entitled to vote on matters of legislation must be calculated purely
from the number of property owners, not from the size of their properties.

Those who possess this right to vote must agree *unanimously* to the law
of public justice, or else a legal contention would arise between those who

---

* He who does a piece of work (*opus*) can sell it to someone else, just as if it were his
own property. But guaranteeing one's labour (*praestatio operae*) is not the same as selling
a commodity. The domestic servant, the shop assistant, the labourer, or even the barber,
are merely labourers (*operarii*), not *artists* (*artifices*, in the wider sense) or members of the
state, and are thus unqualified to be citizens. And although the man to whom I give my
firewood to chop and the tailor to whom I give material to make into clothes both appear
to have a similar relationship towards me, the former differs from the latter in the same
way as the barber from the wig-maker (to whom I may in fact have given the requisite
hair) or the labourer from the artist or tradesman, who does a piece of work which
belongs to him until he is paid for it. For the latter, in pursuing his trade, exchanges his
property with someone else (*opus*), while the former allows someone else to make use of
him.—But I do admit that it is somewhat difficult to define the qualifications which
entitle anyone to claim the status of being his own master.

agree and those who disagree, and it would require yet another higher legal principle to resolve it. An entire people cannot, however, be expected to reach unanimity, but only to show a majority of votes (and not even of direct votes, but simply of the votes of those delegated in a large nation to represent the people). Thus the actual principle of being content with majority decisions must be accepted unanimously and embodied in a contract; and this itself must be the ultimate basis on which a civil constitution is established.

Conclusion

This, then, is an *original contract* by means of which a civil and thus completely lawful constitution and commonwealth can alone be established. But we need by no means assume that this contract (*contractus originarius* or *pactum sociale*), based on a coalition of the wills of all private individuals in a nation to form a common, public will for the purposes of rightful legislation, actually exists as a *fact*, for it cannot possibly be so. Such an assumption would mean that we would first have to prove from history that some nation, whose rights and obligations have been passed down to us, did in fact perform such an act, and handed down some authentic record or legal instrument, orally or in writing, before we could regard ourselves as bound by a pre-existing civil constitution. It is in fact merely an *idea* of reason, which nonetheless has undoubted practical reality; for it can oblige every legislator to frame his laws in such a way that they could have been produced by the united will of a whole nation, and to regard each subject, in so far as he can claim citizenship, as if he had consented within the general will. This is the test of the rightfulness of every public law. For if the law is such that a whole people could not *possibly* agree to it (for example, if it stated that a certain class of *subjects* must be privileged as a hereditary *ruling class*), it is unjust; but if it is at least *possible* that a people could agree to it, it is our duty to consider the law as just, even if the people is at present in such a position or attitude of mind that it would probably refuse its consent if it were consulted.* But this restriction obviously applies only to the judgement of the legislator,

---

* If, for example, a war tax were proportionately imposed on all subjects, they could not claim, simply because it is oppressive, that it is unjust because the war is in their opinion unnecessary. For they are not entitled to judge this issue, since it is at least *possible* that the war is inevitable and the tax indispensable, so that the tax must be deemed rightful in the judgement of the subjects. But if certain estate owners were oppressed with levies for such a war, while others of the same class were exempted, it is easily seen that a whole people could never agree to a law of this kind, and it is entitled at least to make representations against it, since an unequal distribution of burdens can never be considered just.

not to that of the subject. Thus if a people, under some existing legislation, were asked to make a judgement which in all probability would prejudice its happiness, what should it do? Should the people not oppose the measure? The only possible answer is that they can do nothing but obey. For we are not concerned here with any happiness which the subject might expect to derive from the institutions or administration of the commonwealth, but primarily with the rights which would thereby be secured for everyone. And this is the highest principle from which all maxims relating to the commonwealth must begin, and which cannot be qualified by any other principles. No generally valid principle of legislation can be based on happiness. For both the current circumstances and the highly conflicting and variable illusions as to what happiness is (and no-one can prescribe to others how they should attain it) make all fixed principles impossible, so that happiness alone can never be a suitable principle of legislation. The doctrine that *salus publica suprema civitatis lex est*[9] retains its value and authority undiminished; but the public welfare which demands *first* consideration lies precisely in that legal constitution which guarantees everyone his freedom within the law, so that each remains free to seek his happiness in whatever way he thinks best, so long as he does not violate the lawful freedom and rights of his fellow subjects at large. If the supreme power makes laws which are primarily directed towards happiness (the affluence of the citizens, increased population etc.), this cannot be regarded as the end for which a civil constitution was established, but only as a means of *securing the rightful state*, especially against external enemies of the people. The head of state must be authorised to judge for himself whether such measures are necessary for the commonwealth's prosperity, which is required to maintain its strength and stability both internally and against external enemies. The aim is not, as it were, to make the people happy against its will, but only to ensure its continued existence as a commonwealth.* The legislator may indeed err in judging whether or not the measures he adopts are *prudent*, but not in deciding whether or not the law harmonises with the principle of right. For he has ready to hand as an infallible *a priori* standard the idea of an original contract, and he need not wait for experience to show whether the means are suitable, as would be necessary if they were based on the principle of happiness. For so long as it is not self-contra-

* Measures of this kind might include certain restrictions on imports, so that the means of livelihood may be developed for the benefit of the subjects themselves and not as an advantage to foreigners or an encouragement for their industry. For without the prosperity of the people, the state would not have enough strength to resist external enemies or to preserve itself as a commonwealth.

dictory to say that an entire people could agree to such a law, however painful it might seem, then the law is in harmony with right. But if a public law is beyond reproach (i.e. *irreprehensible*) with respect to right, it carries with it the authority to coerce those to whom it applies, and conversely, it forbids them to resist the will of the legislator by violent means. In other words, the power of the state to put the law into effect is also *irresistible*, and no rightfully established commonwealth can exist without a force of this kind to suppress all internal resistance. For such resistance would be dictated by a maxim which, if it became general, would destroy the whole civil constitution and put an end to the only state in which men can possess rights.

It thus follows that all resistance against the supreme legislative power, all incitement of the subjects to violent expressions of discontent, all defiance which breaks out into rebellion, is the greatest and most punishable crime in a commonwealth, for it destroys its very foundations. This prohibition is *absolute*. And even if the power of the state or its agent, the head of state, has violated the original contract by authorising the government to act tyrannically, and has thereby, in the eyes of the subject, forfeited the right to legislate, the subject is still not entitled to offer counterresistance. The reason for this is that the people, under an existing civil constitution, has no longer any right to judge how the constitution should be administered. For if we suppose that it does have this right to judge and that it disagrees with the judgement of the actual head of state, who is to decide which side is right? Neither can act as judge of his own cause. Thus there would have to be another head above the head of state to mediate between the latter and the people, which is self-contradictory.— Nor can a right of necessity (*ius in casu necessitatis*) be invoked here as a means of removing the barriers which restrict the power of the people; for it is monstrous to suppose that we can have a right to do wrong in the direst (physical) distress.* For the head of state can just as readily claim

---

* There is no *casus necessitatis* except where duties, i.e. an *absolute* duty and another which, however pressing, is nevertheless *relative*, come into conflict. For instance, it might be necessary for someone to betray someone else, even if their relationship were that of father and son, in order to preserve the state from catastrophe. This preservation of the state from evil is an absolute duty, while the preservation of the individual is merely a relative duty (i.e. it applies only if he is not guilty of a crime against the state). The first person might denounce the second to the authorities with the utmost unwillingness, compelled only by (moral) necessity. But if a person, in order to preserve his own life, pushes a shipwrecked fellow away from the plank he grasps, it would be quite false to say that (physical) necessity gives him a right to do so. For it is only a relative duty for me to preserve my own life (i.e. it applies only if I can do so without committing a crime). But it is an absolute duty not to take the life of another person who has not offended me and does not even make me risk my own life. Yet the teachers of

that his severe treatment of his subjects is justified by their insubordination as the subjects can justify their rebellion by complaints about their unmerited suffering, and who is to decide? The decision must rest with whoever controls the ultimate enforcement of the public law, i.e. the head of state himself. Thus no-one in the commonwealth can have a right to contest his authority.

Nonetheless, estimable men have declared that the subject is justified, under certain circumstances, in using force against his superiors. I need name only Achenwall,[10] who is extremely cautious, precise and restrained in his theories of natural right.* He says: 'If the danger which threatens the commonwealth as a result of long endurance of injustices from the head of state is greater than the danger to be feared from taking up arms against him, the people may then resist him. It may use this right to abrogate its contract of subjection and to dethrone him as a tyrant.' And he concludes: 'The people, in dethroning its ruler, thus returns to the state of nature.'

I well believe that neither Achenwall nor any others of the worthy men who have speculated along the same lines as he would ever have given their advice or agreement to such hazardous projects if the case had arisen. And it can scarcely be doubted that if the revolutions whereby Switzerland, the United Netherlands or even Great Britain won their much admired constitutions had failed, the readers of their history would regard the execution of their celebrated founders as no more than the deserved punishment of great political criminals. For the result usually affects our judgement of the rightfulness of an action, although the result is uncertain, whereas the principles of right are constant. But it is clear that these peoples have done the greatest degree of wrong in seeking their rights in this way, even if we admit that such a revolution did no injustice to a ruler who had violated a specific basic agreement with the people, such as the *Joyeuse Entrée*.[11] For such procedures, if made into a maxim, make all lawful constitutions insecure and produce a state of complete lawlessness (*status naturalis*) where all rights cease at least to be effectual. In view of this tendency of so many right-thinking authors to plead on behalf of the people (and to its own detriment), I will only remark that such errors arise in part from the usual fallacy of allowing the principle of happiness

general civil law are perfectly consistent in authorising such measures in cases of distress. For the authorities cannot combine a *penalty* with this prohibition, since this penalty would have to be death. But it would be a nonsensical law which threatened anyone with death if he did not voluntarily deliver himself up to death when in dangerous circumstances.

* Ius Naturae. Editio v. Pars posterior, §§203–206.

to influence the judgement, wherever the principle of right is involved; and partly because these writers have assumed that the idea of an original contract (a basic postulate of reason) is something which must have taken place *in reality*, even where there is no document to show that any contract was actually submitted to the commonwealth, accepted by the head oı state, and sanctioned by both parties. Such writers thus believe that the people retains the right to abrogate the original contract at its own discretion, if, in the opinion of the people, the contract has been severely violated.*

It is obvious from this that the principle of happiness (which is not in fact a definite principle at all) has ill effects in political right just as in morality, however good the intentions of those who teach it. The sovereign wants to make the people happy as he thinks best, and thus becomes a despot, while the people are unwilling to give up their universal human desire to seek happiness in their own way, and thus become rebels. If they had first of all asked what is lawful (in terms of *a priori* certainty, which no empiricist can upset), the idea of a social contract would retain its authority undiminished. But it would not exist as a fact (as Danton[13] would have it, declaring that since it does not actually exist, all property and all rights under the existing civil constitution are null and void), but only as a rational principle for judging any lawful public constitution whatsoever. And it would then be seen that, until the general will is there, the people has no coercive right against its ruler, since it can apply coercion legally only through him. But if the will is there, no force can be applied to the ruler by the people, otherwise the people would be the supreme ruler. Thus the people can never possess a right of coercion against the head of state, or be entitled to oppose him in word or deed.

We can see, furthermore, that this theory is adequately confirmed in practice. In the British constitution, of which the people are so proud that they hold it up as a model for the whole world, we find no mention of what the people are entitled to do if the monarch were to violate the contract of 1688.[14] Since there is no law to cover such a case, the people

* Even if an actual contract of the people with the head of state has been violated, the people cannot reply immediately as a *commonwealth*, but only by forming factions. For the hitherto existing constitution has been destroyed by the people, but a new commonwealth has still to be organised. At this point, the state of anarchy supervenes, with all the terrors it may bring with it. And the wrong which is thereby done is done by each faction of the people to the others, as is clear from the case where the rebellious subjects ended up by trying to thrust upon each other a constitution which would have been far more oppressive than the one they abandoned. For they would have been devoured by ecclesiastics and aristocrats, instead of enjoying greater equality in the distribution of political burdens under a single head of state who ruled them all.[12]

tacitly reserve the right to rebel against him if he should violate the contract. And it would be an obvious contradiction if the constitution included a law for such eventualities, entitling the people to overthrow the existing constitution, from which all particular laws are derived, if the contract were violated. For there would then have to be a *publicly constituted** opposing power, hence a second head of state to protect the rights of the people against the first ruler, and then yet a third to decide which of the other two had right on his side. In fact, the leaders (or guardians—call them what you will) of the British people, fearing some such accusation if their plans did not succeed, *invented* the notion of a voluntary abdication by the monarch they forced out, rather than claim a right to depose him (which would have made the constitution self-contradictory).

While I trust that no-one will accuse me of flattering monarchs too much by declaring them inviolable, I likewise hope that I shall be spared the reproach of claiming too much for the people if I maintain that the people too have inalienable rights against the head of state, even if these cannot be rights of coercion.

Hobbes is of the opposite opinion. According to him (*De Cive*, Chap. 7, §14), the head of state has no contractual obligations towards the people; he can do no injustice to a citizen, but may act towards him as he pleases. This proposition would be perfectly correct if injustice were taken to mean any injury which gave the injured party a *coercive right* against the one who has done him injustice. But in its general form, the proposition is quite terrifying.

The non-resisting subject must be able to assume that his ruler has no *wish* to do him injustice. And everyone has his inalienable rights, which he cannot give up even if he wishes to, and about which he is entitled to make his own judgements. But if he assumes that the ruler's attitude is one of good will, any injustice which he believes he has suffered can only have resulted through error, or through ignorance of certain possible consequences of the laws which the supreme authority has made. Thus the citizen must, with the approval of the ruler, be entitled to make public his opinion on whatever of the ruler's measures seem to him to constitute an injustice against the commonwealth. For to assume that the head of state can neither make mistakes nor be ignorant of anything would be to imply that he receives divine inspiration and is more than a human being.

* No right in a state can be tacitly and treacherously included by a secret reservation, and least of all a right which the people claim to be part of the constitution, for all laws within it must be thought of as arising out of a public will. Thus if the constitution allowed rebellion, it would have to declare this right publicly and make clear how it might be implemented.

Thus *freedom of the pen* is the only safeguard of the rights of the people, although it must not transcend the bounds of respect and devotion towards the existing constitution, which should itself create a liberal attitude of mind among the subjects. To try to deny the citizen this freedom does not only mean, as Hobbes maintains, that the subject can claim no rights against the supreme ruler. It also means withholding from the ruler all knowledge of those matters which, if he knew about them, he would himself rectify, so that he is thereby put into a self-stultifying position. For his will issues commands to his subjects (as citizens) only in so far as he represents the general will of the people. But to encourage the head of state to fear that independent and public thought might cause political unrest is tantamount to making him distrust his own power and feel hatred towards his people.

The general principle, however, according to which a people may judge negatively whatever it believes was *not decreed* in good will by the supreme legislation, can be summed up as follows: *Whatever a people cannot impose upon itself cannot be imposed upon it by the legislator either.*

For example, if we wish to discover whether a law which declares permanently valid an ecclesiastical constitution (itself formulated at some time in the past) can be regarded as emanating from the actual will or intention of the legislator, we must first ask whether a people is *authorised* to make a law for itself whereby certain accepted doctrines and outward forms of religion are declared permanent, and whether the people may thus prevent its own descendants from making further progress in religious understanding or from correcting any past mistakes. It is clear that any original contract of the people which established such a law would in itself be null and void, for it would conflict with the appointed aim and purpose of mankind. Thus a law of this kind cannot be regarded as the actual will of the monarch, to whom counter-representations may accordingly be made. In all cases, however, where the supreme legislation did nevertheless adopt such measures, it would be permissible to pass general and public judgements upon them, but never to offer any verbal or active resistance.

In every commonwealth, there must be *obedience* to generally valid coercive laws within the mechanism of the political constitution. There must also be a *spirit of freedom*, for in all matters concerning universal human duties, each individual requires to be convinced by reason that the coercion which prevails is lawful, otherwise he would be in contradiction with himself. Obedience without the spirit of freedom is the effective cause of all *secret societies*. For it is a natural vocation of man to communicate with his fellows, especially in matters affecting mankind as a whole. Thus secret societies would disappear if freedom of this kind were encouraged. And how else can the government itself acquire the knowledge it needs to further its own basic intention, if not by allowing the spirit of freedom, so admirable in its origins and effects, to make itself heard?

Nowhere does practice so readily bypass all pure principles of reason and treat theory so presumptuously as in the question of what is needed for a good political constitution. The reason for this is that a legal constitution of long standing gradually makes the people accustomed to judging both their happiness and their rights in terms of the peaceful *status quo*. Conversely, it does not encourage them to value the existing state of affairs in the light of those concepts of happiness and right which reason provides. It rather makes them prefer this passive state to the dangerous task of looking for a better one, thus bearing out the saying which Hippocrates told physicians to remember: *iudicium anceps, experimentum periculosum.*[15] Thus all constitutions which have lasted for a sufficiently long time, whatever their inadequacies and variations, produce the same result: the people remain content with what they have. If we therefore consider the *welfare of the people*, theory is not in fact valid, for everything depends upon practice derived from experience.

But reason provides a concept which we express by the words *political right*. And this concept has binding force for human beings who coexist in a state of antagonism produced by their natural freedom, so that it has an objective, practical reality, irrespective of the good or ill it may produce (for these can only be known by experience). Thus it is based on *a priori* principles, for experience cannot provide knowledge of what is right, and there is a *theory* of political right to which practice must conform before it can be valid.

The only objection which can be raised against this is that, although men have in their minds the idea of the rights to which they are entitled, their intractability is such that they are incapable and unworthy of being treated as their rights demand, so that they can and ought to be kept under control by a supreme power acting purely from expediency. But this counsel of desperation (*salto mortale*) means that, since there is no appeal to right but only to force, the people may themselves resort to force and thus make every legal constitution insecure. If there is nothing which commands immediate respect through reason, such as the basic rights of man, no influence can prevail upon man's arbitrary will and restrain his freedom. But if both benevolence and right speak out in loud tones, human nature will not prove too debased to listen to their voice with respect. *Tum pietate gravem meritisque si forte virum quem Conspexere, silent arrectisque auribus adstant* (Virgil).[16]

III

ON THE RELATIONSHIP OF THEORY TO PRACTICE IN INTERNATIONAL RIGHT

CONSIDERED FROM A UNIVERSALLY PHILANTHROPIC, I.E. COSMOPOLITAN POINT OF VIEW*

(Against Moses Mendelssohn)[17]

Is the human race as a whole likeable, or is it an object to be regarded with distaste? Must we simply wish it well (to avoid becoming misanthropists) without really expecting its efforts to succeed, and then take no further interest in it? In order to answer such questions, we must first answer the following one: Does man possess natural capacities which would indicate that the race will always progress and improve, so that the evils of the past and present will vanish in the future good? If this were the case, we could at least admire the human species for its constant advance towards the good; otherwise, we should have to hate or despise it, whatever objections might be raised by pretended philanthropists (whose feelings for mankind might at most amount to good will, but not to genuine pleasure).

For however hard we may try to awaken feelings of love in ourselves, we cannot avoid hating that which is and always will be evil, especially if it involves deliberate and general violation of the most sacred rights of man. Perhaps we may not wish to harm men, but shall not want to have any more to do with them than we can help.

Moses Mendelssohn was of the latter opinion (*Jerusalem* §II, pp. 44–47),[18] which he put forward in opposition to his friend Lessing's hypothesis of a divine education of mankind.[19] He regards it as sheer fantasy to say 'that the whole of mankind here on earth must continually progress and become more perfect through the ages'. He continues: 'We see the human race

---

* It is not immediately obvious how a universally *philanthropic* attitude can point the way to a cosmopolitan constitution, and this in turn to the establishment of *international justice* as the only state in which those capacities which make our species worthy of respect can be properly developed. But the conclusion of this essay will make this relationship clear.

as a whole moving slowly back and forth, and whenever it takes a few steps forward, it soon relapses twice as quickly into its former state.' (This is truly the stone of Sisyphus;[20] if we adopt an attitude of this kind, as the Indians do, the earth must strike us as a place of atonement for old and forgotten sins.) 'Man as an individual progresses; but mankind constantly fluctuates between fixed limits. Regarded as a whole, however, mankind maintains roughly the same level of morality, the same degree of religion and irreligion, of virtue and vice, of happiness (?) and misery.' He introduces these assertions with the words (p. 46): 'Do you presume to guess the plan of providence for mankind? Do not invent hypotheses' (he had earlier called these theories); 'just look around at what actually happens, and if you can briefly survey the history of all past ages, look at what has happened from time immemorial. All this is fact; it must have been intended and approved within the plan of higher wisdom, or at least adopted along with it.'

I beg to differ. It is a sight fit for a god to watch a virtuous man grappling with adversity and evil temptations and yet managing to hold out against them. But it is a sight quite unfit not so much for a god, but even for the most ordinary, though right-thinking man, to see the human race advancing over a period of time towards virtue, and then quickly relapsing the whole way back into vice and misery. It may perhaps be moving and instructive to watch such a drama for a while; but the curtain must eventually descend. For in the long run, it becomes a farce. And even if the actors do not tire of it—for they are fools—the spectator does, for any single act will be enough for him if he can reasonably conclude from it that the never-ending play will go on in the same way for ever. If it is only a play, the retribution at the end can make up for the unpleasant sensations the spectator has felt. But in my opinion at least, it cannot be reconciled with the morality of a wise creator and ruler of the world if countless vices, even with intermingled virtues, are in actual fact allowed to go on accumulating.

I may thus be permitted to assume that, since the human race is constantly progressing in cultural matters (in keeping with its natural purpose), it is also engaged in progressive improvement in relation to the moral end of its existence. This progress may at times be *interrupted* but never *broken off*. I do not need to prove this assumption; it is up to the adversary to prove his case. I am a member of a series of human generations, and as such, I am not as good as I ought to be or could be according to the moral requirements of my nature. I base my argument upon my inborn duty of influencing posterity in such a way that it will make constant progress (and I must thus assume that progress is possible), and that this duty may be rightfully handed down from one member of the series to the next. History may well give rise to endless doubts about my hopes, and if these doubts could be proved, they might persuade me to desist from an apparently futile task. But so long as they do not have the force of certainty, I cannot exchange my duty (as a *liquidum*)[21] for a rule of expediency which says that I ought not to attempt the impracticable (i.e. an *illiquidum*,[22] since it is purely hypothetical). And however uncertain I may be and may remain as to whether we can hope for anything better for mankind, this uncertainty cannot detract from the maxim I have adopted, or from the necessity of assuming for practical purposes that human progress is possible.

This hope for better times to come, without which an earnest desire to do something useful for the common good would never have inspired the human heart, has always influenced the activities of right-thinking men. And the worthy Mendelssohn must himself have reckoned on this, since he zealously endeavoured to promote the enlightenment and welfare of the nation to which he belonged. For he could not himself reasonably hope to do this unless others after him continued upon the same path. Confronted by the sorry spectacle not only of those evils which befall mankind from natural causes, but also of those which men inflict upon one another, our spirits can be raised by the prospect of future improvements. This, however, calls for unselfish goodwill on our part, since we shall have been long dead and buried when the fruits we helped to sow are harvested. It is quite irrelevant whether any empirical evidence suggests that these plans, which are founded only on hope, may be unsuccessful. For the idea that something which has hitherto been unsuccessful will therefore never be successful does not justify anyone in abandoning even a pragmatic or technical aim (for example, that of flights with aerostatic balloons). This applies even more to moral aims, which, so long as it is not demonstrably impossible to fulfil them, amount to duties. Besides, various evidence suggests that in our age, as compared with all previous ages, the human race has made considerable moral progress, and short-term hindrances prove nothing to the contrary. Moreover, it can be shown that the outcry about man's continually increasing decadence arises for the very reason that we can see further ahead, because we have reached a higher level of morality. We thus pass more severe judgements on what we are, comparing it with what we ought to be, so that our self-reproach increases in proportion to the number of stages of morality we have advanced through during the whole of known history.

If we now ask what means there are of maintaining and indeed accelerating this constant progress towards a better state, we soon realise that the success of this immeasurably long undertaking will depend not so much upon what *we* do (e.g. the education we impart to younger generations) and upon what methods *we* use to further it; it will rather depend upon what human *nature* may do in and through us, to *compel* us to follow a course which we would not readily adopt by choice. We must look to nature alone, or rather to *providence* (since it requires the highest wisdom to fulfil this purpose), for a successful outcome which will first affect the whole and then the individual parts. The schemes of men, on the other hand, begin with the parts, and frequently get no further than them. For the whole is too great for men to encompass; while they can reach it with their ideas, they cannot actively influence it, especially since their schemes conflict with one another to such an extent that they could hardly reach agreement of their own free volition.

On the one hand, universal violence and the distress it produces must eventually make a people decide to submit to the coercion which reason itself prescribes (i.e. the coercion of public law), and to enter into a *civil* constitution. And on the other hand, the distress produced by the constant wars in which the states try to subjugate or engulf each other must finally lead them, even against their will, to enter into a *cosmopolitan* constitution. Or if such a state of universal peace is in turn even more dangerous to freedom, for it may lead to the most fearful despotism (as has indeed occurred more than once with states which have grown too large), distress must force men to form a state which is not a cosmopolitan commonwealth under a single ruler, but a lawful *federation* under a commonly accepted *international right*.

The increasing culture of the states, along with their growing tendency to aggrandise themselves by cunning or violence at the expense of the others, must make wars more frequent. It must likewise cause increasingly high expenditure on standing armies, which must be kept in constant training and equipped with ever more numerous instruments of warfare. Meanwhile, the price of all necessities will steadily rise, while no-one can hope for any proportionate increase in the corresponding metal currencies. No peace will last long enough for the resources saved during it to meet the expenditure of the next war, while the invention of a national debt, though ingenious, is an ultimately self-defeating expedient. Thus sheer exhaustion must eventually perform what goodwill ought to have done but failed to do: each state must be organised internally in such a way that the head of state, for whom the war actually costs nothing (for he wages it at the expense of others, i.e. the people), must no longer have the deciding vote on whether war is to be declared or not, for the people who pay for it must decide. (This, of course, necessarily presupposes that the idea of an original contract has already been realised.) For the people will not readily place itself in danger of personal want (which would not affect the head of state) out of a mere desire for aggrandisement, or because of some supposed and purely verbal offence. And thus posterity will not be oppressed by any burdens which it has not brought upon itself, and it will be able to make perpetual progress towards a morally superior state. This is not produced by any love on the part of earlier ages for later ones, but only by the love of each age for itself. Each commonwealth, unable to harm the others by force, must observe the laws on its own account, and it may reasonably hope that other similarly constituted bodies will help it to do so.

But this is no more than a personal opinion and hypothesis; it is uncertain, like all judgements which profess to define the appropriate natural cause of an intended effect which is not wholly within our control. And even as such, it does not offer the subject of an existing state any principle by which he could attain the desired effect by force (as has already been demonstrated); only the head of state, who is above coercion, can do so. In the normal order of things, it cannot be expected of human nature to desist voluntarily from using force, although it is not impossible where the circumstances are sufficiently pressing. Thus it is not inappropriate to say of man's moral hopes and desires that, since he is powerless to fulfil them himself, he may look to *providence* to create the circumstances in which they can be fulfilled. The end of *man* as an entire species, i.e. that of fulfilling his ultimate appointed purpose by freely exercising his own powers, will be brought by providence to a successful issue, even although the ends of *men* as individuals run in a diametrically opposite direction. For the very conflict of individual inclinations, which is the source of all evil, gives reason a free hand to master them all; it thus gives predominance not to evil, which destroys itself, but to good, which continues to maintain itself once it has been established.

Nowhere does human nature appear less admirable than in the relationships which exist between peoples. No state is for a moment secure from the others in its independence and its possessions. The will to subjugate the others or to grow at their expense is always present, and the production of armaments for defence, which often makes peace more oppressive and more destructive of internal welfare than war itself, can never be relaxed. And there is no possible way of counteracting this except a state of international right, based upon enforceable public laws to which each state must submit (by analogy with a state of civil or political right among individual men). For a permanent universal peace by means of a so-called *European balance of power* is a pure illusion, like Swift's story of the house which the builder had constructed in such perfect harmony with all the laws of equilibrium that it collapsed as soon as a sparrow alighted on it.[23] But it might be objected that no states will ever submit to coercive laws of this kind, and that a proposal for a universal federation, to whose power all the individual states would voluntarily submit and whose laws they would all obey, may be all very well in the theory of the Abbé St Pierre[24] or of Rousseau, but that it does not apply in practice. For such proposals have always been ridiculed by great statesmen, and even more by heads of state, as pedantic, childish and academic ideas.

For my own part, I put my trust in the theory of what the relationships between men and states *ought to be* according to the principle of right. It recommends to us earthly gods the maxim that we should proceed in our disputes in such a way that a universal federal state may be inaugurated, so that we should therefore assume that it *is possible* (*in praxi*). I likewise rely (*in subsidium*) upon the very nature of things to force men to do what they do not willingly choose (*fata volentem ducunt, nolentem trahunt*).[25] This involves human nature, which is still animated by respect for right and duty. I therefore cannot and will not see it as so deeply immersed in evil that practical moral reason will not triumph in the end, after many unsuccessful attempts, thereby showing that it is worthy of admiration after all. On the cosmopolitan level too, it thus remains true to say that whatever reason shows to be valid in theory, is also valid in practice.

Perpetual Peace
A Philosophical Sketch[1]

'THE PERPETUAL PEACE'

A Dutch innkeeper once put this satirical inscription on his signboard, along with the picture of a graveyard. We shall not trouble to ask whether it applies to men in general, or particularly to heads of state (who can never have enough of war), or only to the philosophers who blissfully dream of perpetual peace. The author of the present essay does, however, make one reservation in advance. The practical politician tends to look down with great complacency upon the political theorist as a mere academic. The theorist's abstract ideas, the practitioner believes, cannot endanger the state, since the state must be founded upon principles of experience; it thus seems safe to let him fire off his whole broadside, and the *worldly-wise* statesman need not turn a hair. It thus follows that if the practical politician is to be consistent, he must not claim, in the event of a dispute with the theorist, to scent any danger to the state in the opinions which the theorist has randomly uttered in public. By this saving clause, the author of this essay will consider himself expressly safeguarded, in correct and proper style, against all malicious interpretation.

FIRST SECTION
Which Contains the Preliminary Articles of a Perpetual Peace Between States

1. 'No conclusion of peace shall be considered valid as such if it was made with a secret reservation of the material for a future war.'

For if this were the case, it would be a mere truce, a suspension of hostilities, not a *peace*. Peace means an end to all hostilities, and to attach the adjective 'perpetual' to it is already suspiciously close to pleonasm. A conclusion of peace nullifies all existing reasons for a future war, even if these are not yet known to the contracting parties, and no matter how acutely and carefully they may later be pieced together out of old docu-

93

ments. It is possible that either party may make a mental reservation with a view to reviving its old pretensions in the future. Such reservations will not be mentioned explicitly, since both parties may simply be too exhausted to continue the war, although they may nonetheless possess sufficient ill will to seize the first favourable opportunity of attaining their end. But if we consider such reservations in themselves, they soon appear as Jesuitical casuistry; they are beneath the dignity of a ruler, just as it is beneath the dignity of a minister of state to comply with any reasoning of this kind.

But if, in accordance with 'enlightened' notions of political expediency, we believe that the true glory of a state consists in the constant increase of its power by any means whatsoever, the above judgement will certainly appear academic and pedantic.

2. 'No independently existing state, whether it be large or small, may be acquired by another state by inheritance, exchange, purchase or gift.'

For a state, unlike the ground on which it is based, is not a possession (*patrimonium*). It is a society of men, which no-one other than itself can command or dispose of. Like a tree, it has its own roots, and to graft it on to another state as if it were a shoot is to terminate its existence as a moral personality and make it into a commodity. This contradicts the idea of the original contract, without which the rights of a people are unthinkable.* Everyone knows what danger the supposed right of acquiring states in this way, even in our own times, has brought upon Europe (for this practice is unknown in other continents). It has been thought that states can marry one another, and this has provided a new kind of industry by which power can be increased through family alliances, without expenditure of energy, while landed property can be extended at the same time. It is the same thing when the troops of one state are hired to another to fight an enemy who is not common to both; for the subjects are thereby used and misused as objects to be manipulated at will.

3. 'Standing armies (*miles perpetuus*) will gradually be abolished altogether.'

For they constantly threaten other states with war by the very fact that they are always prepared for it. They spur on the states to outdo one another in arming unlimited numbers of soldiers, and since the resultant costs eventually make peace more oppressive than a short war, the armies

---

* A hereditary kingdom is not a state which can be inherited by another state. Only the right to rule over it may be bequeathed to another physical person. In this case, the state acquires a ruler, but the ruler as such (i.e. as one who already has another kingdom) does not acquire the state.

are themselves the cause of wars of aggression which set out to end burdensome military expenditure. Furthermore, the hiring of men to kill or to be killed seems to mean using them as mere machines and instruments in the hands of someone else (the state), which cannot easily be reconciled with the rights of man in one's own person. It is quite a different matter if the citizens undertake voluntary military training from time to time in order to secure themselves and their fatherland against attacks from outside. But it would be just the same if wealth rather than soldiers were accumulated, for it would be seen by other states as a military threat; it might compel them to mount preventive attacks, for of the three powers within a state—the *power of the army*, the *power of alliance* and the *power of money*—the third is probably the most reliable instrument of war. It would lead more often to wars if it were not so difficult to discover the amount of wealth which another state possesses.

4. 'No national debt shall be contracted in connection with the external affairs of the state.'

There is no cause for suspicion if help for the national economy is sought inside or outside the state (e.g. for improvements to roads, new settlements, storage of foodstuffs for years of famine, etc.). But a credit system, if used by the powers as an instrument of aggression against one another, shows the power of money in its most dangerous form. For while the debts thereby incurred are always secure against present demands (because not all the creditors will demand payment at the same time), these debts go on growing indefinitely. This ingenious system, invented by a commercial people[2] in the present century, provides a military fund which may exceed the resources of all the other states put together. It can only be exhausted by an eventual tax-deficit, which may be postponed for a considerable time by the commercial stimulus which industry and trade receive through the credit system. This ease in making war, coupled with the warlike inclination of those in power (which seems to be an integral feature of human nature), is thus a great obstacle in the way of perpetual peace. Foreign debts must therefore be prohibited by a preliminary article of such a peace, otherwise national bankruptcy, inevitable in the long run, would necessarily involve various other states in the resultant loss without their having deserved it, thus inflicting upon them a public injury. Other states are therefore justified in allying themselves against such a state and its pretensions.

5. 'No state shall forcibly interfere in the constitution and government of another state.'

For what could justify such interference? Surely not any sense of scandal or offence which a state arouses in the subjects of another state. It should rather serve as a warning to others, as an example of the great evils which a people has incurred by its lawlessness. And a bad example which one free person gives to another (as a *scandalum acceptum*) is not the same as an injury to the latter. But it would be a different matter if a state, through internal discord, were to split into two parts, each of which set itself up as a separate state and claimed authority over the whole. For it could not be reckoned as interference in another state's constitution if an external state were to lend support to one of them, because their condition is one of anarchy. But as long as this internal conflict is not yet decided, the interference of external powers would be a violation of the rights of an independent people which is merely struggling with its internal ills. Such interference would be an active offence and would make the autonomy of all other states insecure.

6. 'No state at war with another shall permit such acts of hostility as would make mutual confidence impossible during a future time of peace. Such acts would include the employment of *assassins* (*percussores*) *or poisoners* (*venefici*), *breach of agreements, the instigation of treason* (*perduellio*) within the enemy state, etc.'

These are dishonourable stratagems. For it must still remain possible, even in wartime, to have some sort of trust in the attitude of the enemy, otherwise peace could not be concluded and the hostilities would turn into a war of extermination (*bellum internecinum*). After all, war is only a regrettable expedient for asserting one's rights by force within a state of nature, where no court of justice is available to judge with legal authority. In such cases, neither party can be declared an unjust enemy, for this would already presuppose a judge's decision; only the *outcome* of the conflict, as in the case of a so-called 'judgement of God', can decide who is in the right. A war of punishment (*bellum punitivum*) between states is inconceivable, since there can be no relationship of superior to inferior among them. It thus follows that a war of extermination, in which both parties and right itself might all be simultaneously annihilated, would allow perpetual peace only on the vast graveyard of the human race. A war of this kind and the employment of all means which might bring it about must thus be absolutely prohibited. But the means listed above would inevitably lead to such a war, because these diabolical arts, besides being intrinsically despicable, would not long be confined to war alone if they were brought into use. This applies, for example, to the employment of spies (*uti exploratoribus*), for it exploits only the dishonesty of others (which can never be completely eliminated). Such practices will be carried over into peacetime and will thus completely vitiate its purpose.

All of the articles listed above, when regarded objectively or in relation to the intentions of those in power, are *prohibitive laws* (*leges prohibitivae*). Yet some of them are of the *strictest* sort (*leges strictae*), being valid irrespective of differing circumstances, and they require that the abuses they prohibit should be abolished *immediately* (Nos. 1, 5, and 6). Others (Nos. 2, 3, and 4), although they are not exceptions to the rule of justice, allow some *subjective* latitude according to the circumstances in which they are applied (*leges latae*). The latter need not necessarily be executed at once, so long as their ultimate purpose (e.g. the *restoration* of freedom to certain states in accordance with the second article) is not lost sight of. But their execution may not be *put off* to a non-existent date (*ad calendas graecas*, as Augustus used to promise), for any delay is permitted only as a means of avoiding a premature implementation which might frustrate the whole purpose of the article. For in the case of the second article, the prohibition relates only to the *mode of acquisition*, which is to be forbidden herefoth, but not to the present *state of political possessions*. For although this present state is not backed up by the requisite legal authority, it was considered lawful in the public opinion of every state at the time of the putative acquisition.*

* It has hitherto been doubted, not without justification, whether there can be permissive laws (*leges permissivae*) in addition to preceptive laws (*leges praeceptivae*) and prohibitive laws (*leges prohibitivae*). For all laws embody an element of objective practical necessity as a reason for certain actions, whereas a permission depends only upon practical contingencies. Thus a *permissive law* would be a compulsion to do something which one cannot be compelled to do, and if the object of the law were the same as that of the permission, a contradiction would result. But in the permissive law contained in the second article above, the initial prohibition applies only to the mode of acquiring a right in the future (e.g. by inheritance), whereas the exemption from this prohibition (i.e. the permissive part of the law) applies to the state of political possessions in the present. For in accordance with a permissive law of natural right, this present state can be allowed to remain even although the state of nature has been abandoned for that of civil society. And even if these present possessions are unlawful, they are nevertheless *honest* (*possessio putativa*). A putative possession is prohibited, however, as soon as it has been recognised as such, both in the state of nature and after the subsequent transition to civil society (if the mode of acquisition is the same). And continued possession could not be permitted if the supposed acquisition had been made in the state of civil society, for it would then

SECOND SECTION

Which Contains the Definitive Articles of a Perpetual Peace Between States

A state of peace among men living together is not the same as the state of nature, which is rather a state of war. For even if it does not involve active hostilities, it involves a constant threat of their breaking out. Thus the state of peace must be *formally instituted*, for a suspension of hostilities is not in itself a guarantee of peace. And unless one neighbour gives a guarantee to the other at his request (which can happen only in a *lawful* state), the latter may treat him as an enemy.*

have to end immediately, as an offence against right, as soon as its unlawfulness had been discovered.

My intention here was merely to point out briefly to exponents of natural right the concept of a permissive law, which automatically presents itself within the systematic divisions of reason. It is especially noteworthy since it is frequently used in civil or statutory law, with the one difference that the prohibitive part of the law exists independently, and the permissive part is not included within the law itself as a limiting condition (as it ought to be), but added to cover exceptional cases. Such laws usually state that this or that is prohibited, *except* in cases 1, 2 or 3, and so on *ad infinitum*, for permissive clauses are only added to the law fortuitously, by a random review of particular cases, and not in accordance with any definite principle. Otherwise, the limiting conditions would have had to be included *in the actual formula of the prohibitive law*, whereby it would have become a permissive law in itself. It is therefore to be regretted that the ingenious but unsolved competition question submitted by that wise and clear-sighted gentleman, Count Windischgrätz,[3] was so soon abandoned, for it might have solved the legal difficulty we are at present discussing. For the possibility of finding a universal formula like those of mathematics is the only true test of consistent legislation, and without it, the so-called *ius certum* must remain no more than a pious hope. Otherwise, we shall only have *general* laws (i.e. laws *valid in general*), but no universal laws (i.e. laws which are *generally valid*) such as the concept of a law seems to demand.

* It is usually assumed that one cannot take hostile action against anyone unless one has already been actively *injured* by them. This is perfectly correct if both parties are living in a *legal civil state*. For the fact that the one has entered such a state gives the required guarantee to the other, since both are subject to the same authority. But man (or an individual people) in a mere state of nature robs me of any such security and injures me by virtue of this very state in which he coexists with me. He may not have injured me actively (*facto*), but he does injure me by the very lawlessness of his state (*statu iniusto*), for he is a permanent threat to me, and I can require him either to enter into a common lawful state along with me or to move away from my vicinity. Thus the postulate on which all the following articles are based is that all men who can at all influence one another must adhere to some kind of civil constitution. But any legal constitution, as far as the persons who live under it are concerned, will conform to one of the three following types:

(1) a constitution based on the *civil right* of individuals within a nation (*ius civitatis*).

(2) a constitution based on the *international right* of states in their relationships with one another (*ius gentium*).

(3) a constitution based on *cosmopolitan right*, in so far as individuals and states, coexisting in an external relationship of mutual influences, may be regarded as

First Definitive Article of a Perpetual Peace :
The Civil Constitution of Every State shall be Republican

A *republican constitution* is founded upon three principles: firstly, the principle of *freedom* for all members of a society (as men); secondly, the principle of the *dependence* of everyone upon a single common legislation (as subjects); and thirdly, the principle of legal *equality* for everyone (as citizens).* It is the only constitution which can be derived from the idea

> citizens of a universal state of mankind (*ius cosmopoliticum*). This classification, with respect to the idea of a perpetual peace, is not arbitrary, but necessary. For if even one of the parties were able to influence the others physically and yet itself remained in a state of nature, there would be a risk of war, which it is precisely the aim of the above articles to prevent.

* *Rightful* (*i.e. external*) *freedom* cannot, as is usually thought, be defined as a warrant to do whatever one wishes unless it means doing injustice to others. For what is meant by a *warrant*? It means a possibility of acting in a certain way so long as this action does not do any injustice to others. Thus the definition would run as follows: freedom is the possibility of acting in ways which do no injustice to others. That is, we do no injustice to others (no matter what we may actually do) if we do no injustice to others. Thus the definition is an empty tautology. In fact, my external and rightful *freedom* should be defined as a warrant to obey no external laws except those to which I have been able to give my own consent. Similarly, external and rightful *equality* within a state is that relationship among the citizens whereby no-one can put anyone else under a legal obligation without submitting simultaneously to a law which requires that he can himself be put under the same kind of obligation by the other person. (And we do not need to define the principle of *legal* dependence, since it is always implied in the concept of a political constitution.) The validity of these innate and inalienable rights, the necessary property of mankind, is confirmed and enhanced by the principle that man may have lawful relations even with higher beings (if he believes in the latter). For he may consider himself as a citizen of a transcendental world, to which the same principles apply. And as regards my freedom, I am not under any obligation even to divine laws (which I can recognise by reason alone), except in so far as I have been able to give my own consent to them; for I can form a conception of the divine will only in terms of the law of freedom of my own reason. As for the principle of equality in relation to the most exalted being I can conceive of, apart from God (e.g. a power such as Aeon),[4] there is no reason, if I and this higher being are both doing our duty in our own stations, why it should be my duty to obey while he should enjoy the right to command. But the reason why this principle of equality (unlike that of freedom) does not apply to a relationship towards God, is that God is the only being for whom the concept of duty ceases to be valid.

But as for the right of equality of all citizens as subjects, we may ask whether a *hereditary aristocracy* is admissible. The answer to this question will depend entirely on whether more importance is attached to the superior *rank* granted by the state to one subject over another than is attached to *merit*, or vice versa. Now it is obvious that if rank is conferred according to birth, it will be quite uncertain whether merit (skill and devotion within one's office) will accompany it; it will be tantamount to conferring a position of command upon a favoured individual without any merit on his part, and this could never be approved by the general will of the people in an original contract, which is, after all, the principle behind all rights. For it does not necessarily follow that a nobleman is also a *noble man*. And as for a nobility of office, i.e. the rank of a *higher magistracy* which can be attained by merit, the rank does not attach as a possession to the person, of an original contract, upon which all rightful legislation of a people must be founded. Thus as far as right is concerned, republicanism is in itself the original basis of every kind of civil constitution, and it only remains to ask whether it is the only constitution which can lead to a perpetual peace.

The republican constitution is not only pure in its origin (since it springs from the pure concept of right); it also offers a prospect of attaining the desired result, i.e. a perpetual peace, and the reason for this is as follows.—If, as is inevitably the case under this constitution, the consent of the citizens is required to decide whether or not war is to be declared, it is very natural that they will have great hesitation in embarking on so dangerous an enterprise. For this would mean calling down on themselves all the miseries of war, such as doing the fighting themselves, supplying the costs of the war from their own resources, painfully making good the ensuing devastation, and, as the crowning evil, having to take upon themselves a burden of debt which will embitter peace itself and which can never be paid off on account of the constant threat of new wars. But under a constitution where the subject is not a citizen, and which is therefore not republican, it is the simplest thing in the world to go to war. For the head of state is not a fellow citizen, but the owner of the state, and a war will not force him to make the slightest sacrifice so far as his banquets, hunts, pleasure palaces and court festivals are concerned. He can thus decide on war, without any significant reason, as a kind of amusement, and unconcernedly leave it to the diplomatic corps (who are always ready for such purposes) to justify the war for the sake of propriety.

The following remarks are necessary to prevent the republican constitution from being confused with the democratic one, as commonly happens. The various forms of state (*civitas*) may be classified either according to the different persons who exercise supreme authority, or according to the way in which the nation is governed by its ruler, whoever he may be. The first classification goes by the form of sovereignty (*forma imperii*), and only three such forms are possible, depending on whether the ruling power is in the hands of an *individual*, of *several persons* in association, or of *all* those who together constitute civil society (i.e. *autocracy*, *aristocracy* and *democracy*—the power of a prince, the power of a nobility, and the power of the people). The second classification depends on the form of

but to the post occupied by the person, and this does not violate the principle of equality. For when a person lays down his office, he simultaneously resigns his rank and again becomes one of the people.

government (*forma regiminis*), and relates to the way in which the state, setting out from its constitution (i.e. an act of the general will whereby the mass becomes a people), makes use of its plenary power. The form of government, in this case, will be either *republican* or *despotic. Republican-ism* is that political principle whereby the executive power (the government) is separated from the legislative power. Despotism prevails in a state if the laws are made and arbitrarily executed by one and the same power, and it reflects the will of the people only in so far as the ruler treats the will of the people as his own private will. Of the three forms of sovereignty, *democracy*, in the truest sense of the word, is necessarily a *despotism*, because it establishes an executive power through which all the citizens may make decisions about (and indeed against) the single individual without his consent, so that decisions are made by all the people and yet not by all the people; and this means that the general will is in contradiction with itself, and thus also with freedom.

For any form of government which is not *representative* is essentially an *anomaly*, because one and the same person cannot at the same time be both the legislator and the executor of his own will, just as the general proposition in logical reasoning cannot at the same time be a secondary proposition subsuming the particular within the general. And even if the other two political constitutions (i.e. autocracy and aristocracy) are always defective in as much as they leave room for a despotic form of government, it is at least possible that they will be associated with a form of government which accords with the *spirit* of a representative system. Thus Frederick II[5] at least *said* that he was merely the highest servant of the state,* while a democratic constitution makes this attitude impossible, because everyone under it wants to be a ruler. We can therefore say that the smaller the number of ruling persons in a state and the greater their powers of representation, the more the constitution will approximate to its republican potentiality, which it may hope to realise eventually by gradual reforms. For this reason, it is more difficult in an aristocracy than in a monarchy to reach this one and only perfectly lawful kind of constitution, while it is possible in a democracy only by means of violent revolution. But the

---

* Many have criticised the high-sounding appellations which are often bestowed on a ruler (e.g. 'the divine anointed', or 'the executor and representative of the divine will on earth') as gross and extravagant flatteries, but it seems to me without reason. Far from making the ruler of the land arrogant, they ought rather to fill his soul with humility. For if he is a man of understanding (which we must certainly assume), he will reflect that he has taken over an office which is too great for a human being, namely that of administering God's most sacred institution on earth, the rights of man; he will always live in fear of having in any way injured God's most valued possession.

people are immensely more concerned with the mode of government* than with the form of the constitution, although a great deal also depends on the degree to which the constitution fits the purpose of the government. But if the mode of government is to accord with the concept of right, it must be based on the representative system. This system alone makes possible a republican state, and without it, despotism and violence will result, no matter what kind of constitution is in force. None of the so-called 'republics' of antiquity employed such a system, and they thus inevitably ended in despotism, although this is still relatively bearable under the rule of a single individual.

Second Definitive Article of a Perpetual Peace: The Right of Nations shall be based on a Federation of Free States

Peoples who have grouped themselves into nation states may be judged in the same way as individual men living in a state of nature, independent of external laws; for they are a standing offence to one another by the very fact that they are neighbours. Each nation, for the sake of its own security, can and ought to demand of the others that they should enter along with it into a constitution, similar to the civil one, within which the rights of each could be secured. This would mean establishing a *federation of peoples*. But a federation of this sort would not be the same thing as an international state. For the idea of an international state is contradictory, since every state involves a relationship between a superior (the legislator) and an inferior (the people obeying the laws), whereas a number of nations forming one state would constitute a single nation. And this contradicts our initial assumption, as we are here considering the right of nations in relation to one another in so far as they are a group of separate states which are not to be welded together as a unit.

We look with profound contempt upon the way in which savages cling to their lawless freedom. They would rather engage in incessant strife

---

* Mallet du Pan,[6] in his flamboyant but hollow and empty style, boasts of having at last, after many years of experience, become convinced of the truth of Pope's famous saying: 'For forms of government let fools contest; Whate'er is best administered is best.'[7] If this means that the best administered government is the best administered, he has cracked a nut (as Swift puts it) and been rewarded with a worm.[8] But if it means that the best administered government is also the best kind of government (i.e. the best constitution), it is completely false, for examples of good governments prove nothing whatsoever about kinds of government. Who, indeed, governed better than a Titus[9] or a Marcus Aurelius[10], and yet the one left a Domitian[11] as his successor, and the other a Commodus.[12] And this could not have happened under a good constitution, since their unsuitability for the post of ruler was known early enough, and the power of their predecessors was great enough to have excluded them from the succession.

than submit to a legal constraint which they might impose upon themselves, for they prefer the freedom of folly to the freedom of reason. We regard this as barbarism, coarseness, and brutish debasement of humanity. We might thus expect that civilised peoples, each united within itself as a state, would hasten to abandon so degrading a condition as soon as possible. But instead of doing so, each *state* sees its own majesty (for it would be absurd to speak of the majesty of a *people*) precisely in not having to submit to any external legal constraint, and the glory of its ruler consists in his power to order thousands of people to immolate themselves for a cause which does not truly concern them, while he need not himself incur any danger whatsoever.* And the main difference between the savage nations of Europe and those of America is that while some American tribes have been entirely eaten up by their enemies, the Europeans know how to make better use of those they have defeated than merely by making a meal of them. They would rather use them to increase the number of their own subjects, thereby augmenting their stock of instruments for conducting even more extensive wars.

Although it is largely concealed by governmental constraints in law-governed civil society, the depravity of human nature is displayed without disguise in the unrestricted relations which obtain between the various nations. It is therefore to be wondered at that the word *right* has not been completely banished from military politics as superfluous pedantry, and that no state has been bold enough to declare itself publicly in favour of doing so. For Hugo Grotius,[13] Pufendorf,[14] Vattel[15] and the rest (sorry comforters as they are) are still dutifully quoted in *justification* of military aggression, although their philosophically or diplomatically formulated codes do not and cannot have the slightest *legal* force, since states as such are not subject to a common external constraint. Yet there is no instance of a state ever having been moved to desist from its purpose by arguments supported by the testimonies of such notable men. This homage which every state pays (in words at least) to the concept of right proves that man possesses a greater moral capacity, still dormant at present, to overcome eventually the evil principle within him (for he cannot deny that it exists), and to hope that others will do likewise. Otherwise the word *right* would never be used by states which intend to make war on one another, unless in a derisory sense, as when a certain Gallic prince declared: 'Nature has given to the strong the prerogative of making the weak obey them.' The

* Thus a Bulgarian prince, replying to the Greek Emperor who had kindly offered to settle his dispute with him by a duel, declared: 'A smith who possesses tongs will not lift the glowing iron out of the coals with his own hands.'

way in which states seek their rights can only be by war, since there is no external tribunal to put their claims to trial. But rights cannot be decided by military victory, and a *peace treaty* may put an end to the current war, but not to that general warlike condition within which pretexts can always be found for a new war. And indeed, such a state of affairs cannot be pronounced completely unjust, since it allows each party to act as judge in its own cause. Yet while natural right allows us to say of men living in a lawless condition that they ought to abandon it, the right of nations does not allow us to say the same of states. For as states, they already have a lawful internal constitution, and have thus outgrown the coercive right of others to subject them to a wider legal constitution in accordance with their conception of right. On the other hand, reason, as the highest legislative moral power, absolutely condemns war as a test of rights and sets up peace as an immediate duty. But peace can neither be inaugurated nor secured without a general agreement between the nations; thus a particular kind of league, which we might call a *pacific federation (foedus pacificum)*, is required. It would differ from a *peace treaty (pactum pacis)* in that the latter terminates *one* war, whereas the former would seek to end *all* wars for good. This federation does not aim to acquire any power like that of a state, but merely to preserve and secure the *freedom* of each state in itself, along with that of the other confederated states, although this does not mean that they need to submit to public laws and to a coercive power which enforces them, as do men in a state of nature. It can be shown that this idea of *federalism*, extending gradually to encompass all states and thus leading to perpetual peace, is practicable and has objective reality. For if by good fortune one powerful and enlightened nation can form a republic (which is by its nature inclined to seek perpetual peace), this will provide a focal point for federal association among other states. These will join up with the first one, thus securing the freedom of each state in accordance with the idea of international right, and the whole will gradually spread further and further by a series of alliances of this kind.

It would be understandable for a people to say: 'There shall be no war among us; for we will form ourselves into a state, appointing for ourselves a supreme legislative, executive and juridical power to resolve our conflicts by peaceful means.' But if this state says: 'There shall be no war between myself and other states, although I do not recognise any supreme legislative power which could secure my rights and whose rights I should in turn secure', it is impossible to understand what justification I can have for placing any confidence in my rights, unless I can rely on some substitute for the union of civil society, i.e. on a free federation. If the concept of international right is to retain any meaning at all, reason must necessarily couple it with a federation of this kind.

The concept of international right becomes meaningless if interpreted as a right to go to war. For this would make it a right to determine what is lawful not by means of universally valid external laws, but by means of one-sided maxims backed up by physical force. It could be taken to mean that it is perfectly just for men who adopt this attitude to destroy one another, and thus to find perpetual peace in the vast grave where all the horrors of violence and those responsible for them would be buried. There is only one rational way in which states coexisting with other states can emerge from the lawless condition of pure warfare. Just like individual men, they must renounce their savage and lawless freedom, adapt themselves to public coercive laws, and thus form an *international state* (*civitas gentium*), which would necessarily continue to grow until it embraced all the peoples of the earth. But since this is not the will of the nations, according to their present conception of international right (so that they reject *in hypothesi* what is true *in thesi*), the positive idea of a *world republic* cannot be realised. If all is not to be lost, this can at best find a negative substitute in the shape of an enduring and gradually expanding *federation* likely to prevent war. The latter may check the current of man's inclination to defy the law and antagonise his fellows, although there will always be a risk of it bursting forth anew. *Furor impius intus—fremit horridus ore cruento* (Virgil).*[16]

Third Definitive Article of a Perpetual Peace: Cosmopolitan Right shall be limited to Conditions of Universal Hospitality

As in the foregoing articles, we are here concerned not with philanthropy, but with *right*. In this context, *hospitality* means the right of a stranger not to be treated with hostility when he arrives on someone else's territory. He can indeed be turned away, if this can be done without causing his

* At the end of a war, when peace is concluded, it would not be inappropriate for a people to appoint a day of atonement after the festival of thanksgiving. Heaven would be invoked in the name of the state to forgive the human race for the great sin of which it continues to be guilty, since it will not accommodate itself to a lawful constitution in international relations. Proud of its independence, each state prefers to employ the barbarous expedient of war, although war cannot produce the desired decision on the rights of particular states. The thanksgivings for individual victories during a war, the hymns which are sung (in the style of the Israelites) to the *Lord of Hosts*, contrast no less markedly with the moral conception of a father of mankind. For besides displaying indifference to the way in which nations pursue their mutual rights (deplorable though it is), they actually rejoice at having annihilated numerous human beings or their happiness.

death, but he must not be treated with hostility, so long as he behaves in a peaceable manner in the place he happens to be in. The stranger cannot claim the *right of a guest* to be entertained, for this would require a special friendly agreement whereby he might become a member of the native household for a certain time. He may only claim a *right of resort*, for all men are entitled to present themselves in the society of others by virtue of their right to communal possession of the earth's surface. Since the earth is a globe, they cannot disperse over an infinite area, but must necessarily tolerate one another's company. And no-one originally has any greater right than anyone else to occupy any particular portion of the earth. The community of man is divided by uninhabitable parts of the earth's surface such as oceans and deserts, but even then, the *ship* or the *camel* (the ship of the desert) make it possible for them to approach their fellows over these ownerless tracts, and to utilise as a means of social intercourse that *right to the earth's surface* which the human race shares in common. The inhospitable behaviour of coastal dwellers (as on the Barbary coast) in plundering ships on the adjoining seas or enslaving stranded seafarers, or that of inhabitants of the desert (as with the Arab Bedouins), who regard their proximity to nomadic tribes as a justification for plundering them, is contrary to natural right. But this natural right of hospitality, i.e. the right of strangers, does not extend beyond those conditions which make it possible for them to *attempt* to enter into relations with the native inhabitants. In this way, continents distant from each other can enter into peaceful mutual relations which may eventually be regulated by public laws, thus bringing the human race nearer and nearer to a cosmopolitan constitution.

If we compare with this ultimate end the *inhospitable* conduct of the civilised states of our continent, especially the commercial states, the injustice which they display in *visiting* foreign countries and peoples (which in their case is the same as *conquering* them) seems appallingly great. America, the negro countries, the Spice Islands, the Cape, etc. were looked upon at the time of their discovery as ownerless territories; for the native inhabitants were counted as nothing. In East India (Hindustan), foreign troops were brought in under the pretext of merely setting up trading posts. This led to oppression of the natives, incitement of the various Indian states to widespread wars, famine, insurrection, treachery and the whole litany of evils which can afflict the human race.

China* and Japan (Nippon), having had experience of such guests,

---

* If we wish to give this great empire the name by which it calls itself (i.e. *China*, not *Sina* or any similar form), we need only consult Georgi's[17] *Alphabetum Tibetanum*,

have wisely placed restrictions on them. China permits contact with her territories, but not entrance into them, while Japan only allows contact with a single European people, the Dutch, although they are still segregated from the native community like prisoners. The worst (or from the point of view of moral judgements, the best) thing about all this is that the commercial states do not even benefit by their violence, for all their trading companies are on the point of collapse. The Sugar Islands, that stronghold of the cruellest and most calculated slavery, do not yield any real profit; they serve only the indirect (and not entirely laudable) purpose of training sailors for warships, thereby aiding the prosecution of wars in Europe. And all this is the work of powers who make endless ado about their piety, and who wish to be considered as chosen believers while they live on the fruits of iniquity.

The peoples of the earth have thus entered in varying degrees into a universal community, and it has developed to the point where a violation

pp. 651–654, note b in particular. According to Professor Fischer[18] of Petersburg, it actually has no fixed name which it might apply to itself; the commonest one is still the word *Kin*, which means gold (the Tibetans, however, call this *Ser*), which explains why the emperor is called King of Gold (i.e. of the fairest land in the world). The word is apparently pronounced *Chin* in the land itself, but expressed as *Kin* by the Italian missionaries, who cannot pronounce the correct guttural sound. It can also be seen that what the Romans called the land of the people of *Ser* was in fact China, and silk was brought from there to Europe via Greater Tibet (probably crossing Lesser Tibet, Bukhara[19] and Persia). This led to numerous speculations on the antiquity of this extraordinary state as compared with that of Hindustan, and on its relations with Tibet as well as with Japan. But the name Sina or Tschina, which neighbouring countries allegedly use of it, leads nowhere.

Perhaps the ancient but hitherto obscure community between Europe and Tibet can be explained from what Hesychius[20] has recorded of the hierophant's[21] cry Κονξ Ὄμπαξ (*Konx Ompax*)[22] in the Eleusinian Mysteries[23] (cf. *Journey of the Younger Anacharsis*, Part V, p. 447 *et seq.*).[24] For according to Georgi's *Alphabetum Tibetanum*, the word *Concioa* means god, and it markedly resembles *Konx*, while *Pah-cio* (*ibid.* p. 520), which the Greeks might easily have pronounced *pax*, means *promulgator legis*, the divinity which pervades the whole of nature (also called *Cencresi*, p. 177). But *Om*, which La Croze[25] translates as *benedictus* (blessed), can scarcely mean anything other than *beatific* if applied to the deity (p. 507). When P. Francisco Orazio[26] asked the Tibetan lamas how they conceived of god (*Concioa*), he always received the answer: '*God is the community of all the holy ones*' (i.e. the community of blessed souls, at last reunited in the deity by being reborn as lamas after numerous migrations through all kinds of bodies, and thereby transformed into beings worthy of adoration—p. 223). Thus the mysterious name *Konx Ompax* might designate that *holy* (*Konx*), *heavenly* (*Om*) and *wise* (*Pax*) supreme being who pervades the whole world, i.e. nature personified. As used in the Greek mysteries, it may well have signified *monotheism* to the epopts,[27] as distinct from the *polytheism* of the uninitiated mass, although it savoured of atheism to P. Orazio (*loc. cit.*). Our earlier considerations should help to explain how this mysterious name reached the Greeks from Tibet; conversely, this influence makes it appear probable that Europe at an early date had contact with China by way of Tibet, perhaps even earlier than with India.[28]

of rights in *one* part of the world is felt *everywhere*. The idea of a cosmopolitan right is therefore not fantastic and overstrained; it is a necessary complement to the unwritten code of political and international right, transforming it into a universal right of humanity. Only under this condition can we flatter ourselves that we are continually advancing towards a perpetual peace.

First Supplement: On the Guarantee of a Perpetual Peace

Perpetual peace is *guaranteed* by no less an authority than the great artist *Nature* herself (*natura daedala rerum*).[29] The mechanical process of nature visibly exhibits the purposive plan of producing concord among men, even against their will and indeed by means of their very discord. This design, if we regard it as a compelling cause whose laws of operation are unknown to us, is called *fate*. But if we consider its purposive function within the world's development, whereby it appears as the underlying wisdom of a higher cause, showing the way towards the objective goal of the human race and predetermining the world's evolution, we call it *providence*.* We cannot actually observe such an agency in the artifices

---

* In the mechanism of nature, of which man (as a sensory being) is a part, there is evident a fundamental form on which its very existence depends. This form becomes intelligible to us only if we attribute it to the design of a universal creator who has determined it in advance. We call this predetermining influence divine *providence*, and further define it as *original providence* in so far as it is active from the earliest times onwards (*providentia conditrix*; *semel iussit, semper parent*—Augustine).[30] In as much as it sustains the course of nature in accordance with purposive universal laws, we call it *ruling providence* (*providentia gubernatrix*). If it realises particular ends which man could not have foreseen and whose existence can only be guessed at from the results, it is termed *guiding providence* (*providentia directrix*). And finally, if individual events are regarded as divinely intended, we no longer speak of providence but of a *special dispensation* (*directio extraordinaria*). But it is foolish presumption for man to claim that he can recognise this as such, since it implies that a miracle has taken place, even if the events are not specifically described as miraculous. For however pious and humble it may sound, it is absurd and self-conceited for anyone to conclude from a single event that the efficient cause is governed by a special principle, or that the event in question is an end in itself and not just the natural and mechanical consequence of another end which is completely unknown to us. Similarly, it is false and self-contradictory to classify providence in terms of worldly objects (*materialiter*), dividing it up into *general* and *particular*, as occurs in the doctrine that providence takes care to preserve the various species of creatures, but leaves chance to look after the individuals; for the whole point of saying that providence applies in general is that no single object should be excepted from it. This classification, however, was probably meant to indicate that the intentions of providence are carried out *in different ways* (*formaliter*). These might be *ordinary* (e.g. the annual death and revival of nature with the changes of seasons) or *extraordinary* (e.g. the transporting of wood by Ocean currents to Arctic coasts where it cannot grow, thus providing for the native inhabitants, who could not live without it). In the latter case, while we can well explain the physico-mechanical cause of the phenomena in question (e.g. by the fact that the riverbanks in temperate lands are

of nature, nor can we even *infer* its existence from them. But as with all relations between the form of things and their ultimate purposes, we can and must *supply it mentally* in order to conceive of its possibility by analogy with human artifices. Its relationship to and conformity with the end which reason directly prescribes to us (i.e. the end of morality) can only be conceived of as an idea. Yet while this idea is indeed far-fetched in *theory*, it does possess dogmatic validity and has a very real foundation in *practice*, as with the concept of *perpetual peace*, which makes it our duty to promote it by using the natural mechanism described above. But in contexts such as this, where we are concerned purely with theory and not with religion, we should also note that it is more in keeping with the limitations of human reason to speak of *nature* and not of *providence*, for reason, in dealing with cause and effect relationships, must keep within the bounds of possible experience. *Modesty* forbids us to speak of providence as something we can recognise, for this would mean donning the wings of Icarus and presuming to approach the mystery of its inscrutable intentions.

But before we define this guarantee more precisely, we must first examine the situation in which nature has placed the actors in her great spectacle, for it is this situation which ultimately demands the guarantee of peace. We may next enquire in what manner the guarantee is provided.

Nature's provisional arrangement is as follows. Firstly, she has taken

covered in forests, so that the trees may fall into the rivers and be carried further afield by currents like the Gulf Stream), we must not on the other hand overlook teleology, which indicates the foresight of a wise agency governing nature. But the conception, current in the academic world, of a divine *participation* or *collaboration* (*concursus*) in effects experienced in the world of the senses, is superfluous. For *firstly*, it is self-contradictory to try to harness disparates together (*gryphes iungere equis*),[31] and to imply that a being who is himself the complete cause of the world's developments has to *supplement* his own predetermining providence during the course of world events (so that it must originally have been inadequate); for example, it is absurd to say that after God, the doctor acted as an assistant in curing the patient—*causa solitaria non iuvat*.[32] God is the creator of the doctor and of all his medicaments, so that the effect must be ascribed *entirely* to him if we are to ascend to that supreme original cause which is theoretically beyond our comprehension. Alternatively, it can be ascribed *entirely* to the doctor, in so far as we treat the event in question as belonging to the order of nature and as capable of explanation within the causal series of earthly occurrences. And *secondly*, if we adopt such attitudes, we are deprived of all definite principles by which we might judge effects. But the concept of a divine *concursus* is completely acceptable and indeed necessary in the moral and practical sense, which refers exclusively to the transcendental world. For example, we may say that we should never cease to strive towards goodness, for we believe that God, even by means which we cannot comprehend, will make up for our own lack of righteousness so long as our attitude is sincere. It is, however, self-evident that no-one should use such arguments to *explain* a good deed, regarded as a secular event, for this would presuppose theoretical knowledge of the transcendental, which it is absurd for us to claim.

care that human beings are able to live in all the areas where they are settled. Secondly, she has driven them in all directions by means of *war*, so that they inhabit even the most inhospitable regions. And thirdly, she has compelled them by the same means to enter into more or less legal relationships. It is in itself wonderful that moss can still grow in the cold wastes around the Arctic Ocean; the *reindeer* can scrape it out from beneath the snow, and can thus itself serve as nourishment or as a draft animal for the Ostiaks or Samoyeds. Similarly, the sandy salt deserts contain the *camel*, which seems as if it had been created for travelling over them in order that they might not be left unutilised. But evidence of design in nature emerges even more clearly when we realise that the shores of the Arctic Ocean are inhabited not only by fur-bearing animals, but also by seals, walrusses and whales, whose flesh provides food and whose fat provides warmth for the native inhabitants. Nature's care arouses most admiration, however, by carrying driftwood to these treeless regions, without anyone knowing exactly where it comes from. For if they did not have this material, the natives would not be able to construct either boats or weapons, or dwellings in which to live. And they have enough to do making war on the animals to be able to live in peace among themselves. But it was probably nothing but war which *drove* them into these regions. And the first *instrument of war* among all the animals which man learned to domesticate in the course of peopling the earth was the *horse*. For the elephant belongs to that later age of luxury which began after states had been established. The same applies to the art of cultivating certain kinds of grasses known as *cereals*, whose original nature is now unknown to us, and to the production and refinement of various *fruits* by transplanting and grafting (in Europe, perhaps only two species were involved, the crab-apple and the wild pear). Such arts could arise only within established states in which landed property was secure, after men had made the transition to an *agricultural* way of life, abandoning the lawless freedom they had enjoyed in their previous existence as hunters,* fishers and shepherds. *Salt* and *iron* were next discovered, and were perhaps the

---

* Of all ways of life, that of the hunter is undoubtedly most at odds with a civilised constitution. For families, having to live in separation, soon become strangers to each other, and subsequently, being scattered about in wide forests, they treat each other with hostility, since each requires a large area to provide itself with food and clothing. The command addressed to Noah forbidding the eating of blood (Genesis 9, 4–6) seems to have been originally nothing else but a prohibition of the hunter's way of life. For this must often involve eating uncooked meat, and if the latter is forbidden, the first is automatically ruled out too. This prohibition, often reiterated, was a condition later imposed by the Jewish Christians upon the newly accepted Christians of heathen origin, albeit with a different intention (Acts 15,20 and 21,25).

first articles of trade between nations to be in demand everywhere. In this way, nations first entered into *peaceful relations* with one another, and thus achieved mutual understanding, community of interests and peaceful relations, even with the most distant of their fellows.

In seeing to it that men *could* live everywhere on earth, nature has at the same time despotically willed that they *should* live everywhere, even against their own inclinations. And this obligation does not rest upon any concept of duty which might bind them to fulfil it in accordance with a moral law; on the contrary, nature has chosen war as a means of attaining this end.

We can observe nations which reveal the unity of their descent by the unity of their language. This is the case with the *Samoyeds* on the Arctic Ocean and another people with a similar language living two hundred miles away in the Altai Mountains; another people of Mongol extraction, given to horsemanship and hence to warlike pursuits, has pushed its way between them, thus driving the one part of the tribe far away from the other into the most inhospitable Arctic regions, where it would certainly not have gone by its own inclinations.* In the same way, the Finns in the northernmost region of Europe (where they are known as Lapps) are now far separated from the Hungarians, to whom they are linguistically related, by Gothic and Sarmatian peoples who have pushed their way in between them. And what else but war, nature's means of peopling the whole earth, can have driven the Eskimos so far North—for they are quite distinct from all other American races, and are perhaps descended from European adventurers of ancient times; the Pesherae have been driven South into Tierra del Fuego in the same manner. War itself, however, does not require any particular kind of motivation, for it seems to be ingrained in human nature, and even to be regarded as something noble to which man is inspired by his love of honour, without selfish motives. Thus warlike courage, with the American savages as with their European counterparts in medieval times, is held to be of great and immediate value—and not just *in times of* war (as might be expected), but also *in order that* there may be war. Thus wars are often started merely to display this quality, so

---

* The following question might be raised. If nature intended that these frozen shores should not remain uninhabited, what will happen to their inhabitants if nature, as indeed may well happen, ceases to provide them with driftwood? For we may well believe that the natives of temperate zones, as their culture progresses, will make better use of the wood which grows on the banks of their rivers, and will not allow it to fall into them and be swept out to sea. I should reply that those who live on the Ob, the Yenisei, the Lena etc. will supply them with it commercially, bartering it for the animal products in which the Arctic coasts are so plentiful—but only after nature has compelled them to live in peace with one another.

that war itself is invested with an inherent *dignity*; for even philosophers have eulogised it as a kind of ennobling influence on man, forgetting the Greek saying that 'war is bad in that it produces more evil people than it destroys'. So much, then, for what nature does to further *her own end* with respect to the human race as an animal species.

We now come to the essential question regarding the prospect of perpetual peace. What does nature do in relation to the end which man's own reason prescribes to him as a duty, i.e. how does nature help to promote his *moral purpose*? And how does nature guarantee that what man *ought* to do by the laws of his freedom (but does not do) will in fact be done through nature's compulsion, without prejudice to the free agency of man? This question arises, moreover, in all three areas of public right—in *political, international* and *cosmopolitan right*. For if I say that nature *wills* that this or that should happen, this does not mean that nature imposes on us a *duty* to do it, for duties can only be imposed by practical reason, acting without any external constraint. On the contrary, nature does it herself, whether we are willing or not: *fata volentem ducunt, nolentem trahunt.*[33]

1. Even if people were not compelled by internal dissent to submit to the coercion of public laws, war would produce the same effect from outside. For in accordance with the natural arrangement described above, each people would find itself confronted by another neighbouring people pressing in upon it, thus forcing it to form itself internally into a *state* in order to encounter the other as an armed *power*. Now the *republican* constitution is the only one which does complete justice to the rights of man. But it is also the most difficult to establish, and even more so to preserve, so that many maintain that it would only be possible within a state of *angels*, since men, with their self-seeking inclinations, would be incapable of adhering to a constitution of so sublime a nature. But in fact, nature comes to the aid of the universal and rational human will, so admirable in itself but so impotent in practice, and makes use of precisely those self-seeking inclinations in order to do so. It only remains for men to create a good organisation for the state, a task which is well within their capability, and to arrange it in such a way that their self-seeking energies are opposed to one another, each thereby neutralising or eliminating the destructive effects of the rest. And as far as reason is concerned, the result is the same as if man's selfish tendencies were non-existent, so that man, even if he is not morally good in himself, is nevertheless compelled to be a good citizen. As hard as it may sound, the problem of setting up a state can be solved even by a nation of devils (so long as they possess understanding). It may be stated as follows: 'In order to organise a group of

rational beings who together require universal laws for their survival, but of whom each separate individual is secretly inclined to exempt himself from them, the constitution must be so designed that, although the citizens are opposed to one another in their private attitudes, these opposing views may inhibit one another in such a way that the public conduct of the citizens will be the same as if they did not have such evil attitudes.' A problem of this kind must be soluble. For such a task does not involve the moral improvement of man; it only means finding out how the mechanism of nature can be applied to men in such a manner that the antagonism of their hostile attitudes will make them compel one another to submit to coercive laws, thereby producing a condition of peace within which the laws can be enforced. We can even see this principle at work among the actually existing (although as yet very imperfectly organised) states. For in their external relations, they have already approached what the idea of right prescribes, although the reason for this is certainly not their internal moral attitudes. In the same way, we cannot expect their moral attitudes to produce a good political constitution; on the contrary, it is only through the latter that the people can be expected to attain a good level of moral culture. Thus that mechanism of nature by which selfish inclinations are naturally opposed to one another in their external relations can be used by reason to facilitate the attainment of its own end, the reign of established right. Internal and external peace are thereby furthered and assured, so far as it lies within the power of the state itself to do so. We may therefore say that nature *irresistibly wills* that right should eventually gain the upper hand. What men have neglected to do will ultimately happen of its own accord, albeit with much inconvenience. As Bouterwek[34] puts it: 'If the reed is bent too far, it breaks; and he who wants too much gets nothing.'

2. The idea of international right presupposes the separate existence of many independent adjoining states. And such a state of affairs is essentially a state of war, unless there is a federal union to prevent hostilities breaking out. But in the light of the idea of reason, this state is still to be preferred to an amalgamation of the separate nations under a single power which has overruled the rest and created a universal monarchy. For the laws progressively lose their impact as the government increases its range, and a soulless despotism, after crushing the germs of goodness, will finally lapse into anarchy. It is nonetheless the desire of every state (or its ruler) to achieve lasting peace by thus dominating the whole world, if at all possible. But *nature* wills it otherwise, and uses two means to separate the nations and prevent them from intermingling—*linguistic* and

*religious** differences. These may certainly occasion mutual hatred and provide pretexts for wars, but as culture grows and men gradually move towards greater agreement over their principles, they lead to mutual understanding and peace. And unlike that universal despotism which saps all man's energies and ends in the graveyard of freedom, this peace is created and guaranteed by an equilibrium of forces and a most vigorous rivalry.

3. Thus nature wisely separates the nations, although the will of each individual state, even basing its arguments on international right, would gladly unite them under its own sway by force or by cunning. On the other hand, nature also unites nations which the concept of cosmopolitan right would not have protected from violence and war, and does so by means of their mutual self-interest. For the *spirit of commerce* sooner or later takes hold of every people, and it cannot exist side by side with war. And of all the powers (or means) at the disposal of the power of the state, *financial power* can probably be relied on most. Thus states find themselves compelled to promote the noble cause of peace, though not exactly from motives of morality. And wherever in the world there is a threat of war breaking out, they will try to prevent it by mediation, just as if they had entered into a permanent league for this purpose; for by the very nature of things, large military alliances can only rarely be formed, and will even more rarely be successful.

In this way, nature guarantees perpetual peace by the actual mechanism of human inclinations. And while the likelihood of its being attained is not sufficient to enable us to *prophesy* the future theoretically, it is enough for practical purposes. It makes it our duty to work our way towards this goal, which is more than an empty chimera.

Second Supplement: Secret Article of a Perpetual Peace

In transactions involving public right, a secret article (regarded objectively or in terms of its content) is a contradiction. But in subjective terms, i.e. in relation to the sort of person who dictates it, an article may well contain a secret element, for the person concerned may consider it prejudicial to his own dignity to name himself publicly as its originator.

The only article of this kind is embodied in the following sentence:

---

* *Religious differences*—an odd expression! As if we were to speak of different *moralities*. There may certainly be different historical *confessions*, although these have nothing to do with religion itself but only with changes in the means used to further religion, and are thus the province of historical research. And there may be just as many different religious *books* (the Zend-Avesta, the Vedas, the Koran, etc.). But there can only be *one religion* which is valid for all men and at all times. Thus the different confessions can scarcely be more than the vehicles of religion; these are fortuitous, and may vary with differences in time or place.

'*The maxims of the philosophers on the conditions under which public peace is possible shall be consulted by states which are armed for war.*'

Although it may seem humiliating for the legislative authority of a state, to which we must naturally attribute the highest degree of wisdom, to seek instruction from *subjects* (the philosophers) regarding the principles on which it should act in its relations with other states, it is nevertheless extremely advisable that it should do so. The state will therefore invite their help *silently*, making a secret of it. In other words, it will *allow them to speak* freely and publicly on the universal maxims of warfare and peace-making, and they will indeed do so of their own accord if no-one forbids their discussions. And no special formal arrangement among the states is necessary to enable them to agree on this issue, for the agreement already lies in the obligations imposed by universal human reason in its capacity as a moral legislator. This does not, however, imply that the state must give the principles of the philosopher precedence over the pronouncements of the jurist (who represents the power of the state), but only that the philosopher should be given a *hearing*. The jurist, who has taken as his symbol the scales of right and the sword of justice, usually uses the latter not merely to keep any extraneous influences away from the former, but will throw the *sword* into one of the *scales* if it refuses to sink (*vae victis!*).[35] Unless the jurist is at the same time a philosopher, at any rate in moral matters, he is under the greatest temptation to do this, for his business is merely to apply existing laws, and not to enquire whether they are in need of improvement. He acts as if this truly low rank of his faculty were in fact one of the higher ones, for the simple reason that it is accompanied by power (as is also the case with two of the other faculties). But the philosophical faculty occupies a very low position in face of the combined power of the others. Thus we are told, for instance, that philosophy is the *handmaid* of theology, and something similar in relation to the others. But it is far from clear whether this handmaid bears the torch before her gracious lady, or carries the train behind.

It is not to be expected that kings will philosophise or that philosophers will become kings; nor is it to be desired, however, since the possession of power inevitably corrupts the free judgement of reason. Kings or sovereign peoples (i.e. those governing themselves by egalitarian laws) should not, however, force the class of philosophers to disappear or to remain silent, but should allow them to speak publicly. This is essential to both in order that light may be thrown on their affairs. And since the class of philosophers is by nature incapable of forming seditious factions or clubs, they cannot incur suspicion of disseminating propaganda.

Appendix

I

ON THE DISAGREEMENT BETWEEN MORALS AND POLITICS IN RELATION TO PERPETUAL PEACE

Morality, as a collection of absolutely binding laws by which our actions *ought* to be governed, belongs essentially, in an objective sense, to the practical sphere. And if we have once acknowledged the authority of this concept of duty, it is patently absurd to say that we *cannot* act as the moral laws require. For if this were the case, the concept of duty would automatically be dropped from morals (*ultra posse nemo obligatur*).[36] Hence there can be no conflict between politics, as an applied branch of right, and morality, as a theoretical branch of right (i.e. between theory and practice); for such a conflict could occur only if morality were taken to mean a general doctrine of expediency, i.e. a theory of the maxims by which one might select the most useful means of furthering one's own advantage—and this would be tantamount to denying that morality exists.

If politics were to say: '*Be ye therefore wise as serpents*', morality might add, by way of qualification: '*and harmless as doves*'.[37] If these two precepts cannot exist together within a single commandment, then there is indeed a disagreement between politics and morality. But if the two are to be united, it is absurd to suppose that they are in opposition, and the question of how such a conflict could be resolved cannot even be posed as a mental exercise. It is true, alas, that the saying '*Honesty is the best policy*' embodies a theory which is frequently contradicted by practice. Yet the equally theoretical proposition '*Honesty is better than any policy*' infinitely transcends all objections, and it is indeed an indispensable condition of any policy whatsoever. The god of morality does not yield to Jupiter, the custodian of violence, for even Jupiter is still subject to fate. In short, reason is not sufficiently enlightened to discover the whole series of predetermining causes which would allow it to predict accurately the happy or unhappy consequences of human activities as dictated by the mechanism of nature; it can only hope that the result will meet with its wishes. But reason at all times shows us clearly enough what we have to do in order to remain in the paths of duty, as the rules of wisdom require, and thus shows us the way towards our ultimate goal.

But the man of practice, to whom morality is pure theory, coldly repudiates our well-intentioned hopes, even if he does concede that we *can* do what we *ought* to do. He bases his argument on the claim that we can tell in advance from human nature that man will never *want* to do what is necessary in order to attain the goal of eternal peace. It is perfectly true that the will of all *individual* men to live in accordance with principles of freedom within a lawful constitution (i.e. the *distributive* unity of the will of all) is not sufficient for this purpose. Before so difficult a problem can be solved, all men *together* (i.e. the *collective* unity of the combined will) must desire to attain this goal; only then can civil society exist as a single whole. Since an additional unifying cause must therefore overrule the differences in the particular wishes of all individuals before a common will can arise, and since no single individual can create it, the only conceivable way of executing the original idea *in practice*, and hence of inaugurating a state of right, is by *force*. On its coercive authority, public right will subsequently be based.

We can certainly expect in advance that there will be considerable deviations in actual experience from the original theoretical idea. For we cannot assume that the moral attitude of the legislator will be such that, after the disorderly mass has been united into a people, he will leave them to create a lawful constitution by their own common will.

It might thus be said that, once a person has the power in his own hands, he will not let the people prescribe laws for him. Similarly, a state which is self-governing and free from all external laws will not let itself become dependent on the judgement of other states in seeking to uphold its rights against them. And even a whole continent, if it feels itself in a superior position to another one, will not hesitate to plunder it or actually to extend its rule over it, irrespective of whether the other is in its way or not. In this way, all the plans which theory lays for political, international or cosmopolitan right dissolve into empty and impracticable ideals; but a practice which is based on empirical principles of human nature, and which does not consider it beneath its dignity to shape its maxims according to the way of the world, can alone hope to find a solid foundation for its system of political opportunism.

If, of course, there is neither freedom nor any moral law based on freedom, but only a state in which everything that happens or can happen simply obeys the mechanical workings of nature, politics would mean the art of utilising nature for the government of men, and this would constitute the whole of practical wisdom; the concept of right would then be only an empty idea. But if we consider it absolutely necessary to couple the concept of right with politics, or even to make it a limiting condition of politics, it must be conceded that the two are compatible. And I can indeed imagine a *moral politician*, i.e. someone who conceives of the principles of political expediency in such a way that they can co-exist with morality, but I cannot imagine a *political moralist*, i.e. one who fashions his morality to suit his own advantage as a statesman.

The moral politician will make it a principle that, if any faults which could not have been prevented are discovered in the political constitution or in the relations between states, it is a duty, especially for heads of state, to see to it that they are corrected as soon as possible; it should be ensured that these political institutions are made to conform to natural right, which stands before us as a model in the idea of practical reason, and this should be done even if selfish interests have to be sacrificed. It would be contrary to all political expediency, which in this case agrees with morality, to destroy any of the existing bonds of political or cosmopolitan union before a better constitution has been prepared to take their place. And while it would be absurd to demand that their faults be repaired at once and by violent measures, it can still be required of the individual in power that he should be intimately aware of the maxim that changes for the better are necessary, in order that the constitution may constantly approach the optimum end prescribed by laws of right. A state may well *govern* itself in a republican way, even if its existing constitution provides for a despotic *ruling power*; and it will gradually come to the stage where the people can be influenced by the mere idea of the law's authority, just as if it were backed up by physical force, so that they will be able to create for themselves a legislation ultimately founded on right. If, however, a more lawful constitution were attained by unlawful means, i.e. by a violent *revolution* resulting from a previous bad constitution, it would then no longer be permissible to lead the people back to the original one, even although everyone who had interfered with the old constitution by violence or conspiracy would rightly have been subject to the penalties of rebellion during the revolution itself. But as for the external relationship between states, no state can be required to relinquish its constitution, even if the latter is despotic (and hence stronger in relation to external enemies), so long as this state is in danger of being engulfed at any moment by other states; hence while plans must be made for political improvement, it must be permissible to delay their execution until a better opportunity arises.*

---

* These are permissive laws of reason, which allow a state of public right to continue, even if it is affected by injustice, until all is ripe for a complete revolution or has been prepared for it by peaceful means. For any *legal* constitution, even if it is only in small measure *lawful*, is better than none at all, and the fate of a premature reform would be anarchy. Thus political prudence, with things as they are at present, will make it a duty

It may well be the case that despotic moralists, i.e. those who err in practice, frequently act contrary to political prudence by adopting or recommending premature measures, yet experience must gradually bring them out of their opposition to nature and make them adopt better ways. But moralising politicians, for what they are worth, try to cover up political principles which are contrary to right, under the pretext that human nature is *incapable* of attaining the good which reason prescribes as an idea. They thereby make progress *impossible*, and eternalise the violation of right.

Instead of applying the correct practice they boast of, these worldly-wise politicians resort to despicable tricks, for they are only out to exploit the people (and if possible the whole world) by influencing the current ruling power in such a way as to ensure their own private advantage. They are just like lawyers (i.e. those for whom law is a profession, not a matter of legislation) who have found their way into politics. For since it is not their business to argue over legislation itself, but to fulfil the present instructions of the law of the land, they will always regard the existing legal constitution (or if this is altered by a higher authority, the subsequent one) as the best, because everything in it will follow a proper mechanical order. But this skill in being all things to all men may give them the illusion that they can also pass judgement, in accordance with concepts of right (i.e. *a priori*, not empirically), on the principles of any *political constitution* whatsoever. And they may boast that they know *men* (which is certainly to be expected, since they have to do with so many of them), although they do not know *man* and his potentialities, for this requires a higher anthropological vantage-point.

Armed with concepts such as these, they proceed to take up political and international law as prescribed by reason. But they cannot take this step except in a spirit of chicanery, for they will follow their usual procedure of applying despotically formulated coercive laws in a mechanical manner, even in a sphere where the concepts of reason only allow for lawful coercion, in keeping with the principles of freedom, which alone makes possible a rightfully established political constitution. The supposed practitioner believes he can solve this problem empirically, ignoring the idea of reason and drawing on experience of how the (largely unlawful) constitutions which have hitherto survived best were organised. And the

to carry out reforms appropriate to the ideal of public right. But where revolutions are brought about by nature alone, it will not use them as a good excuse for even greater oppression, but will treat them as a call of nature to create a lawful constitution based on the principles of freedom, for a thorough reform of this kind is the only one which will last.

maxims which he employs for this purpose, although he does not make them public, can roughly be expressed in the following sophistries:

1. *Fac et excusa.*[38] Seize any favourable opportunity of arbitrarily expropriating a right which the state enjoys over its own or over a neighbouring people; the justification can be presented far more easily and elegantly and the use of violence can be glossed over far more readily *after the fact* than if one were to think out convincing reasons in advance and then wait for counter-arguments to be offered. This is particularly true of the first case, where the highest power in the state is also the legislative authority which must be obeyed without argument. Such audacity itself gives a certain appearance of inner conviction that the deed is right and just, and the god of success (*bonus eventus*) will then be the best of advocates.

2. *Si fecisti, nega.*[39] If you have committed a crime, for instance, in order to lead your people to desperation and thence to rebellion, deny that the guilt is yours. Maintain instead that it arose from the intransigence of the subjects; or if you have seized control of a neighbouring people, say that the very nature of man is responsible, for if he does not anticipate others in resorting to violence, he may count on it that they will anticipate and overpower him.

3. *Divide et impera.*[40] That is, if there are certain privileged persons among the people who have chosen you for their ruler merely as *primus inter pares*,[41] make sure to disunite them among themselves and set them at odds with the people. And if you back up the people with false promises of greater freedom, everything will be dependent on your absolute will. Or if you are dealing with foreign states, to stir up discord among them is a fairly certain method of subjugating them one by one while merely appearing to lend support to the weaker.

No-one, it must be confessed, will be taken in by these political maxims, for they are all generally known. And it is not the case that men are ashamed of them, as if their injustice were all too obviously visible. For great powers are never embarrassed about how the common mass might judge them, but only about one another's opinions. And as for the principles listed above, the powers will feel no shame if they become publicly known, but only if they *fail to succeed*, for they are all agreed on the moral status of the maxims. They are left with *political honour*, on which they can always rely if they *enlarge their power* by whatever means they care to use.*

---

* It might be doubted whether any inherent wickedness rooted in human nature influences *men* who live together within a single state, for one might instead (with some plausibility) adduce the deficiencies of their as yet underdeveloped culture (i.e. their

From all these twists and turns of an immoral and opportunistic doctrine of how to create peace among men out of the warlike state of nature, this much at least is clear: men can as little escape the concept of right in their private relations as in their public ones, and they will not openly dare to base their politics on opportunistic machinations alone and thus to refuse altogether to obey any concept of public right (which is particularly remarkable in the case of international right). Instead, they pay such concepts all the honour they deserve, even although they may also devise a hundred excuses and subterfuges to get out of observing them in practice and to pretend that brute force and cunning can possess that authority which is the source and unifying bond of all right.

In order to end this sophistry (if not the actual injustice which it covers over) and to make the false representatives of those who wield power on earth confess that they are advocating might instead of right (adopting as they do the tone of persons entitled to give orders), it will be well to discover the ultimate principle from which the end of perpetual peace is derived, and thus to destroy the illusions with which men deceive themselves and others. It must likewise be demonstrated that all the evil which stands in the way of perpetual peace results from the fact that the political moralist starts out from the very point at which the moral politician rightly stops; he thus makes his principles subordinate to his end (i.e. puts the cart before the horse), thereby defeating his own purpose of reconciling politics with morality.

To ensure that practical philosophy is at one with itself, it is first necessary to resolve the question of whether, in problems of practical

barbarism) as the cause of the unlawful elements in their thinking. But in the external relationships between *states*, this wickedness is quite undisguisedly and irrefutably apparent. Within each individual state, it is concealed by the coercion embodied in the civil laws, for the citizens' inclination to do violence to one another is counteracted by a more powerful force—that of the government. This not only gives the whole a veneer of morality (*causae non causae*),[42] but by putting an end to outbreaks of lawless proclivities, it genuinely makes it much easier for the moral capacities of men to develop into an immediate respect for right. For each individual believes of himself that he would by all means maintain the sanctity of the concept of right and obey it faithfully, if only he could be certain that all the others would do likewise, and the government in part guarantees this for him; thus a great step is taken *towards* morality (although this is still not the same as a moral step), towards a state where the concept of duty is recognised for its own sake, irrespective of any possible gain in return. But since each individual, despite his good opinion of himself, assumes bad faith in everyone else, men thereby pass judgement on one another to the effect that they are all in point of *fact* of little worth— although it is a moot point why this should be so, since we cannot blame it on the *nature* of man as a free being. Since, however, that respect for the concept of right which man is absolutely incapable of renouncing gives the most solemn sanction to the theory that man is also capable of conforming to this concept, everyone can see that he must himself act in accordance with it, no matter how others may behave.

reason, we should begin with its *material* principle, i.e. its *end*, as an object of the will, or with its *formal* principle, i.e. the principle which rests on man's freedom in his external relations and which states: 'Act in such a way that you can wish your maxim to become a universal law (irrespective of what the end in view may be).'

The latter principle must undoubtedly take precedence. For as a principle of right, it has absolute necessity, whereas the former is necessary only if the empirical conditions which permit the proposed end to be realised can be assumed to exist. And if this end were also a duty, as with the end of perpetual peace, it would itself have to be deduced from the formal principle of the maxims governing external action. Now the former (i.e. material) principle is that of the *political moralist*, and it treats the problems of political, international and cosmopolitan right as mere *technical tasks*; but the latter (i.e. formal) principle is that of the *moral politician*, for whom it is a *moral task*, totally different in its execution from technical problems, to bring about perpetual peace, which is desirable not just as a physical good, but also as a state of affairs which must arise out of recognising one's duty.

For the solution of the first problem (that of political expediency), much knowledge of nature is required, so that one can use its mechanism to promote the intended end. Nevertheless, all this is uncertain so far as its repercussions on perpetual peace are concerned, no matter which of the three departments of public right one considers. For it is uncertain whether the obedience and prosperity of the people can be better maintained over a long period by strict discipline or by appeals to their vanity, by conferring supreme power upon a single individual or upon several united leaders, or perhaps merely by means of an aristocracy of office or by popular internal government. History offers examples of the opposite effect being produced by all forms of government, with the single exception of genuine republicanism, which, however, could be the object only of a moral politician. And it is even more uncertain in the case of an *international right* supposedly based on statutes worked out by ministers, for it is in fact a mere word with nothing behind it, since it depends upon treaties which contain in the very act of their conclusion the secret reservation that they may be violated. On the other hand, the solution of the second problem, that of *political wisdom*, presents itself as it were automatically; it is obvious to everyone, it defeats all artifices, and leads straight to its goal, so long as we prudently remember that it cannot be realised by violent and precipitate means, but must be steadily approached as favourable opportunities present themselves.

We may therefore offer the following advice: 'Seek ye first the kingdom of pure practical reason and its *righteousness*, and your object (the blessing of perpetual peace) will be added unto you.' For morality, with regard to its principles of public right (hence in relation to a political code which can be known *a priori*), has the peculiar feature that the less it makes its conduct depend upon the end it envisages (whether this be a physical or moral advantage), the more it will in general harmonise with this end. And the reason for this is that it is precisely the general will as it is given *a priori*, within a single people or in the mutual relationships of various peoples, which alone determines what is right among men. But this union of the will of all, if only it is put into practice in a consistent way, can also, within the mechanism of nature, be the cause which leads to the intended result and gives effect to the concept of right. For example, it is a principle of moral politics that a people should combine to form a state in accordance with freedom and equality as its sole concepts of right, and this principle is based not on expediency, but on duty. Political moralists, on the other hand, do not deserve a hearing, however much they argue about the natural mechanism of a mass of people who enter into society, or claim that this mechanism would invalidate the above principles and frustrate their fulfilment, or try to prove their assertions by citing examples of badly organised constitutions of ancient and modern times (e.g. of democracies without a system of representation). Such theories are particularly damaging, because they may themselves produce the very evil they predict. For they put man into the same class as other living machines, which only need to realise consciously that they are not free beings for them to become in their own eyes the most wretched of all earthly creatures.

The proverbial saying *fiat iustitia, pereat mundus*[43] (i.e. let justice reign, even if all the rogues in the world must perish) may sound somewhat inflated, but it is nonetheless true. It is a sound principle of right, which blocks up all the devious paths followed by cunning or violence. But it must not be misunderstood, or taken, for example, as a permit to apply one's own rights with the utmost rigour (which would conflict with ethical duty), but should be seen as an obligation of those in power not to deny or detract from the rights of anyone out of disfavour or sympathy for others. And this requires above all that the state should have an internal constitution organised in accordance with pure principles of right, and also that it unite with other neighbouring or even distant states to arrive at a lawful settlement of their differences by forming something analogous to a universal state. This proposition simply means that whatever the physical consequences may be, the political maxims adopted must not be influenced by the prospect of any benefit or happiness which might accrue to the state if it followed them, i.e. by the end which each state takes as the object of its will (as the highest *empirical* principle of political wisdom); they should be influenced only by the pure concept of rightful duty, i.e. by an obligation whose principle is given *a priori* by pure reason. The world will certainly not come to an end if there are fewer bad men. Moral evil has by nature the inherent quality of being self-destructive and self-contradictory in its aims (especially in relations between persons of a like mind), so that it makes way for the moral principle of goodness, even if such progress is slow.

Thus in *objective* or theoretical terms, there is no conflict whatsoever between morality and politics. In a *subjective* sense, however (i.e. in relation to the selfish disposition of man, which, since it is not based on maxims of reason, cannot however be called practice), this conflict will and ought to remain active, since it serves as a whetstone of virtue. The true courage of virtue, according to the principle *tu ne cede malis, sed contra audentior ito*,[44] does not so much consist, in the present case, in resolutely standing up to the evils and sacrifices which must be encountered, as in facing the evil principle within ourselves and overcoming its wiles. For this principle is far more dangerous, since it is deceitful, treacherous, and liable to exploit the weakness of human nature in order to justify any violation of justice.

The political moralist may indeed say that the ruler and people, or one people and another people, do no injustice to *each other* if they enter into mutual conflict through violence or cunning, although they act completely unjustly in refusing to respect the concept of right, which would alone be capable of establishing perpetual peace. For if one party violates his duty towards another who is just as lawlessly disposed towards him, that which actually *happens* to them in wearing each other out is perfectly just, and enough of their kind will always survive to keep this process going without interruption into the most distant future, so that later generations may take them as a warning example. Providence is justified in disposing the course of world events in this way; for the moral principle in man is never extinguished, and reason, which is pragmatically capable of applying the ideas of right according to this principle, constantly increases with the continuous progress of culture, while the guilt attending violations of right increases proportionately. If we suppose that mankind never can and will be in a better condition, it seems impossible to justify by any kind of theodicy the mere fact that such a race of corrupt beings could have been created on earth at all. But this kind of judgement is far too exalted for us; we cannot theoretically attribute our conception of wisdom to the supreme power whose nature is beyond our understanding.

Such are the desperate conclusions to which we are inevitably driven if we do not assume that the pure principles of right have an objective reality, i.e. that they can be applied in practice. And whatever empirical politics may say to the contrary, the people within the state, as well as the states in their relations with one another, must act accordingly. A true system of politics cannot therefore take a single step without first paying tribute to morality. And although politics in itself is a difficult art, no art is required to combine it with morality. For as soon as the two come into conflict, morality can cut through the knot which politics cannot untie.

The rights of man must be held sacred, however great a sacrifice the ruling power may have to make. There can be no half measures here; it is no use devising hybrid solutions such as a pragmatically conditioned right halfway between right and utility. For all politics must bend the knee before right, although politics may hope in return to arrive, however slowly, at a stage of lasting brilliance.

II

ON THE AGREEMENT BETWEEN POLITICS AND MORALITY ACCORDING TO THE TRANSCENDENTAL CONCEPT OF PUBLIC RIGHT

If, in considering public right as the jurists usually conceive of it, I abstract from all its *material* aspects (as determined by the various empirically given relationships of men within a state, or of states with one another), I am left with the *formal attribute of publicness*. For every claim upon right potentially possesses this attribute, and without it, there can be no justice (which can only be conceived of as *publicly knowable*) and therefore no right, since right can only come from justice.

Every claim upon right must have this public quality, and since it is very easy to judge whether or not it is present in a particular instance, i.e. whether or not it can be combined with the principles of the agent concerned, it provides us with a readily applicable criterion which can be discovered *a priori* within reason itself. If it cannot be reconciled with the agent's principles, it enables us to recognise at once the falseness (i.e. unrightfulness) of the claim (*praetensio iuris*) in question, as if by an experiment of pure reason.

After we have abstracted in this way from all the empirical elements contained within the concept of political and international right (including that evil aspect of human nature which makes coercion necessary), we may specify the following proposition as the *transcendental formula* of public right: 'All actions affecting the rights of other human beings are wrong if their maxim is not compatible with their being made public.'

This principle should be regarded not only as *ethical* (i.e. pertaining to the theory of virtue) but also as *juridical* (i.e. affecting the rights of man). For a maxim which I may not *declare openly* without thereby frustrating my own intention, or which must at all costs be *kept secret* if it is to succeed, or which I cannot *publicly acknowledge* without thereby inevitably arousing the resistance of everyone to my plans, can only have stirred up this necessary and general (hence *a priori* foreseeable) opposition against me because it is itself unjust and thus constitutes a threat to everyone. Besides, this is a purely *negative* test, i.e. it serves only as a means of detecting what is *not* right in relation to others. Like any axiom, it is valid without demonstration, and besides, it is easy to apply, as can be seen from the following examples of public right.

1. In the *internal right of a state* (*ius civitatis*), a question may arise which many people consider difficult to answer, although it can be resolved quite easily by means of the transcendental principle of publicness. It runs as follows: 'Is rebellion a rightful means for a people to use in order to overthrow the oppressive power of a so-called tyrant (*non titulo, sed exercitio talis*)?' The rights of the people have been violated, and there can be no doubt that the tyrant would not be receiving unjust treatment if he were dethroned. Nevertheless, it is in the highest degree wrong if the subjects pursue their rights in this way, and they cannot in the least complain of injustice if they are defeated in the ensuing conflict and subsequently have to endure the most severe penalties.

Much can be said in arguments both for and against such a course of action if we try to settle the matter by dogmatic deduction of the principles of right. But the transcendental principle of publicness in questions of right can get round such long-winded discussion. According to this principle, the people, before establishing the civil contract, asks itself whether it dares to make public the maxim of its intention to rebel on certain occasions. It is easily seen that if one were to make it a condition of founding a political constitution that force might in certain eventualities be used against the head of state, the people would have to claim rightful authority over its ruler. But if this were so, the ruler would not be the head of state; or if *both* parties were given authority as a prior condition of establishing the state, the existence of the state itself, which it was the people's intention to establish, would become impossible. The injustice of rebellion is thus apparent from the fact that if the maxim upon which it would act *were publicly acknowledged*, it would defeat its own purpose. This maxim would therefore have to be kept secret.

But it would not be necessary for the head of state to conceal his intentions. He may say quite openly that he will punish any rebellion by putting the ringleaders to death, even if they believed that he was himself the first to infringe the fundamental law. For if he is aware that he possesses *irresistible* supreme power (and this must be assumed in any civil constitution, for a ruler who does not have sufficient power to protect each individual among the people against the others cannot have the right to give the people orders either), he does not have to worry that his own aims might be frustrated if his maxim became generally known. And it is perfectly consistent with this argument that if the people were to rebel successfully, the head of state would revert to the position of a subject; but he would not be justified in starting a new rebellion to restore his former position, nor should he have to fear being called to account for his previous administration.

2. We now come to *international right.*—We can speak of international right only on the assumption that some kind of lawful condition exists, i.e. that external circumstances are such that a man can genuinely be accorded his rights. For as a form of public right, it implies by definition that there is a general will which publicly assigns to each individual that which is his due. And this *status iuridicus* must be derived from some sort of contract, which, unlike that from which a state originates, must not be based on coercive laws, but may at most be a state of *permanent and free association* like the above-mentioned federation of different states. For without some kind of *lawful condition* which actively links together the various physical or moral persons (as is the case in the state of nature), the only possible form of right is a private one. This again involves a conflict between politics and morality (the latter in the shape of a theory of right). The criterion of publicness in the relevant maxims can, however, once again be easily applied, but only on condition that the contract binds the states for the single purpose of preserving peace amongst themselves and in relation to other states, and on no account with a view to military conquest. We can thus envisage the following instances of an antinomy between politics and morality, along with the appropriate solution in each case.

(*a*) 'If one of these states has promised something to another, whether it be assistance, cession of certain territories, subsidies, or the like, it may be asked whether this state, on occasions when its own welfare is at stake, may free itself from the obligation to keep its word, maintaining that it[45] ought to be regarded as a dual person—on the one hand, as a *sovereign* who is not responsible to anyone within the state, and on the other, merely as the highest political *official* who is responsible to the state; and the conclusion to be drawn from this is that the state (or its ruler) can be exempted in the latter capacity from obligations it incurred in the first.' But if the ruler of a state were to let it be known that this was his maxim, everyone else would naturally flee from him, or unite with others in order to resist his pretensions; which proves that such a system of politics, for all its cunning, would defeat its own purpose if it operated on a public footing, so that the above maxim must be wrong.

(*b*) 'If a neighbouring power which has grown to a formidable size (*potentia tremenda*) gives cause for anxiety, can one assume that it will *wish* to oppress other states because is *is able* to do so, and does this give the less powerful party a right to mount a concerted attack upon it, even if no offence has been offered?' If a state were to *let it be known* that it affirmed this maxim, it would merely bring about more surely and more quickly the very evil it feared. For the greater power would anticipate the lesser ones, and the possibility that they might unite would be but a feeble reed against one who knew how to use the tactics of *divide et impera*. Thus this maxim of political expediency, if acknowledged publicly, necessarily defeats its own purpose and is consequently unjust.

(*c*) 'If a smaller state, by its geographical situation, constitutes a gap in the territory of a larger state, and this larger state requires the intrusive territory for its own preservation, is not the larger state justified in subjugating the smaller one and in annexing its territory?' One can easily see that the larger state must on no account let it be known that it has adopted such a maxim. For the smaller states would either unite in good time, or other powerful states would quarrel over the proposed prey, so that the plan would be rendered impracticable if it were made public. This is a sign that it is unjust, and it would in fact be an injustice of very great magnitude; for the fact that the object of an injustice is small does not mean that the injustice done to it may not be very great.

3. As for *cosmopolitan right*, I pass over it here in silence, for its maxims are easy to formulate and assess on account of its analogy with international right.

In the principle that the maxims of international right may be incompatible with publicity, we thus have a good indication that politics and morality (in the sense of a theory of right) are *not in agreement*. But it is also necessary that we should know what the condition is under which its maxims will agree with international right. For we cannot simply conclude by a reverse process that all maxims which can be made public are therefore also just, because the person who has decisive supremacy has no need to conceal his maxims. The condition which must be fulfilled before any kind of international right is possible is that a *lawful state* must already be in existence. For without this, there can be no public right, and any right which can be conceived of outside it, i.e. in a state of nature, will be merely a private right. Now we have already seen above that a federative association of states whose sole intention is to eliminate war is the only *lawful* arrangement which can be reconciled with their *freedom*. Thus politics and morality can only be in agreement within a federal union, which is therefore necessary and given *a priori* through the principles of right. And the rightful basis of all political prudence is the founding of such a union in the most comprehensive form possible; for without this aim, all its reasonings are unwisdom and veiled injustice. This kind of false politics has its own *casuistry* to match that of the best Jesuit scholars. For it includes the *reservatio mentalis* whereby public contracts are formulated in terms which one can interpret to one's own advantage as required (for example, the distinction between the *status quo* of fact and the *status quo* of right); it also includes the *probabilismus*, i.e. it tries to think out evil intentions which it might attribute to others, or uses the likelihood of their gaining predominance as a legal justification for undermining other peaceful states; and finally, it has the principle of the philosophical sin (*peccatum philosophicum, peccatillum,* or *bagatelle*), whereby it can be regarded as a readily pardonable trifle to seize a *small* state if a much *larger* state gains in the process, to the supposed advantage of the world in general.*

All this is occasioned by the duplicity of politics in relation to morality, for it makes use of whatever branch of morality suits its purposes. But *both* aspects, philanthropy and respect for the *rights* of man, are obligatory. And while the former is only a *conditional* duty, the latter is an *unconditional* and absolutely imperative one; anyone must first be completely sure that he has not infringed it if he wishes to enjoy the sweet sense of

---

* One can find examples of such maxims in Garve's[46] treatise *Über die Verbindung der Moral mit der Politik*[47] (*On Combining Morality with Politics*), 1788. This estimable scholar admits from the very outset that he is unable to offer a satisfactory answer to this question. But to condone such procedures while admitting that one cannot fully answer the objections which can be raised against them seems to constitute a greater concession to those who are most inclined to misuse it than it is advisable for anyone to make.

having acted justly. Politics can easily be reconciled with morality in the former sense (i.e. as ethics), for both demand that men should give up their rights to their rulers. But when it comes to morality in its second sense (i.e. as the theory of right), which requires that politics should actively defer to it, politics finds it advisable not to enter into any contract at all, preferring to deny that the theory of right has any reality and to reduce all duties to mere acts of goodwill. This subterfuge of a secretive system of politics could, however, easily be defeated if philosophy were to make its maxims public, would it but dare to allow the philosopher to publicise his own maxims.

With this in mind, I now put forward another transcendental and affirmative principle of public right. It might be formulated as follows: 'All maxims which *require* publicity if they are not to fail in their purpose can be reconciled both with right and with politics.'

For if they can only attain their end by being publicised, they must conform to the universal aim of the public (which is happiness), and it is the particular task of politics to remain in harmony with the aim of the public through making it satisfied with its condition. But if this end is to be attained *only* through publicity (i.e. by dispelling all distrust of the maxims employed), the maxims in question must also be in harmony with public right; for only within this right is it possible to unite the ends of everyone. I must, however, postpone the further elaboration and discussion of this principle until another occasion, although it can already be seen that it is a transcendental formula if one removes all the empirical conditions relating to happiness, i.e. the substance of the law, and looks exclusively to the form of universal lawfulness.

If it is a duty to bring about in reality a state of public right (albeit by an infinite process of gradual approximation), and if there are also good grounds for hoping that we shall succeed, then it is not just an empty idea that *perpetual peace* will eventually replace what have hitherto been wrongly called peace treaties (which are actually only truces). On the contrary, it is a task which, as solutions are gradually found, constantly draws nearer fulfilment, for we may hope that the periods within which equal amounts of progress are made will become progressively shorter.

The Metaphysics of Morals[1]

This work begins with a preface and a general introduction. Its main body falls into two parts—*The Metaphysical Elements of the Theory of Right* and *The Metaphysical Elements of the Theory of Virtue*. The extracts included in the present edition are taken only from *The Metaphysical Elements of the Theory of Right*. They include the most important paragraphs from the introduction to this part of the work, and its second main section, which deals with *The Theory of Public Right*. In order to place the relevant passages in their proper context, I have provided a brief summary of the other sections preceding *The Theory of Public Right*.

In the preface to *The Metaphysics of Morals*, Kant points out that a complete metaphysics of right is impossible because completeness in an account of empirical matters is impossible. He refers only to *The Metaphysical Elements of the Theory of Right* because the second part, *The Metaphysical Elements of the Theory of Virtue*, was published at a later date. Kant also states that, in his treatise, he has put into the body of the text those arguments relating to the system of right which were arrived at by *a priori* reasoning and has relegated those relating to specific empirical cases to the notes. Kant then defends the apparent obscurity of his style by saying that it is impossible to aim at popularity in a work involving a system of criticism of the faculty of reason.

In his general introduction to the *Metaphysics of Morals*, Kant discusses the fundamental terms and presuppositions of this work, pointing out that science can make progress without explicit reference to *a priori* laws, but that the case of morality is different. Moral laws are laws only in so far as they have an *a priori* basis and are necessary. He explains why he distinguishes between legal and moral laws: the former admit of no incentive except that of duty, the latter do not.

A full account of this introduction would be too long to justify inclusion here. Kant proceeds to provide definitions for many of the terms which he uses, thus supplying a brief account of the principles underlying his moral philosophy (cf. my introduction pp. 17–21 for a brief discussion of his moral philosophy). In the course of the argument Kant also states that a collision of duties is impossible, because two opposing rules involving the objective-practical necessity of an action cannot exist side by side. If there are conflicting obligations, the stronger obligation always prevails.

This introduction is followed by *The Metaphysical Elements of the Theory of Right*.

INTRODUCTION TO THE THEORY OF RIGHT[2]

§ A

Definition of the Theory of Right

The sum total of those laws which can be incorporated in external legislation is termed the *theory of right* (*Ius*). If legislation of this kind actually exists, the theory is one of *positive right*. If a person who is conversant with it or has studied it (*Iuriconsultus*) is acquainted with the external laws in their external function, i.e. in their application to instances encountered in experience, he is said to be *experienced in matters of right* (*Iurisperitus*). This body of theory may amount to the same as *jurisprudence* (*Iurisprudentia*), but it will remain only the *science of right* (*Iuriscientia*) unless both its elements are present. The latter designation applies to a *systematic* knowledge of the theory of natural right (*Ius naturae*), although it is the student of natural right who has to supply the immutable principles on which all positive legislation must rest.

§ B

What is Right?

The *jurist*, if he does not wish to lapse into tautology or to base his answer on the laws of a particular country at a particular time instead of offering a comprehensive solution, may well be just as perplexed on being asked this as the logician is by the notorious question: '*What is truth?*' He will certainly be able to tell us what is legally right (*quid sit iuris*) within a given context, i.e. what the laws say or have said in a particular place and at a particular time: but whether their provisions are also in keeping with right, and whether they constitute a universal criterion by which we may recognise in general what is right and what is unjust (*iustum et iniustum*), are questions whose answers will remain concealed from him unless he abandons such empirical principles for a time and looks for the sources of these judgements in the realm of pure reason. This will enable him to lay the foundations of all possible positive legislations. And while empirical laws may give him valuable guidance, a purely empirical theory of right, like the wooden head in Phaedrus'[3] fable, may have a fine appearance, but will unfortunately contain no brain.

The concept of right, in so far as it is connected with a corresponding obligation (i.e. the moral concept of right), applies within the following conditions. *Firstly*, it applies only to those relationships between one person and another which are both external and practical, that is, in so far as their actions can in fact influence each other either directly or indirectly. But *secondly*, it does not concern the relationship between the will[4] of one person and the *desires* of another (and hence only the latter's needs, as in acts of benevolence or hardheartedness); it concerns only the relationship between the will of the first and the *will* of the second. And *thirdly*, the will's *material* aspect, i.e. the end which each party intends to accomplish by means of the object of his will, is completely irrelevant in this mutual relationship; for example, we need not ask whether someone who buys goods from me for his own commercial use will gain anything in the process. For we are interested only in the *form* of the relationship between the two wills, in so far as they are regarded as *free*, and in whether the action of one of the two parties can be reconciled with the freedom of the other in accordance with a universal law.

Right is therefore the sum total of those conditions within which the will of one person can be reconciled with the will of another in accordance with a universal law of freedom.

§ C

The Universal Principle of Right

'Every action which by itself or by its maxim enables the freedom of each individual's will to co-exist with the freedom of everyone else in accordance with a universal law is *right*.'

Thus if my action or my situation in general can co-exist with the freedom of everyone in accordance with a universal law, anyone who hinders me in either does me an injustice; for this hindrance or resistance cannot co-exist with freedom in accordance with universal laws.

It also follows from this that I cannot be required to make this principle of all maxims my own maxim, i.e. *to make it the maxim of my own actions*; for each individual can be free so long as I do not interfere with his freedom by my *external actions*, even although his freedom may be a matter of total indifference to me or although I may wish in my heart to deprive him of it. That I should make it my maxim to *act* in accordance with right is a requirement laid down for me by ethics.

Thus the universal law of right is as follows: let your external actions be such that the free application of your will can co-exist with the freedom of everyone in accordance with a universal law. And although this law imposes an obligation on me, it does not mean that I am in any way expected, far less required, to restrict my freedom *myself* to these conditions purely for the sake of this obligation. On the contrary, reason merely says that individual freedom *is* restricted in this way by virtue of the idea behind it, and that it may also be actively restricted by others; and it states this as a postulate which does not admit of any further proof.

If it is not our intention to teach virtue, but only to state what is *right*, we may not and should not ourselves represent this law of right as a possible motive for actions.

§ D

Right entails the Authority to use Coercion

Any resistance which counteracts the hindrance of an effect helps to promote this effect and is consonant with it. Now everything that is contrary to right is a hindrance to freedom based on universal laws, while coercion is a hindrance or resistance to freedom. Consequently, if a certain use to which freedom is put is itself a hindrance to freedom in accordance with universal laws (i.e. if it is contrary to right), any coercion which is used against it will be a *hindrance* to a *hindrance of freedom*, and will thus be consonant with freedom in accordance with universal laws—that is, it will be right. It thus follows by the law of contradiction that right entails the authority to apply coercion to anyone who infringes it.

§ E

In its 'strict' Sense, Right can also be envisaged as the Possibility of a general and reciprocal Coercion consonant with the Freedom of Everyone in accordance with Universal Laws

This proposition implies that we should not conceive of right as being composed of two elements, namely the obligation imposed by a law, and the authority which someone who obligates another party through his will possesses to coerce the latter into carrying out the obligation in question. Instead, the concept of right should be seen as consisting immediately of the possibility of universal reciprocal coercion being combined with the freedom of everyone. For just as the only object of right in general is the external aspect of actions, right in its strict sense, i.e. right unmixed with any ethical considerations, requires no determinants of the will apart from purely external ones; for it will then be pure and will not be confounded with any precepts of virtue. Thus only a completely external right can be called right in the *strict* (or narrow) sense. This right is certainly based on each individual's awareness of his obligations within the law; but if it is to remain pure, it may not and cannot appeal to this awareness as a motive which might determine the will to act in accordance with it, and it therefore depends rather on the principle of the possibility of an external coercion which can coexist with the freedom of everyone in accordance with universal laws.

Thus when it is said that a creditor has a right to require the debtor to pay his debt, it does not mean that he can make the latter feel that his reason itself obliges him to act in this way. It means instead that the use of coercion to compel everyone to do this can very well be reconciled with everyone's freedom, hence also with the debtor's freedom, in accordance with a universal external law: thus right and the authority to apply coercion mean one and the same thing.

The law of reciprocal coercion, which is necessarily consonant with the freedom of everyone within the principle of universal freedom, is in a sense the *construction* of the concept of right: that is, it represents this concept in pure *a priori* intuition by analogy with the possibility of free movement of bodies within the law of the *equality of action and reaction*. Just as the qualities of an object of pure mathematics cannot be directly deduced from the concept but can only be discovered from its construction, it is not so much the *concept* of right but rather a general, reciprocal and uniform coercion, subject to universal laws and harmonising with the concept itself, which makes any representation of the concept possible. But while this concept of dynamics (i.e. that of the equality of action and reaction) is based upon a purely formal concept of pure mathematics (e.g. of geometry), reason has taken care that the understanding is likewise as fully equipped as possible with *a priori* intuitions for the construction of the concept of right.

In geometry, the term 'right' (*rectum*), in the sense of '*straight*', can be used either as the opposite of '*curved*' or of '*oblique*'. In the first sense, it applies to a line whose *intrinsic nature* is such that there can be only *one* of its kind between two given *points*. But in the second sense, it applies to an *angle* between two intersecting or coincident *lines* whose nature is such that there can be only *one* of its kind (a right angle) between the given lines. The perpendicular line which forms a right angle will not incline more to one side than to the other, and will divide the area on either side of it into two equal parts. By this analogy, the theory of right will also seek an assurance that each individual receives (with mathematical precision) *what is his due*. This cannot be expected of *ethics*, however, for it cannot refuse to allow some room for exceptions (*latitudinem*).[5]

Kant then adds some remarks on 'equivocal right'. He does not mean right in the strict sense, but in the wider sense of the word. Only two aspects of right arise here: equity and the right of necessity. Kant remarks of equity that it concerns only such cases as are outside strict right, i.e. where there is no case in law at all. The right of necessity applies to cases where one acts against someone else (for instance, by taking someone else's life because one's own life is in danger). A man cannot be punished with any greater punishment than the loss of life itself. There can be therefore no law punishing a man who acts out of necessity.

Kant explains the division of the theory of right into private and public right. He also distinguishes between innate and acquired rights. In his view, freedom (i.e. independence from the coercive will of another), in so far as it can coexist with the freedom of everyone else in accordance with a universal law, is the sole original right. It belongs to every man by virtue of his humanity. Equality, honesty and the right to act towards others in such a way that their rights are not infringed all derive from this right of freedom. Kant also provides a general division of the metaphysics of morals, distinguishing between those duties which are duties of right and those which are duties of virtue.

In the first section of *The Metaphysical Elements of Right*, Kant deals with private right which is concerned with property. There are two kinds of property: property which one possesses directly through physical possession and property which one only possesses indirectly. Kant examines the philosophical foundations of the law of property, deducing it from the idea of original communal possession of the soil. He also argues that external possession of things of which we are not in physical possession is possible only because we are noumenal beings, not necessarily bound by the limits of mere empirical (phenomenal) possessions. Kant goes on to argue that external possessions are possible only in a state of civil society, whereas in a state of nature, such possession can have only a provisional character.

Subsequently, Kant deals with the right of acquiring things and with various other rights, such as the rights of persons, marriage, parentage, landlords, contract, money, books, inheritance, etc. His discussion of the theory of private right is followed by a discussion of the theory of public right, which is printed below.

THE THEORY OF RIGHT, PART II: PUBLIC RIGHT[6]

SECTION I: POLITICAL RIGHT

§ 43

Public right is the sum total of those laws which require to be made universally public in order to produce a state of right. It is therefore a system of laws for a people, i.e. an aggregate of human beings, or for an aggregate of peoples. Since these individuals or peoples must influence one another, they need to live in a state of right under a unifying will: that is, they require a *constitution* in order to enjoy their rights.

A condition in which the individual members of a people are related to each other in this way is said to be a *civil* one (*status civilis*), and when considered as a whole in relation to its own members, it is called a *state* (*civitas*). Since the state takes the form of a union created by the common interest of everyone in living in a state of right, it is called a *commonwealth* (*res publica latius sic dicta*). In relation to other peoples, however, it is simply called a *power* (*potentia*—hence the word 'potentate'); and if it claims to be united by heredity, it may also call itself a *congeneric nation* (*gens*). Within the general concept of public right, we must therefore include not only *political right* but also *international right* (*ius gentium*). And since the earth's surface is not infinite but limited by its own configuration, these two concepts taken together necessarily lead to the idea of an *international political right* (*ius gentium*) or a *cosmopolitan right* (*ius cosmopoliticum*). Consequently, if even only one of these three possible forms of rightful state lacks a principle which limits external freedom by means of laws, the structure of all the rest must inevitably be undermined, and finally collapse.

§ 44

Experience teaches us the maxim that human beings act in a violent and malevolent manner, and that they tend to fight among themselves until an external coercive legislation supervenes. But it is not experience or any kind of factual knowledge which makes public legal coercion necessary. On the contrary, even if we imagine men to be as benevolent and law-abiding as we please, the *a priori* rational idea of a non-lawful state will still tell us that before a public and legal state is established, individual men, peoples and states can never be secure against acts of violence from one another, since each will have his own right to do *what seems right and good to him*, independently of the opinion of others. Thus the first decision the individual is obliged to make, if he does not wish to renounce all concepts of right, will be to adopt the principle that one must abandon the state of nature in which everyone follows his own desires, and unite with everyone else (with whom he cannot avoid having intercourse) in order to submit to external, public and lawful coercion. He must accordingly enter into a state wherein that which is to be recognised as belonging to each person is allotted to him *by law* and guaranteed to him by an adequate power (which is not his own, but external to him). In other words, he should at all costs enter into a state of civil society.

The state of nature need not necessarily be a *state of injustice* (*iniustus*) merely because those who live in it treat one another solely in terms of the amount of power they possess. But it is a *state devoid of justice* (*status iustitia vacuus*), for if a *dispute* over rights (*ius controversum*) occurs in it, there is no competent judge to pronounce legally valid decisions. Anyone may thus use force to impel the others to abandon this state for a state of right. For although each individual's *concepts of right* may imply that an external object can be acquired by occupation or by contract, this acquisition is only *provisional* until it has been sanctioned by a public law, since it is not determined by any public (distributive) form of justice and is not guaranteed by any institution empowered to exercise this right.

If no-one were willing to recognise any acquisition as rightful, not even provisionally so, before a civil state had been established, the civil state would itself be impossible. For in relation to their form, the laws relating to property contain exactly the same things in a state of nature as they would prescribe in a civil state, in so far as we conceive of this state only in terms of concepts of pure reason. The only difference is that in the second case, the conditions under which the laws are applied (in accordance with distributive justice) are given. Thus if there were not even a *provisional* system of external property in the state of nature, there would not be any rightful duties in it either, so that there could not be any commandment to abandon it.

§ 45

A state (*civitas*) is a union of an aggregate of men under rightful laws. In so far as these laws are necessary *a priori* and follow automatically from concepts of external right in general (and are not just set up by statute), the form of the state will be that of a state in the absolute sense, i.e. as the idea of what a state ought to be according to pure principles of right. This idea can serve as an internal guide (*norma*) for every actual case where men unite to form a commonwealth.

Every state contains three powers, i.e. the universally united will is made up of three separate persons (*trias politica*). These are the *ruling power* (or sovereignty) in the person of the legislator, the *executive power* in the person of the individual who governs in accordance with the law, and the *judicial power* (which allots to everyone what is his by law) in the person of the judge (*potestas legislatoria, rectoria et iudiciaria*). They can be likened to the three propositions in a practical operation of reason: the major premise, which contains the *law* of the sovereign will, the minor premise, which contains the *command* to act in accordance with the law (i.e. the principle of subsumption under the general will), and the conclusion, which contains the *legal decision* (the sentence) as to the rights and wrongs of each particular case.

§ 46

The legislative power can belong only to the united will of the people. For since all right is supposed to emanate from this power, the laws it gives must be absolutely *incapable* of doing anyone an injustice. Now if someone makes dispositions for *another* person, it is always possible that he may thereby do him an injustice, although this is never possible in the case of decisions he makes for himself (for *volenti non fit iniuria*).[7] Thus only the unanimous and combined will of everyone whereby each decides the same for all and all decide the same for each—in other words, the general united will of the people—can legislate.

The members of such a society (*societas civilis*) or state who unite for the purpose of legislating are known as *citizens* (*cives*), and the three rightful attributes which are inseparable from the nature of a citizen as such are as follows: firstly, lawful *freedom* to obey no law other than that to which he has given his consent; secondly, civil *equality* in recognising no-one among the people as superior to himself, unless it be someone whom he is just as morally entitled to bind by law as the other is to bind him; and thirdly, the attribute of civil *independence* which allows him to owe his existence and sustenance not to the arbitrary will of anyone else among the people, but purely to his own rights and powers as a member of the commonwealth (so that he may not, as a civil personality, be represented by anyone else in matters of right).

Fitness to vote is the necessary qualification which every citizen must possess. To be fit to vote, a person must have an independent position among the people. He must therefore be not just a part of the commonwealth, but a member of it, i.e. he must by his own free will actively participate in a community of other people. But this latter quality makes it necessary to distinguish between the *active* and the *passive* citizen, although the latter concept seems to contradict the definition of the concept of a citizen altogether. The following examples may serve to overcome this difficulty. Apprentices to merchants or tradesmen, servants who are not employed by the state, minors (*naturaliter vel civiliter*),[8] women in general and all those who are obliged to depend for their living (i.e. for food and protection) on the offices of others (excluding the state)— all of these people have no civil personality, and their existence is, so to speak, purely inherent. The woodcutter whom I employ on my premises; the blacksmith in India who goes from house to house with his hammer, anvil and bellows to do work with iron, as opposed to the European carpenter or smith who can put the products of his work up for public sale; the domestic tutor as opposed to the academic, the tithe-holder as opposed to the farmer; and so on—they are all mere auxiliaries to the commonwealth, for they have to receive orders or protection from other individuals, so that they do not possess civil independence.

This dependence upon the will of others and consequent inequality does not, however, in any way conflict with the freedom and equality of all men as *human beings* who together constitute a people. On the contrary, it is only by accepting these conditions that such a people can become a state and enter into a civil constitution. But all are not equally qualified within this constitution to possess the right to vote, i.e. to be citizens and not just subjects among other subjects. For from the fact that as passive members of the state, they can demand to be treated by all others in accordance with laws of natural freedom and equality, it does not follow that they also have a right to influence or organise the state itself as *active* members, or to co-operate in introducing particular laws. Instead, it only means that the positive laws to which the voters agree, of whatever sort they may be, must not be at variance with the natural laws of freedom and with the corresponding equality of all members of the people whereby they are allowed to work their way up from their passive condition to an active one.

§ 47

All of the three powers within the state are dignities, and since they necessarily follow from the general idea of a state as elements essential for its establishment (constitution), they are *political dignities*. They involve a relationship between a universal *sovereign* (who, if considered in the light of laws of freedom, can be none other than the united people itself) and the scattered mass of the people as subjects, i.e. a relationship of *commander* (*imperans*) to him who *obeys* (*subditus*). The act by which the people constitutes a state for itself, or more precisely, the mere idea of such an act (which alone enables us to consider it valid in terms of right), is the *original contract*. By this contract, all members of the people (*omnes et singuli*)[9] give up their external freedom in order to receive it back at once as members of a commonwealth, i.e. of the people regarded as a state (*universi*). And we cannot say that men within a state have sacrificed a *part* of their inborn external freedom for a specific purpose; they have in fact completely abandoned their wild and lawless freedom, in order to find again their entire and undiminished freedom in a state of lawful dependence (i.e. in a state of right), for this dependence is created by their own legislative will.

§48

The three powers in the state are related to one another in the following ways. Firstly, as moral persons, they are co-ordinate (*potestates coordinatae*), i.e. each is complementary to the others in forming the complete constitution of the state (*complementum ad sufficientiam*). But secondly, they are also *subordinate* (*subordinatae*) to one another, so that the one cannot usurp any function of the others to which it ministers; for each has its own principle, so that although it issues orders in the quality of a distinct person, it does so under the condition of a superior person's will. Thirdly, the combination of both relationships described above assures every subject of his rights.

It can be said of these powers, considered in their appropriate dignity, that the will of the *legislator* (*legislatoris*) in relation to external property cannot be reproached (i.e. it is irreprehensible), that the executive power of the supreme *ruler* (*summi rectoris*) cannot be opposed (i.e. it is irresistible), and that the verdict of the supreme *judge* (*supremi iudicis*) cannot be altered (i.e. it is without appeal).

§49

The *ruler* of the state (*rex, princeps*) is that moral or physical person who wields the executive power (*potestas executoria*). He is the *agent* of the state who appoints the magistrates, and who prescribes rules for the people so that each may acquire something or retain what is his by law (i.e. by subsuming individual cases under the law). If the ruler is taken to be a moral person, he is called the *directory* or government. His *commands* to the people, the magistrates, and their superiors (ministers) who are responsible for *administering the state* (*gubernatio*), are not laws but ordinances or decrees; for they depend upon decisions in particular cases and are issued subject to revision. A *government* which were also to make *laws* would be called a *despotic* as opposed to a *patriotic* government. This is not to be confused with a *paternal* government (*regimen paternale*); the latter is the most despotic kind of all, for it treats the citizens like children. A patriotic government (*regimen civitatis et patriae*) means that although the state itself (*civitas*) treats its subjects as if they were members of one family, it also treats them as citizens of the state, i.e. in accordance with laws guaranteeing their own independence. Thus each is responsible for himself and does not depend upon the absolute will of anyone equal or superior to him.

The sovereign of the people (the legislator) cannot therefore also be the *ruler*, for the ruler is subject to the law, through which he is consequently beholden to *another* party, i.e. the sovereign. The sovereign may divest the ruler of his power, depose him, or reform his administration, but he cannot *punish* him. (And that is the real meaning of the common English saying that the king—i.e. the supreme executive authority—can do no wrong.) For to punish the ruler would in turn be an act of the executive power, which alone possesses the supreme authority to apply *coercion* in accordance with the law, and such a punishment would mean subjecting the executive power itself to coercion, which is self-contradictory.

Finally, neither the sovereign nor the ruler may *pass judgement*; they can only appoint judges as magistrates. The people judge themselves, through those fellow-citizens whom they have nominated as their representatives, by free election, for each particular juridical act. For a legal decision or sentence is a particular act of public justice (*iustitiae distributivae*) by an administrator of the state (a judge or court of law) upon a subject, i.e. one who belongs to the people, and it does not carry the necessary authority to grant or assign to the subject that which is his. Now since each member of the people is purely passive in his relationship to the supreme authority, it would be possible for either the legislative or the executive power to do him an injustice in any decision it might make in a controversial case involving that which belongs to the subject; for it would not be an action of the people themselves in pronouncing a fellow citizen *guilty* or *not guilty*. After the facts of a legal suit have thus been established, the court of law has the judicial authority to put the law into practice and to ensure, by means of the executive authority, that each person receives his due. Thus only the *people*, albeit through the indirect means of the representatives they have themselves appointed (i.e. the jury), can pass judgement upon anyone of their own number. Besides, it would be beneath the dignity of the head of state to act the part of a judge, i.e. to put himself in a position where he could do some injustice, and thus give cause for an appeal to some higher authority (*a rege male informato ad regem melius informandum*).[10]

There are thus three distinct powers (*potestas legislatoria, executoria, iudiciaria*) which give the state (*civitas*) its autonomy, that is, which enable the state to establish and maintain itself in accordance with laws of freedom. The *welfare* of the state consists in the union of these powers (*salus reipublicae suprema lex est*).[11] But this welfare must not be understood as synonymous with the *well-being* and *happiness* of the citizens, for it may well be possible to attain these in a more convenient and desirable way within a state of nature (as Rousseau declares), or even under a despotic regime. On the contrary, the welfare of the state should be seen as that condition in which the constitution most closely approximates to the principles of right; and reason, *by a categorical imperative*, obliges us to strive for its realisation.

General Remarks On the Legal Consequences of the Nature of the Civil Union

A

The origin of the supreme power, for all practical purposes, is *not discoverable* by the people who are subject to it. In other words, the subject *ought not* to indulge in *speculations* about its origin with a view to acting upon them, as if its right to be obeyed were open to doubt (*ius controversum*). For since the people must already be considered as united under a general legislative will before they can pass rightful judgement upon the highest power within the state (*summumim perium*), they cannot and may not pass any judgement other than that which is willed by the current head of state (*summus imperans*). Whether in fact an actual contract originally preceded their submission to the state's authority (*pactum subiectionis civilis*), whether the power came first and the law only appeared after it, or whether they ought to have followed this order—these are completely futile arguments for a people which is already subject to civil law, and they constitute a menace to the state. For if the subject, having delved out the ultimate origin, were then to offer resistance to the authority currently in power, he might by the laws of this authority (i.e. with complete justice) be punished, eliminated or banished as an outlaw (*exlex*). A law which is so sacred (i.e. inviolable) that it is practically a crime even to cast doubt upon it and thus to suspend its effectiveness for even an instant, cannot be thought of as coming from human beings, but from some infallible supreme legislator. That is what is meant by the saying that 'all authority comes from God', which is not a *historical derivation* of the civil constitution, but an idea expressed as a practical principle of reason, requiring men to obey the legislative authority now in power, irrespective of its origin.

From this there follows the proposition that the sovereign of a state has only rights in relation to the subject, and no (coercive) duties. Furthermore, if the organ of the sovereign, the ruler, does anything against the laws (e.g. if he infringes the law of equal distribution of political burdens in taxation, recruiting, or the like), the subject may lodge *complaints* (*gravamina*) about this injustice, but he may not offer resistance.

Indeed, even the actual constitution cannot contain any article which might make it possible for some power within the state to resist or hold in check the supreme executive in cases where he violates the constitutional laws. For a person who is supposed to hold the power of the state in check must have more power than (or at least as much power as) the one who is held in check; and if, as a rightful commander, he ordered the subjects to offer resistance, he would also have to be able to *protect* them and to pass legally valid judgements in each particular case which arose, so that he would have to be able to order resistance publicly. But if this were so, the latter instead of the former would be the supreme executive, which is self-contradictory. In such a case, the sovereign would simultaneously be acting through his minister as a ruler, i.e. despotically, and any attempt to pretend that the people (whose power is purely legislative) can hold the executive in check through their deputies cannot conceal the underlying despotism successfully enough to prevent it becoming apparent in the means which the minister employs. The people, who are represented in parliament by their deputies, have in these men guarantors of their freedom and their rights. These deputies, however, will also be actively interested in themselves and their own families, and they will depend upon the minister to supply them with positions in the army, navy or civil service. And even disregarding the fact that there would have to be a pre-arranged agreement among the people before any resistance could be publicly proclaimed (although such agreements are impermissible in times of peace), we can thus see that the deputies, instead of offering resistance to the pretensions of the government, will always be ready to play into its hands. A so-called 'moderate' political constitution, as a constitution regulating the internal rights of the state, is therefore an absurdity. Far from harmonising with right, it is merely a clever expedient, designed to make it as easy as possible for the powerful transgressor of popular rights to exercise his arbitrary influence upon the government, disguising this influence as a right of opposition to which the people are entitled.

There can thus be no rightful resistance on the part of the people to the legislative head of state.[12] For a state of right becomes possible only through submission to his universal legislative will. Thus there can be no right of *sedition* (*seditio*), and still less a right of *rebellion* (*rebellio*), least of all a right to *lay hands on* the person of the monarch as an individual, or to take his life on the pretext that he has misused his power (*monarcho-machismus sub specie tyrannicidii*). The least attempt to do so is *high treason* (*proditio eminens*), and a traitor of this kind, as one who has tried to *destroy his fatherland* (*parricida*), may be punished with nothing less than death.

The reason why it is the duty of the people to tolerate even what is apparently the most intolerable misuse of supreme power is that it is impossible ever to conceive of their resistance to the supreme legislation as being anything other than unlawful and liable to nullify the entire legal constitution. For before such resistance could be authorised, there would have to be a public law which permitted the people to offer resistance: in other words, the supreme legislation would have to contain a provision to the effect that it is not supreme, so that in one and the same judgement, the people as subjects would be made sovereign over the individual to whom they are subject. This is self-contradictory, and the contradiction is at once obvious if we ask who would act as judge in this dispute between the people and the sovereign (for in terms of right, they are still two distinct moral persons). It then becomes clear that the people would set themselves up as judges of their own cause.*

* It is possible to conceive of a monarch's *dethronement* as a *voluntary* abdication of the crown and a renunciation of his power by giving it back to the people, or as a forfeiture of power, without violation of the monarch's person, whereby he is simply relegated to the rank of a private citizen. And while one might at least appeal to a supposed *right of necessity* (*casus necessitatis*) as an excuse for the people's action in forcibly dethroning the head of state, they can never have the slightest right to punish him for his previous administration. For everything which he previously did in his capacity as head of state must be considered to have been outwardly in keeping with right, and he himself, regarded as the source of all laws, is incapable of any unjust action. But of all the outrages attending a revolution through rebellion, even the *murder* of the monarch is not the worst; for it is still possible to imagine that the people did it because they *feared* that if he were allowed to survive, he might recover his power and mete out to the people the punishment they deserved, in which case their behaviour would not be an act of penal justice but simply an act of self-preservation. It is the formal *execution* of a monarch which must arouse dread in any soul imbued with ideas of human right, and this feeling will recur whenever one thinks of events like the fate of Charles I or Louis XVI. But how are we to explain this feeling? It is not aesthetic (like that sympathy which comes from imagining oneself placed in the sufferer's situation), but rather moral, being our reaction to the complete reversal of all concepts of right. It is seen as a crime which must always remain as such and which can never be effaced (*crimen immortale, inexpiabile*), and it might be likened to that sin which the theologians maintain can never be forgiven either in this world or the next. The explanation of this phenomenon of the human psyche would seem to lie in the following reflections concerning our own nature, reflections which also cast some light on the principles of political right.

Every transgression of the law can and must be explained only as the result of a maxim of the criminal whereby he makes a rule out of misdeeds like the one in question. For if we were to explain such transgressions in terms of a motive of the senses, the deed could not have been committed by the criminal as a free being, and he could not consequently be held responsible for it. But it is absolutely impossible to explain how the subject is able to formulate a maxim contrary to the clear prohibition of legislative reason, for only those events which follow the mechanism of nature are capable of explanation. Now the criminal can commit his misdeed either by adopting a maxim based on an assumed objective rule (as if it were universally valid), or merely as an exception to the rule (by exempting himself from it as the occasion requires). In the *latter* case, he merely

Any alteration to a defective political constitution, which may certainly be necessary at times, can thus be carried out only by the sovereign himself through *reform*, but not through revolution by the people. And if any such alteration takes place, it can only affect the *executive power*, not the legislature.

A constitution may be arranged in such a way that the people, through their representatives in parliament, are lawfully able to *resist* the executive power and its representative (the minister). This is known as a limited constitution. But even a constitution of this kind cannot permit any active resistance (i.e. an arbitrary association of the people designed to force the government to adopt a certain mode of action, and hence an attempt by the people themselves to act as the executive power). The people may offer only a *negative* form of resistance, in that they may *refuse* in parliament to comply on all occasions with those demands which the executive says must necessarily be met for administrative purposes. In fact, if the people were to comply on all occasions, it would be a sure indication that they were decadent, their representatives venal, the head of the government a despot through his minister, and the minister himself a traitor to the people.

deviates (albeit deliberately) from the law, for he may at the same time deplore his own transgression and simply wish to get round the law without formally terminating his obedience to it. But in the *former* case, he rejects the authority of the law itself (although he cannot deny its validity in the light of his own reason), and makes it his rule to act in opposition to it; his maxim is thus at variance with the law not simply through *deficiency* (*negative*); it is actually *contrary* to the law (*contrarie*), or, so to speak, diametrically opposed to it as a contradiction (i.e. virtually hostile to it). So far as can be seen, it is impossible for men to commit a crime of such formal and completely futile malice, although no system of morality should omit to consider it, if only as a pure idea representing ultimate evil.

Thus the reason why the thought of the formal execution of a monarch *by his people* inspires us with dread is that, while his *murder* must be regarded merely as an exception to the rule which the people have taken as their maxim, his *execution* must be seen as a complete *reversal* of the principles which govern the relationship between the sovereign and the people. For it amounts to making the people, who owe their existence purely to the legislation of the sovereign, into rulers over the sovereign, thereby brazenly adopting violence as a deliberate principle and exalting it above the most sacred canons of right. And this, like an abyss which engulfs everything beyond hope of return, is an act of suicide by the state, and it would seem to be a crime for which there can be no atonement. There are therefore grounds for assuming that agreements to perform such executions do not really proceed from any supposed principle of right, but from the people's fear of revenge from the state if it should ever recover, and that such formalities are introduced only in order to give the deed an air of penal justice and of *rightful procedure* (with which murder, on the other hand, could not be reconciled). But this disguise is futile, since any such presumption on the part of the people is more atrocious than murder itself, for it in fact embodies a principle which must make it impossible for an overthrown state to be reconstituted.

Furthermore, if a revolution has succeeded and a new constitution has been established, the unlawfulness of its origin and success cannot free the subjects from the obligation to accommodate themselves as good citizens to the new order of things, and they cannot refuse to obey in an honest way the authority now in power. The dethroned monarch, if he survives such a revolution, cannot be taken to task for his earlier management of the state, far less punished for it. This applies so long as he has retired to the status of a citizen, preferring his own peace and that of the state to the hazards of abandoning his position and embarking as a pretender on the enterprise of restoration, whether through secretly instigated counter-revolution or the support of other powers. But if he prefers the latter course, his right to his property remains intact, since the rebellion which deprived him of it was unjust. It must, however, be left to international right to decide whether other powers have the right to join in an association for the benefit of this fallen monarch simply in order that the people's crime should not go unpunished or remain as a scandal in the eyes of other states, and whether they are entitled or called upon to overthrow a constitution established in any other state by revolution, and to restore the old one by forcible means.

B

Can the sovereign be regarded as the supreme proprietor of the land, or must he be regarded only as one who exercises supreme command over the people by means of laws? Since the land is the ultimate condition under which it is alone possible to possess external objects as one's own, while the possession and use of such objects in turn constitutes the primary hereditary right, all such rights must be derived from the sovereign as *lord of the land*, or rather as the supreme proprietor (*dominus territorii*). The people, as a mass of subjects, also belong to him (i.e. they are his people), although they do not belong to him as an owner by the right of property, but as a supreme commander by the right of persons.

But this supreme ownership is only an idea of the civil union, designed to represent through concepts of right the need to unite the private property of all members of the people under a universal public owner; for this makes it possible to define particular ownership by means of the necessary formal principle of *distribution* (division of the land), rather than by principles of *aggregation* (which proceeds empirically from the parts to the whole). The principles of right require that the supreme proprietor should not possess any land as private property (otherwise he would become a private person), for all land belongs exclusively to the people (not collectively, but distributively). Nomadic peoples, however, would be an exception to this rule, for they do not have any private property in the shape of land. Thus the supreme commander cannot own any *domains*, i.e. land reserved for his private use or for the maintenance of his court. For since the extent of his lands would then depend on his own discretion, the state would run the risk of finding all landed property in the hands of the government, and all the subjects would be treated as serfs bound to the soil (*glebae adscripti*) or holders of what always remained the property of someone else; they would consequently appear devoid of all freedom (*servi*). One can thus say of a lord of the land that he *possesses nothing* of his own (except his own person). For if he owned something on equal terms with anyone else in the state, he could conceivably come into conflict with this other person without there being any judge to settle it. But it can also be said that he *possesses everything*, because he has the right to exercise command over the people, to whom all external objects (*divisim*) belong, and to give each person whatever is his due.

It follows from this that there can be no corporation, class or order within the state which may as an owner hand down land indefinitely, by appropriate statutes, for the exclusive use of subsequent generations. The state can at all times repeal such statutes, with the one condition that it must compensate those still alive. The *order of knights* (either as a corporation or simply as a class of eminently distinguished individual persons) and the *order of the clergy* (i.e. the church) can never acquire ownership of land to pass on to their successors by virtue of the privileges with which they have been favoured; they may acquire only the temporary use of it. Either the land tenure of the military orders or the estates of the church can be suspended without hesitation, so long as the above-named condition is fulfilled. This could happen to the military orders if public opinion no longer wished to use *military honour* as a means of protecting the state against indifference in matters of defence, or alternatively to the church if the public no longer wished to use masses for the dead, prayers and a host of men employed as spiritual advisers as means of urging on the citizens to preserve them from eternal fire. Those who are affected by such a reform cannot complain of being expropriated, for *public opinion* was the only ground on which their previous possessions were based, and they remained legitimate so long as this opinion remained constant. But as soon as public opinion changes (above all in the judgement of those who, by virtue of their merit, have the strongest claim to lead it), the pretended ownership must cease as if by public appeal to the state (*a rege male informato ad regem melius informandum*).[13]

From this basic right of ownership as it was originally acquired, the supreme commander (as the supreme proprietor or lord of the land) derives his right to *tax* the private landowners, i.e. to impose levies in the shape of land taxes, excises and customs duties, or to require work such as military service. But it must be done in such a way that the people tax themselves, for this alone would be in keeping with laws of right. It is therefore done through the corps of deputies of the people, although it may be permissible to impose an enforced loan (i.e. a loan not provided for in the law as it has hitherto stood) by the right of majesty in cases where the state is threatened with dissolution.

From the same source, the rights of economic and financial administration and of the police force are derived. The police look after public *security*, *convenience* and also *propriety*; for it makes it much easier for the government to perform its business of governing the people by laws if the public sense of propriety (*sensus decori*—a negative taste) is not dulled by affronts to the moral sense such as begging, uproar in the streets, offensive smells and public prostitution (*venus volgivaga*).

A third kind of right is necessary for the preservation of the state—the right of *inspection* (*ius inspectionis*). This requires that no association which could influence the *public* welfare of society (*publicum*), such as an association of political or religious *illuminati*, may be kept secret; at the request of the police, it must not refuse to disclose its constitution. But only in cases of emergency may the police search anyone's private residence, and in each case, they must be authorised to do so by a higher authority.

C

Indirectly, i.e. in so far as he takes the duty of the people upon himself, the supreme commander has the right to impose taxes upon the people for their own preservation, e.g. for the *care of the poor*, for *foundling hospitals* and *church activities*, or for what are otherwise known as charitable or pious institutions.

For the general will of the people has united to form a society which must constantly maintain itself, and to this end, it has subjected itself to the internal power of the state so as to preserve those members of the society who cannot do so themselves. The nature of the state thus justifies the government in compelling prosperous citizens to provide the means of preserving those who are unable to provide themselves with even the most rudimentary necessities of nature. For since their existence itself is an act of submission to the protection of the commonwealth and to the care it must give them to enable them to live, they have committed themselves in such a way that the state has a right to make them contribute their share to maintaining their fellow citizens. This may be done by taxing the citizens' property or their commercial transactions, or by instituting funds and using the interest from them—not for the needs of the state (for it is rich), but for the needs of the people. The contributions should not be purely *voluntary* (for we are here concerned only with the *rights* of the state as against the subjects), they must in fact be compulsory political impositions. Some voluntary contributions such as lotteries, which are made from profit-seeking motives, should not be permitted, since they create greater than usual numbers of poor who become a danger to public property.

It might at this point be asked whether the poor ought to be provided for by *current contributions* so that each generation would support its own members, or by gradually accumulated *capital funds* and *pious foundations* at large (such as widows' homes, hospitals, etc.). Funds must certainly not be raised by begging, which has close affinities with robbery, but by lawful taxation. The first arrangement (that of current contributions) must be considered the only one appropriate to the rights of the state, for no-one who wishes to be sure of his livelihood can be exempt from it. These contributions increase with the numbers of poor, and they do not make poverty a means of support for the indolent (as is to be feared in the case of pious foundations), so that the government need not impose an *unjust* burden on the people.

As for the support of children abandoned through need or through shame (and who may even be murdered for such reasons), the state has a right to make it a duty for the people not to let them perish knowingly, even although they are an unwelcome increase to the state's population. But whether this can justly be done by taxing bachelors of both sexes (i.e. single persons of *means*) as a class which is partly responsible for the situation, using the proceeds to set up foundling hospitals, or whether any other method is preferable (although it is scarcely likely that any means of preventing the evil can be found)—this is a problem which has not yet been successfully solved without prejudice to right or to morality.

The *church*, as an institution for public *divine service* among the people whose opinions or convictions created it, must be carefully distinguished from religion, which is an inward attitude of mind quite outside the sphere of influence of the civil power. As such, the church fulfils a genuine political necessity, for it enables the people to regard themselves as subjects of an *invisible* supreme power to which they must pay homage and which may often come into very unequal conflict with the civil power. The state certainly has no right to legislate on the internal constitution of the church, to arrange church affairs to suit its own advantage, or to issue directions and commands to the people in matters of faith and liturgical forms (*ritus*); for all this must be left entirely to the teachers and supervisors whom the people have themselves elected. It has only a *negative* right to prevent the public teachers of religion from exercising any influence on the *visible* political commonwealth such as might threaten the public peace, and to ensure that internal conflicts within the church or conflicts between different churches do not endanger civil concord. That is, it has a right like that of the police. It would be *beneath the dignity* of the ruling authority to interfere in church affairs by requiring that a church should have a certain belief and by laying down which belief it should have, or by demanding that it should preserve this belief without alteration and never attempt to reform itself. For by becoming involved in a scholastic quarrel, the supreme power would be placing itself on an equal footing with the subjects and the monarch setting himself up as a priest. The subjects may tell him outright that he does not understand the affairs in question, especially if he attempts to prohibit internal reforms, for anything which the entire people cannot decide for itself cannot be decided for the people by the legislator either. But no people can decide never to make further progress in opinions relating to its faith (i.e. in enlightenment), nor can it decide never to undertake reforms in affairs of the church, for this would be contrary to humanity as represented in the person of the people, hence also to the people's highest rights. Thus no ruling authority may make such a decision for the people. But for precisely the same reason, the onus of paying the costs of maintaining the church cannot fall upon the state; they must be met by that portion of the people which follows one or other particular creed, i.e. by the congregation.

D

The rights of the supreme commander in the state also include (1) the distribution of *offices* as jobs involving remuneration; (2) the distribution of *dignities*, i.e. distinctions of rank without remuneration, based purely on honour, giving rise to a division between the superior or commanding class and the inferior class which, although free and bound only by public law, is predetermined to obey the former; (3) *penal right* (over and above the more or less benevolent rights already described).

If we consider civil offices, we are faced with the question of whether the sovereign has a right to take away an office at his discretion without any misdemeanour on the part of the person to whom he had given it. I reply in the negative. For a decision which the united will of the people would never make about a civil official cannot be made by the head of state either. Now the people (who will have to bear the costs incurred in appointing an official) will undoubtedly wish this official to be fully qualified to perform the work he is given. But he cannot be fully qualified unless he has been able to devote a sufficient period to extended preparation and training, during which period he will have sacrificed the time he could have spent learning some other profession as a means of supporting himself. Thus if people were dismissed without reason, the office would as a rule be filled with individuals who had not acquired the necessary skill or achieved through practice a mature faculty of judgement. But this is contrary to the intention of the state; and besides, the state also requires that every individual should be able to rise from a lower office to higher ones (which would otherwise fall into the hands of utterly unsuitable persons), and hence to count on receiving a livelihood throughout his life.

As for civil *dignities*, the *nobility* includes not only those positions to which an office is attached, but also those which make the holder a member of a higher class, even if he performs no particular services. The nobility is distinct from the civil status occupied by the people, for it is inherited by the male descendants. Through the latter, it can also be conferred upon female relatives of ignoble birth, although a woman of noble birth cannot in turn confer noble status upon a husband who was not born a nobleman, but must herself revert to the purely civil status of the people. The question which now arises is whether the sovereign is entitled to create a nobility as a *hereditary* class between himself and the rest of the citizens. The answer will not, however, depend upon whether it suits the sovereign's policies for furthering his own or the people's advantage, but simply upon whether it is in keeping with right that anyone should have above him a class of persons who, although themselves subjects, will in relation to the people be commanders by birth, or at least possess greater privileges than they do.

As before, the answer to this question will be found in the principle that anything which the people (i.e. the entire mass of subjects) cannot decide for themselves and their fellows cannot be decided for the people by the sovereign either. Now a *hereditary* nobility is a distinction bestowed before it is earned, and since it gives no grounds for hoping that it will be earned, it is wholly unreal and fanciful. For if an ancestor has earned his position through merit, he still cannot pass on his merit to his descendants. On the contrary, the latter must always earn it themselves, for nature is not such that the talent and will which enable a person to serve the state meritoriously can be *inherited*. Now since it cannot be assumed of anyone that he will throw his freedom away, it is impossible for the universal will of the people to agree to so groundless a prerogative; thus the sovereign cannot make it valid either.

It may be, however, that an anomaly of this sort has crept into the mechanism of government in past ages (as with the feudal system, which was almost entirely geared to making war), so that some subjects claim that they are more than citizens and are entitled by birth to official posts (a hereditary professorship, let us say). In this case, the state can make good its mistake of unrightfully bestowing hereditary privileges only by a gradual process, by allowing the posts to fall vacant and omitting to fill them again. The state thus has a provisional right to allow such dignities to persist as titles until public opinion itself realises that the hierarchy of sovereign, nobility and people should give way to the more natural division of sovereign and people.

No human being in the state can be totally without a position of dignity, for each at least has that of a citizen, unless he has forfeited it through some *crime* of his own doing. If the latter is the case, he may indeed be kept alive, but he will be made a mere instrument of another person (either the state or another citizen). Anyone in this position is a *bondsman or slave* (*servus in sensu stricto*) and is part of the *property* (*dominium*) of someone else, who is therefore not just his *master* (*herus*), but also his *owner* (*dominus*); the latter may accordingly make him over to anyone else as a chattel or use him as he wishes (except for infamous purposes), and he may *dispose of* his powers, although not of his life and limbs, at his own discretion. No-one can enter by contract into such a state of dependence and thus cease to be a person; for only as a person is he able to make a contract. Now it may seem that in return for payment, food or protection, a man can bind himself to another person by a contract of hire (*locatio conductio*) whereby he must perform certain services of a permissible nature but of an *indeterminate amount*, and that this will merely make him a *servant* (*subiectus*) but not a *slave* (*servus*). But this is an illusion. For if the master is authorised to use the powers of his servant as he pleases, he may (as happens with the negroes in the West Indies) exhaust him to the point of death or despair, and the servant will really have made himself over to his master as property, which is impossible. The servant can thus hire himself out only for work which is determinate both in nature and in quantity, either as a day labourer or a resident servant. In the latter case, he will not receive a wage, but will be allowed to use his master's land; and he will fulfil his side of the contract of tenure partly by serving on this land and partly by paying definite sums (i.e. a rent) for his own use of it. He can do this without making himself a *serf of the soil (glebae adscriptus)* and thereby forfeiting his personality, and he may enter into a temporary or hereditary leasehold. He may, however, have become a *personal* subject through some misdemeanour he has committed, but he cannot *inherit* any such position of servitude, for he can acquire this status only through his own guilt. And it is in no way more permissible for anyone to claim ownership of a bondsman's offspring on account of the costs incurred in educating him, for education is an absolute natural duty of parents, and if the parents' status is servile, it is in turn the duty of the masters, since the latter cannot take possession of their bondsmen without also taking over their duties.

E

The Right of Punishment and the Right of Pardon

I

The *right of punishment* is the right of the commander as against the subject to inflict pain on him for some crime he has committed. Thus the supreme authority in the state cannot be punished; a subject may at most withdraw from his rule. An infringement of the public law which renders the guilty person incapable of citizenship is known as a *crime (crimen)* in the absolute sense, or alternatively, as a public crime *(crimen publicum)*. The former (a private crime) will be dealt with by a court of civil justice, the latter (a public crime) by a court of criminal justice. *Embezzlement* (i.e. misappropriation of money or goods entrusted to someone for commercial purposes) and fraudulent dealings in buying and selling under the eyes of another party are private crimes. On the other hand, counterfeiting money or bills of exchange, theft, robbery, and the like are public crimes, because they endanger the commonwealth and not merely an individual person. Such crimes might in turn be divided into those of *base* motivation *(indolis abiectae)* and those of *violent* motivation *(indolis violentae)*.

Judicial punishment (poena forensis) should be distinguished from *natural punishment (poena naturalis)*; the latter is found where vice punishes itself, and is thus no concern of the legislator. Judicial punishment can never be merely a means of furthering some extraneous good for the criminal himself or for civil society, but must always be imposed on the criminal simply *because he has committed a crime*. For a human being can never be manipulated just as a means of realising someone else's intentions, and is not to be confused with the objects of the law of kind. He is protected against this by his inherent personality, although he may well be sentenced to forfeit his civil personality. He must first be found worthy of punishment before any thought is given to the possible utility which he or his fellow citizens might derive from his punishment. The penal law is a categorical imperative, and woe betide anyone who winds his way through the labyrinth of the theory of happiness in search of some possible advantage to be gained by releasing the criminal from his punishment or from any part of it, or who acts in the spirit of the pharisaical saying: 'It is better that one man should die than that the whole people should go to ruin.' For if justice perishes, there is no further point in men living on earth. What then are we to think of the proposal that the life of a condemned criminal should be spared if he agrees to let dangerous experiments be carried out on him in order that the doctors may gain new information of value to the commonwealth, and is fortunate enough to survive? A court of justice would dismiss with contempt any medical institution which made such a proposal; for justice ceases to be justice if it can be bought at a price.

But what kind and what degree of punishment does public justice take as its principle and norm? None other than the principle of equality in the movement of the pointer on the scales of justice, the principle of not inclining to one side more than to the other. Thus any undeserved evil which you do to someone else among the people is an evil done to yourself. If you slander him, you slander yourself; if you rob him, you rob yourself; if you strike him, you strike yourself; and if you kill him, you kill yourself. But it should be understood that only the *law of retribution (ius talionis)* can determine exactly what quality and quantity of punishment is required, and it must do so in court, not within your private judgement. All other criteria are inconstant; they cannot be reconciled with the findings of pure and strict justice, because they introduce other outside considerations.

Now it may well appear that class differences do not allow for the principle of retribution whereby like is exchanged for like. But although it is impossible according to the letter, it may still remain valid in terms of effect if we consider the sensibilities of the more distinguished classes. Thus a monetary fine on account of a verbal injury, for example, bears no relation to the actual offence, for anyone who has plenty of money could allow himself such an offence whenever he pleased. But the injured honour of one individual might well be closely matched by the wounded pride of the other, as would happen if the latter were compelled by judgement and right not only to apologise publicly, but also, let us say, to kiss the hand of the former, even though he were of lower station. The same would apply if a high-ranking individual convicted of violence were sentenced, in return for the blows he had dealt an inferior but guiltless citizen, not only to make an apology but also to undergo a period of painful solitary confinement; for apart from the resultant discomfort, the perpetrator's vanity would also be painfully affected, and this humiliation would provide an appropriate repayment of like with like.

But what does it mean to say: 'If you rob him, you rob yourself'? Anyone who steals makes the property of everyone else insecure; by the right of retribution, he thus robs himself of the security of all possible ownership. He has nothing and he cannot acquire anything, but he still wishes to live, and this is possible only if others provide him with sustenance. But since the state will not do this for nothing, he must place his powers at the state's disposal for whatever tasks it chooses (i.e. hard labour), and he is relegated to the status of a slave for a certain period or even permanently, according to circumstances. But if he has committed murder, he must *die*. In this case, no possible substitute can satisfy justice. For there is no *parallel* between death and even the most miserable life, so that there is no equality of crime and retribution unless the perpetrator is judicially put to death (at all events without any maltreatment which might make humanity an object of horror in the person of the sufferer). Even if civil society were to dissolve itself with the consent of all its members (for example, if a people who inhabited an island decided to separate and to disperse to other parts of the world), the last murderer in prison would first have to be executed in order that each should receive his deserts and that the people should not bear the guilt of a capital crime through failing to insist on its punishment; for if they do not do so, they can be regarded as accomplices in the public violation of justice.

This equality of punishments is therefore possible only if the judge passes the death sentence in accordance with the strict law of retribution. It will be a sign of such equality if the death sentence is pronounced on all criminals in proportion to their inner *malice* (even if the crime in question is not murder, but some other crime against the state which can only be effaced by death). Let us take the case of the last Scottish rebellion, in which various participants (such as Balmerino[14] and others) considered that they were only fulfilling a duty they owed to the house of Stuart, while others were furthering their personal aims. If the supreme court had passed judgement to the effect that each should be free to choose between death and penal servitude, I say that the honourable man would choose death and the scoundrel penal servitude; for such is the nature of man. The former knows something which he values more highly than life itself, namely *honour*; but the latter considers even a life of disgrace better than no life at all (*animam praeferre pudori*—Juvenal).[15] Now the first is unquestionably less culpable than the second, so that if they are both condemned to death, they each receive punishment proportionate to their deserts; for the first will be punished mildly in relation to his own sensibility, and the second severely in relation to his. On the other hand, if both were sentenced to penal servitude, the first would be punished too severely, and the second too mildly for the degree of his baseness. Thus in sentencing a number of criminals who have joined in a conspiracy, the most balanced solution in terms of public justice is once again the *death penalty*. Besides, no-one has ever heard of a criminal condemned to death for murder complaining that the punishment was excessive and therefore unjust; everyone would laugh in his face if he said so. Otherwise, it would have to be assumed that although no injustice is done to the criminal according to the law, the legislative power in the state is not authorised to impose this sort of penalty, and that if it does so, it is in contradiction with itself.

All murderers, whether they have themselves done the deed, ordered it to be done, or acted as accomplices, must suffer the death penalty. This is what justice, as the idea of judicial power, wills in accordance with universal laws of *a priori* origin. But the number of accomplices (*correi*) in such a deed might be so great that the state, in order to rid itself of such criminals, would soon reach the stage of having no more subjects, and yet it would not wish to dissolve itself and revert to the state of nature, for the latter, devoid of all external justice, is much worse still. And above all, the state will not wish to blunt the people's feelings by a spectacle of mass slaughter. The sovereign must therefore have the power to act as judge himself in such an emergency (*casus necessitatis*), and to pass a sentence which imposes a penalty other than death on the criminals so that the community of people may be preserved (e.g. a sentence of deportation). This procedure, however, may not be adopted in consequence of any public law, but only as a peremptory order, i.e. an act based on the right of majesty; and this, as a right of mercy, may only be exercised in isolated cases.

But the Marchese Beccaria,[16] from motives of compassionate sentimentality and affected humanity (*compassibilitas*), has set up in opposition to this view his claim that capital punishment is always *contrary to right*. For he maintains that it could not have been contained in the original civil contract, since this would have compelled each individual to agree to forfeit his life if he were to murder anyone else (among his own people), and such an agreement is impossible because no-one can dispose of his own life.

This is pure sophistry and distortion of the principles of right. For a person does not suffer punishment because he wished to have *the punishment itself*, but because he wished to commit a *punishable deed*. After all, it is not a punishment if a person is subjected to something which he wishes, and it is impossible to *wish* to be punished. To say: 'I wish to be punished if I murder anyone' means nothing more than 'I submit along with the rest of the people to the laws, which, if there are criminals among the people, will naturally include penal laws.' As a co-legislator who dictates the *penal law*, I cannot possibly be the same person who, as a subject, is punished in accordance with the law. For in the latter capacity, i.e. as a criminal, I cannot possibly have a say in the legislation, since the legislator is holy. Thus if I promulgate a penal law against myself as a criminal, it is the pure rightful and legislative reason within me (*homo noumenon*) which subjects me as a person capable of crime, hence as one person (*homo phaenomenon*) along with all the others within the civil union, to the penal law. In other words, it is not the people (i.e. all individuals) who dictate the death penalty, but the court of public justice, i.e. someone other than the criminal; and the social contract does not contain a promise by anyone to let himself be punished and hence to dispose of himself and his own life. For if the authority to impose punishments had to depend upon a *promise* on the part of the malefactor to *will* his own punishment, it would also have to be left to him to declare himself culpable, and the criminal would thus be his own judge. The cardinal error (πρῶτον ψεῦδος) in this sophistry consists in regarding the criminal's own judgement that he must forfeit his life (a judgement which one must necessarily attribute to his *reason*) as a decision on the part of his *will* to take his own life: this amounts to representing the execution of right and the adjudication of right as united in one and the same person.

There are, however, two further crimes worthy of the death penalty, but it remains doubtful whether the *legislature* has the authority to impose this penalty upon them. Both of them are actuated by a sense of honour, but the first involves *sexual honour* whereas the second involves *military honour*. Both are true forms of honour, and it is a duty of the two classes of people involved (women and soldiers respectively) to uphold them.

The first crime is *infanticide* by the mother (*infanticidium maternale*), and the second is *murder of a comrade in arms* (*commilitonicidium*) in a duel. No legislation can remove the disgrace of an illegitimate birth; nor can it efface the stain which is left when suspicions of cowardice fall upon a subordinate officer who does not react to a humiliating encounter with a vigour surpassing the fear of death. It therefore appears that in cases of this kind, men find themselves in a state of nature. And while their *killing* of each other (*homicidium*) should not then be called *murder* (*homicidium dolosum*), it still remains punishable, although the supreme power cannot punish it with death. The child born outside marriage is outside the law (for marriage is a lawful institution), and it is therefore also outside the protection of the law. It has found its way into the commonwealth by stealth, so to speak, like contraband goods, so that the commonwealth can ignore its existence and hence also its destruction, for it ought not to have come into existence at all in this way; and no decree can remove the mother's disgrace if the illegitimate birth becomes known. In the same way, if a military man with the rank of a junior officer is offered an affront, he finds himself compelled by the universal opinion of his equals to seek satisfaction and to punish the offender, although not through the workings of the law in a court of justice, but by means of a duel as in the state of nature. He thereby risks losing his own life in order to prove his martial courage, on which the honour of his profession is essentially based; and even if it involves *killing* his opponent, the deed may not actually be called *murder* (*homicidium dolosum*), because it occurred in a public conflict to which both parties (however unwillingly) consented.

What, then, are the rights and wrongs of these two cases in so far as they are subject to criminal justice? Penal justice is here faced with a very difficult problem, for it must either declare that the concept of honour, which in the present case is no mere illusion, is null and void before the law and ought to be punished by death, or it must exempt the crimes in question from the death penalty. And while the first course would be cruel, the second would be over-indulgent. The solution to this dilemma is that the categorical imperative of penal justice (whereby the unlawful killing of another person must be punished by death) remains in force, although the legislation itself (hence also the civil constitution), so long as it remains barbarous and undeveloped, is to blame for the fact that the motives of honour obeyed by the people are subjectively incompatible with those measures which are objectively suited to their realisation, so that public justice as dispensed by the state is *injustice* in the eyes of the people.

II

The *right of pardon* (*ius aggratiandi*), whereby the criminal's punishment is either mitigated or completely remitted, is certainly the most equivocal of all the rights exercised by the sovereign; for while it may confirm the aura of his majesty, it can at the same time do a great deal of injustice. In cases involving crimes of the subjects against one another, the sovereign should on no account exercise this right, for exemption from punishment (*impunitas criminis*) in such cases means doing the greatest injustice to the subjects. Thus he can only make use of it when *he himself* has been done an injury (*crimen laesae maiestatis*), and he may not do so even then if a remittance of punishment might endanger the security of the people. This right is the only one which deserves to be called a right of majesty.

On the Relationship of the Citizen to his own and other Countries with Regard to Right

§ 50

A country (*territorium*) whose inhabitants are fellow citizens of one and the same commonwealth by the very nature of the constitution (i.e. without having to exercise any particular right, so that they are already citizens by birth) is called the *fatherland* of these citizens. Lands in which this condition of citizenship does not apply to them are *foreign countries*. And a country which is part of a wider system of government is called a *province* (in the sense in which the Romans used this word); since it is not, however, an integrated part of an empire (*imperii*) whose inhabitants are all fellow-citizens, but is only a *possession* and *subordinate realm* of the empire, it must respect the territory of the ruling state as its *motherland* (*regio domina*).

1. The *subject* (considered also as a citizen) has the right of emigration, for the state could not hold him back as it might a piece of property. But he can take only his mobile belongings with him; he cannot take his fixed possessions, as would indeed be the case if he were authorised to sell the land he had hitherto possessed and to take the money he received for it with him.

2. The *lord of the land* has the right to encourage the immigration and settlement of foreigners (colonists), even though the native subjects should look askance at it. But he must see to it that private ownership of the land by the native subjects is not diminished.

3. If a subject should commit a crime which makes it a danger to the state for him to associate with his fellow citizens, the lord of the land has

the right to *banish* him to a foreign province where he will not share any of the rights of a citizen, i.e. he has a right to *deport* him.

4. The lord indeed has the right to exile him completely (*ius exilii*), to send him out into the world at large, i.e. to foreign countries (for which the old German word was 'Elend', the same word as that denoting misery). And since the lord of the land thereby withdraws his protection from him, it is tantamount to making him an outlaw within his own frontiers.

§ 51

The three powers within the state, which emerge from the general concept of a *commonwealth* (*res publica latius dicta*), are simply so many relationships within the united will of the people (which is derived *a priori* from reason itself), and are likewise a pure idea of the supreme head of state, which also has objective and practical reality. But this head of state (the sovereign) is only an abstraction (representing the entire people) so long as there is no physical person to represent the highest power in the state and to make this idea influence the will of the people. Now the relationship between the head of state and the people can be envisaged in three different ways. Either *one* person within the state will rule over everyone, or *several* persons of equal rank will unite to rule over all others, or *all* will rule collectively over each (hence also over themselves). That is, the *form of the state* will either be *autocratic*, *aristocratic*, or *democratic*. (The expression 'monarchic' instead of 'autocratic' does not properly cover the concept here intended, for a *monarch* is one who has the *highest* power, while an *autocrat* or absolute ruler is one who has *all* the power; the latter is the sovereign, whereas the former merely represents him.)

It can readily be seen that the autocratic form is the *simplest* form of state, for it involves only a relationship between one individual (the king) and the people, and the legislator is a single person. An aristocratic state is *composite*, involving two kinds of relationship: that of the aristocrats (as legislators) towards one another, thereby constituting the sovereign, and then the relationship between this sovereign and the people. But the democratic form is the most composite of all. For it must first unite the will of all in order to make a people; it must then unite the will of the citizens to make a commonwealth; and finally, it must unite their will to place at the head of the commonwealth a sovereign, who is simply this united will itself.* As far as the actual *manipulation* of right within the

---

* I make no mention here of perversions of these forms by the interference of unauthorised rulers (as in *oligarchy* and *ochlocracy*), nor of so-called *mixed* constitutions, since this would go beyond the scope of the present work.

state is concerned, the simplest form is of course also the best, but in relation to *right* itself, it is the most dangerous from the point of view of the people, for it is extremely conducive to despotism. Simplification is certainly the most rational maxim for the mechanical process of uniting the people by means of coercive laws, so long as all the people are passive and obedient to a single individual above them—but this would mean that no subjects could be *citizens*. Perhaps, however, the people are supposed to content themselves with the consolation that monarchy (in this case, autocracy) is the best political constitution *if the monarch is a good one* (i.e. if he has not only the will but also the necessary insight to be one). But this saying is a tautology, for it merely means that the best constitution is that *by which* the administrator of the state is made into the best ruler, i.e. that the best constitution is that which is best.

§ 52

It is futile to hunt for *historical documentation* of the origins of this mechanism. That is, we cannot reach back to the time at which civil society first emerged (for savages do not set up any formal instruments in submitting themselves to the law, and it can easily be gathered from the nature of uncivilised man that they must have initially used violent means). But it would be quite culpable to undertake such researches with a view to forcibly changing the constitution at present in existence. For this sort of change could only be effected by the people by means of revolutionary conspiracy, and not by the legislature. But revolution under an already existing constitution means the destruction of all relationships governed by civil right, and thus of right altogether. And this is not a change but a dissolution of the civil constitution; and the transition to a better one would not then be a metamorphosis but a palingenesis, for it would require a new social contract on which the previous one (which is now dissolved) could have no influence. But it must still be possible for the sovereign to alter the existing constitution if it cannot readily be reconciled with the idea of the original contract, and yet in so doing to leave untouched that basic form which is essential if the people are to constitute a state. This alteration cannot be such that the state abandons one of the three fundamental forms and reconstitutes itself in accordance with one of the two remaining ones, as would happen, for example, if the aristocrats agreed to submit to an autocracy or to disband and create a democracy or vice versa. This would imply that it depended on the sovereign's own free choice and discretion to subject the people to whatever constitution he wished. For even if the sovereign decided to go over to democracy, he might still be doing the people an injustice; for they might themselves detest this form of constitution and find one of the two others more congenial.

The three forms of state are merely the *letter* (*littera*) of the original legislation within civil society, and they may therefore remain as part of the mechanism of the constitution for as long as they are considered necessary by old and long established custom (i.e. purely subjectively). But the *spirit* of the original contract (*anima pacti originarii*) contains an obligation on the part of the constitutive power to make the *mode of government* conform to the original idea, and thus to alter the mode of government by a gradual and continuous process (if it cannot be done at once) until it accords *in its effects* with the only rightful constitution, that of a pure republic. The old empirical (and statutory) forms, which serve only to effect the *subjection* of the people, should accordingly resolve themselves into the original (rational) form which alone makes *freedom* the principle and indeed the condition of all *coercion*. For coercion is required for a just political constitution in the truest sense, and this will eventually be realised in letter as well as in spirit.

This, then, is the only lasting political constitution in which the *law* is the sole ruler, independent of all particular persons; it is the ultimate end of all public right, and the only condition in which each individual can be given his due *peremptorily*. But as long as the various forms of the state are supposed to be represented literally by an equivalent number of distinct moral persons invested with supreme power, only a *provisional* internal right instead of an absolute condition of right can obtain within civil society.

Any true republic, however, is and cannot be anything other than a *representative system* of the people whereby the people's rights are looked after on their behalf by deputies who represent the united will of the citizens. But as soon as a head of state in person (whether this head of state be a king, a nobility, or the whole populace as a democratic association) also allows himself to be represented, the united people then does not merely represent the sovereign, but actually *is* the sovereign itself. For the supreme power originally rests with the people, and all the rights of individuals as mere subjects (and particularly as state officials) must be derived from this supreme power. Once it has been established, the republic will therefore no longer need to release the reins of government from its own hands and to give them back to those who previously held them, for they might then destroy all the new institutions again by their absolute and arbitrary will.

It was thus a great error of judgement on the part of a certain powerful ruler in our own times when he tried to relieve himself of the embarrassment of large national debts by leaving it to the people to assume and distribute this burden at their own discretion.[17] It was thus natural that the people should acquire legislative powers not only in matters of taxation but also in matters of government, for they had to ensure that the government would incur no new debts by extravagance or by war. The monarch's ruling authority thus disappeared completely; for it was not merely suspended but actually passed over to the people, to whose legislative will the property of every subject was now submitted. Nor is it possible to say that we must postulate a tacit yet contractual promise on the part of the national assembly not to take over the sovereignty, but only to administer the sovereign's business and to hand back the reins of government to the monarch after the business had been completed. For a contract of this kind would in itself be null and void. The right of the supreme legislation in the commonwealth is not alienable; on the contrary, it is the most personal right of all. Whoever possesses it can only exercise control over the people through the people's collective will, but not over the collective will itself, the original foundation of all public contracts. A contract which obliged the people to give back their authority would not be in accord with the people's function as a legislative power. And this, according to the proposition that no man can serve two masters, is self-contradictory.

SECTION II: INTERNATIONAL RIGHT

§ 53

The human beings who make up a nation can, as natives of the country, be represented as analogous to descendants from a common ancestry (*congeniti*) even if this is not in fact the case. But in an intellectual sense or for the purposes of right, they can be thought of as the offspring of a common mother (the republic), constituting, as it were, a single family (*gens, natio*) whose members (the citizens) are all equal by birth. These citizens will not intermix with any neighbouring people who live in a state of nature, but will consider them ignoble, even though such savages for their own part may regard themselves as superior on account of the lawless freedom they have chosen. The latter likewise constitute national groups, but they do not constitute states.

What we are now about to consider under the name of international right or the right of nations is the right of *states* in relation to one another (although it is not strictly correct to speak, as we usually do, of the *right of nations*; it should rather be called the *right of states—ius publicum civitatum*). The situation in question is that in which one state, as a moral person, is considered as existing in a state of nature in relation to another state, hence in a condition of constant war. International right is thus concerned partly with the right to make war, partly with the right of war itself, and partly with questions of right after a war, i.e. with the right of states to compel each other to abandon their warlike condition and to create a constitution which will establish an enduring peace. A state of nature among individuals or families (in their relations with one another) is different from a state of nature among entire nations, because inter-national right involves not only the relationship between one state and another within a larger whole, but also the relationship between individual persons in one state and individuals in the other or between such individuals and the other state as a whole. But this difference between international right and the right of individuals in a mere state of nature is easily deducible from the latter concept without need of any further definitions.

§ 54

The elements of international right are as follows. Firstly, in their external relationships with one another, states, like lawless savages, exist in a condition devoid of right. Secondly, this *condition* is one of war (the right of the stronger), even if there is no actual war or continuous active fighting (i.e. hostilities). But even although neither of two states is done any injustice by the other in this condition, it is nevertheless in the highest degree unjust in itself, for it implies that neither wishes to experience anything better. Adjacent states are thus bound to abandon such a condition. Thirdly, it is necessary to establish a federation of peoples in accordance with the idea of an original social contract, so that states will protect one another against external aggression while refraining from interference in one another's internal disagreements. And fourthly, this association must not embody a sovereign power as in a civil constitution, but only a partner-ship or *confederation*. It must therefore be an alliance which can be terminated at any time, so that it has to be renewed periodically. This right is derived *in subsidium* from another original right, that of preventing oneself from lapsing into a state of actual war with one's partners in the confederation (*foedus Amphictyonum*).

§ 55

If we consider the original right of free states in the state of nature to make war upon one another (for example, in order to bring about a condition closer to that governed by right), we must first ask what right the state has *as against its own subjects* to employ them in a war on other states, and to expend or hazard their possessions or even their lives in the process. Does it not then depend upon their own judgement whether they wish to go to war or not? May they simply be sent thither at the sovereign's supreme command?

This right might seem an obvious consequence of the right to do what one wishes with one's own property. Whatever someone has himself substantially *made* is his own undisputed property. These are the premises from which a mere jurist would deduce the right in question.

A country may yield various *natural products*, some of which, because of their very *abundance*, must also be regarded as *artefacts* of the state. For the country would not yield them in such quantities if there were no state or proper government in control and if the inhabitants still lived in a state of nature. For example, domestic poultry (the most useful kind of fowl), sheep, pigs, cattle, etc. would be completely unknown in the country I live in (or would only rarely be encountered) if there were no government to guarantee the inhabitants their acquisitions and possessions. The same applies to the number of human beings, for there can only be few of them in a state of nature, as in the wilds of America, even if we credit them with great industry (which they do not have). The inhabitants would be very sparsely scattered, for no-one could spread very far afield with his household in a land constantly threatened with devastation by other human beings, wild animals, or beasts of prey. There would thus be no adequate support for so large a population as now inhabits a country.

Now one can say that vegetables (e.g. potatoes) and domestic animals, in quantity at least, are *made* by human beings, and that they may therefore be used, expended or consumed (i.e. killed) at will. One might therefore appear justified in saying that the supreme power in the state, the sovereign, has the right to lead his subjects to war as if on a hunt, or into battle as if on an excursion, simply because they are for the most part produced by the sovereign himself.

But while this legal argument (of which monarchs are no doubt dimly aware) is certainly valid in the case of animals, which can be the *property* of human beings, it is absolutely impermissible to apply it to human beings themselves, particularly in their capacity as citizens. For a citizen must always be regarded as a co-legislative member of the state (i.e. not just as a means, but also as an end in himself), and he must therefore give his free consent through his representatives not only to the waging of war in general, but also to every particular declaration of war. Only under this limiting condition may the state put him to service in dangerous enterprises.

We shall therefore have to derive the right under discussion from the *duty* of the sovereign towards the people, not vice versa. The people must be seen to have given their consent to military action, and although they remain passive in this capacity (for they allow themselves to be directed), they are still acting spontaneously and they represent the sovereign himself.

§ 56

In the state of nature, the *right to make war* (i.e. to enter into hostilities) is the permitted means by which one state prosecutes its rights against another. Thus if a state believes that it has been injured by another state, it is entitled to resort to violence, for it cannot in the state of nature gain satisfaction through *legal proceedings*, the only means of settling disputes in a state governed by right. Apart from an actively inflicted injury (the first aggression, as distinct from the first hostilities), a state may be subjected to *threats*. Such threats may arise either if another state is the first to make *military preparations*, on which the right of *anticipatory attack* (*ius praeventionis*) is based, or simply if there is an alarming increase of power (*potentia tremenda*) in another state which has acquired new territories. This is an injury to the less powerful state by the mere fact that the other state, even without offering any active offence, is *more powerful*; and any attack upon it is legitimate in the state of nature. On this is based the right to maintain a balance of power among all states which have active contact with one another.

Those *active injuries* which give a state the *right to make war* on another state include any unilateral attempt to gain satisfaction for an affront which the people of one state have offered to the people of the other. Such an act of *retribution* (*retorsio*) without any attempt to obtain compensation from the other state by peaceful means is similar in form to starting war without prior declaration. For if one wishes to find any rights in wartime, one must assume the existence of something analogous to a contract; in other words, one must assume that the other party has *accepted* the declaration of war and that both parties therefore wish to prosecute their rights in this manner.

§ 57

The most problematic task in international right is that of determining rights in wartime. For it is very difficult to form any conception at all of such rights and to imagine any law whatsoever in this lawless state without involving oneself in contradictions (*inter arma silent leges*).[18] The only possible solution would be to conduct the war in accordance with principles which would still leave the states with the possibility of abandoning the state of nature in their external relations and of entering a state of right.

No war between independent states can be a *punitive* one (*bellum punitivum*). For a punishment can only occur in a relationship between a superior (*imperantis*) and a subject (*subditum*), and this is not the relationship which exists between states. Nor can there be a *war of extermination* (*bellum internecinum*) or a *war of subjugation* (*bellum subiugatorium*); for these would involve the moral annihilation of a state, and its people would either merge with those of the victorious state or be reduced to bondage. Not that this expedient, to which a state might resort in order to obtain peace, would in itself contradict the rights of a state. But the fact remains that the only concept of antagonism which the idea of international right includes is that of an antagonism regulated by principles of external freedom. This requires that violence be used only to preserve one's existing property, but not as a method of further acquisition; for the latter procedure would create a threat to one state by augmenting the power of another.

The attacked state is allowed to use any means of defence except those whose use would render its subjects unfit to be citizens. For if it did not observe this condition, it would render itself unfit in the eyes of international right to function as a person in relation to other states and to share equal rights with them. It must accordingly be prohibited for a state to use its own subjects as spies, and to use them, or indeed foreigners, as poisoners or assassins (to which class the so-called sharpshooters who wait in ambush on individual victims also belong), or even just to spread false reports. In short, a state must not use such treacherous methods as would destroy that confidence which is required for the future establishment of a lasting peace.

It is permissible in war to impose levies and contributions on the conquered enemy, but not to plunder the people, i.e. to force individual persons to part with their belongings (for this would be robbery, since it was not the conquered people who waged the war, but the state of which they were subjects which waged it *through them*). Bills of receipt should be issued for any contributions that are exacted, so that the burden imposed on the country or province can be distributed proportionately when peace is concluded.

§ 58

The right which applies *after* a war, i.e. with regard to the peace treaty at the time of its conclusion and also to its later consequences, consists of the following elements. The victor sets out the conditions, and these are drawn up in a *treaty* on which agreement is reached with the defeated party in order that peace may be concluded. A treaty of this kind is not determined by any pretended right which the victor possesses over his opponent because of an alleged injury the latter has done him; the victor should not concern himself with such questions, but should rely only on his own power for support. Thus he cannot claim compensation for the costs of the war, for he would then have to pronounce his opponent unjust in waging it. And even if this argument should occur to him, he could not make use of it, or else he would have to maintain that the war was a punitive one, which would in turn mean that he had committed an offence in waging it himself. A peace treaty should also provide for the exchange of prisoners without ransom, whether the numbers on both sides are equal or not.

The vanquished state and its subjects cannot forfeit their civil freedom through the conquest of the country. Consequently, the former cannot be degraded to the rank of a colony or the latter to the rank of bondsmen. Otherwise, the war would have been a punitive one, which is self-contradictory.

A *colony* or province is a nation which has its own constitution, legislation and territory, and all members of any other state are no more than foreigners on its soil, even if the state to which they belong has supreme *executive* power over the colonial nation. The state with executive power is called the *mother state*. The daughter state is *ruled* by it, although it *governs* itself through its own parliament, which in turn functions under the presidency of a viceroy (*civitas hybrida*). The relationship of Athens to various islands was of this kind, as is that of Great Britain towards Ireland at the present moment.

It is even less possible to infer the rightful existence of *slavery* from the military conquest of a people, for one would then have to assume that the war had been a punitive one. Least of all would this justify hereditary slavery, which is completely absurd, for the guilt of a person's crime cannot be inherited.

It is implicit in the very concept of a peace treaty that it includes an *amnesty*.

§ 59

The *rights of peace* are as follows: firstly, the right to remain at peace when nearby states are at war (i.e. the right of *neutrality*); secondly, the right to secure the continued maintenance of peace once it has been concluded (i.e. the right of *guarantee*); and thirdly, the right to form *alliances* or confederate leagues of several states for the purpose of communal defence against any possible attacks from internal or external sources—although these must never become leagues for promoting aggression and internal expansion.

§ 60

The rights of a state against an *unjust enemy* are unlimited in quantity or degree, although they do have limits in relation to quality. In other words, while the threatened state may not employ *every* means to assert its own rights, it may employ any intrinsically permissible means to whatever degree its own strength allows. But what can the expression 'an unjust enemy' mean in relation to the concepts of international right, which requires that every state should act as judge of its own cause just as it would do in a state of nature? It must mean someone whose publicly expressed will, whether expressed in word or in deed, displays a maxim which would make peace among nations impossible and would lead to a perpetual state of nature if it were made into a general rule. Under this heading would come violations of public contracts, which can be assumed to affect the interests of all nations. For they are a threat to their freedom, and a challenge to them to unite against such misconduct and to deprive the culprit of the power to act in a similar way again. But this does *not* entitle them *to divide up the offending state among themselves* and to make it disappear, as it were, from the face of the earth. For this would be an injustice against the people, who cannot lose their original right to unite into a commonwealth. They can only be made to accept a new constitution of a nature that is unlikely to encourage their warlike inclinations.

Besides, the expression 'an unjust enemy' is a *pleonasm* if applied to any situation in a state of nature, for this state is itself one of injustice. A just enemy would be one whom I could not resist without injustice. But if this were so, he would not be my enemy in any case.

§61

Since the state of nature among nations (as among individual human beings) is a state which one ought to abandon in order to enter a state governed by law, all international rights, as well as all the external property of states such as can be acquired or preserved by war, are purely *provisional* until the state of nature has been abandoned. Only within a universal *union of states* (analogous to the union through which a nation becomes a state) can such rights and property acquire *peremptory* validity and a true *state of peace* be attained. But if an international state of this kind extends over too wide an area of land, it will eventually become impossible to govern it and thence to protect each of its members, and the multitude of corporations this would require must again lead to a state of war. It naturally follows that *perpetual peace*, the ultimate end of all international right, is an idea incapable of realisation. But the political principles which have this aim, i.e. those principles which encourage the formation of international alliances designed to *approach* the idea itself by a continual process, are not impracticable. For this is a project based upon duty, hence also upon the rights of man and of states, and it can indeed be put into execution.

Such a *union of several states* designed to preserve peace may be called a *permanent congress of states*, and all neighbouring states are free to join it. A congress of this very kind (at least as far as the formalities of international right in relation to the preservation of peace are concerned) found expression in the assembly of the States General at The Hague in the first half of this century.[19] To this assembly, the ministers of most European courts and even of the smallest republics brought their complaints about any aggression suffered by one of their number at the hands of another. They thus thought of all Europe as a single federated state, which they accepted as an arbiter in all their public disputes. Since then, however, international right has disappeared from cabinets, surviving only in books, or it has been consigned to the obscurity of the archives as a form of empty deduction after violent measures have already been employed.

In the present context, however, a *congress* merely signifies a voluntary gathering of various states which can be *dissolved* at any time, not an association which, like that of the American states, is based on a political constitution and is therefore indissoluble. For this is the only means of realising the idea of public international right as it ought to be instituted, thereby enabling the nations to settle their disputes in a civilised manner by legal proceedings, not in a barbaric manner (like that of the savages) by acts of war.

SECTION III: COSMOPOLITAN RIGHT

§62

The rational idea, as discussed above, of a *peaceful* (if not exactly amicable) international community of all those of the earth's peoples who can enter into active relations with one another, is not a philanthropic principle of ethics, but a principle of *right*. Through the spherical shape of the planet they inhabit (*globus terraqueus*), nature has confined them all within an area of definite limits. Accordingly, the only conceivable way in which anyone can possess habitable land on earth is by possessing a part within a determinate whole in which everyone has an original right to share. Thus all nations are *originally* members of a community of the land. But this is not a *legal community* of possession (*communio*) and utilisation of the land, nor a community of ownership. It is a community of reciprocal action (*commercium*), which is physically possible, and each member of it accordingly has constant relations with all the others. Each may *offer* to have commerce with the rest, and they all have a right to make such overtures without being treated by foreigners as enemies. This right, in so far as it affords the prospect that all nations may unite for the purpose of creating certain universal laws to regulate the intercourse they may have with one another, may be termed *cosmopolitan* (*ius cosmopoliticum*).

The oceans may appear to cut nations off from the community of their fellows. But with the art of navigation, they constitute the greatest natural incentive to international commerce, and the greater the number of neighbouring coastlines there are (as in the Mediterranean), the livelier this commerce will be. Yet these visits to foreign shores, and even more so, attempts to settle on them with a view to linking them with the mother-land, can also occasion evil and violence in one part of the globe with ensuing repercussions which are felt everywhere else. But although such abuses are possible, they do not deprive the world's citizens of the right to *attempt* to enter into a community with everyone else and to *visit* all regions of the earth with this intention. This does not, however, amount to a right to *settle* on another nation's territory (*ius incolatus*), for the latter would require a special contract.

But one might ask whether a nation may establish a *settlement alongside another nation* (*accolatus*) in newly discovered regions, or whether it may take possession of land in the vicinity of a nation which has already settled in the same area, even without the latter's consent. The answer is that the right to do so is incontestable, so long as such settlements are established sufficiently far away from the territory of the original nation for neither

THE METAPHYSICS OF MORALS

party to interfere with the other in their use of the land. But if the nations involved are pastoral or hunting peoples (like the Hottentots, the Tunguses, and most native American nations) who rely upon large tracts of wasteland for their sustenance, settlements should not be established by violence, but only by treaty; and even then, there must be no attempt to exploit the ignorance of the natives in persuading them to give up their territories. Nevertheless, there are plausible enough arguments for the use of violence on the grounds that it is in the best interests of the world as a whole. For on the one hand, it may bring culture to uncivilised peoples (this is the excuse with which even Büsching[20] tries to extenuate the bloodshed which accompanied the introduction of Christianity into Germany); and on the other, it may help us to purge our country of depraved characters, at the same time affording the hope that they or their offspring will become reformed in another continent (as in New Holland). But all these supposedly good intentions cannot wash away the stain of injustice from the means which are used to implement them. Yet one might object that the whole world would perhaps still be in a lawless condition if men had had any such compunction about using violence when they first created a law-governed state. But this can as little annul the above condition of right as can the plea of political revolutionaries that the people are entitled to reform constitutions by force if they have become corrupt, and to act completely unjustly for once and for all, in order to put justice on a more secure basis and ensure that it flourishes in the future.

Conclusion

If a person cannot prove that a thing exists, he may attempt to prove that it does not exist. If neither approach succeeds (as often happens), he may still ask whether it is *in his interest to assume* one or other possibility as a hypothesis, either from theoretical or from practical considerations. In other words, he may wish on the one hand simply to explain a certain phenomenon (as the astronomer, for example, may wish to explain the sporadic movements of the planets), or on the other, to achieve a certain end which may itself be either *pragmatic* (purely technical) or *moral* (i.e. an end which it is our duty to take as a maxim). It is, of course, self-evident that no-one is duty-bound to make an *assumption* (*suppositio*) that the end in question can be realised, since this would involve a purely theoretical and indeed problematic judgement; for no-one can be obliged to accept a given belief. But we can have a duty to act in accordance with the idea of such an end, even if there is not the slightest theoretical probability of its realisation, provided that there is no means of demonstrating that it cannot be realised either.

Now, moral-practical reason within us pronounces the following irresistible veto: *There shall be no war*, either between individual human beings in the state of nature, or between separate states, which, although internally law-governed, still live in a lawless condition in their external relationships with one another. For war is not the way in which anyone should pursue his rights. Thus it is no longer a question of whether perpetual peace is really possible or not, or whether we are not perhaps mistaken in our theoretical judgement if we assume that it is. On the contrary, we must simply act as if it could really come about (which is perhaps impossible), and turn our efforts towards realising it and towards establishing that constitution which seems most suitable for this purpose (perhaps that of republicanism in all states, individually and collectively). By working towards this end, we may hope to terminate the disastrous practice of war, which up till now has been the main object to which all states, without exception, have accommodated their internal institutions. And even if the fulfilment of this pacific intention were forever to remain a pious hope, we should still not be deceiving ourselves if we made it our maxim to work unceasingly towards it, for it is our duty to do so. To assume, on the other hand, that the moral law within us might be misleading, would give rise to the execrable wish to dispense with all reason and to regard ourselves, along with our principles, as subject to the same mechanism of nature as the other animal species.

It can indeed be said that this task of establishing a universal and lasting peace is not just a part of the theory of right within the limits of pure reason, but its entire ultimate purpose. For the condition of peace is the only state in which the property of a large number of people living together as neighbours under a single constitution can be guaranteed by *laws*. The rule on which this constitution is based must not simply be derived from the experience of those who have hitherto fared best under it, and then set up as a norm for others. On the contrary, it should be derived *a priori* by reason from the absolute ideal of a rightful association of men under public laws. For all particular examples are deceptive (an example can only illustrate a point, but does not prove anything), so that one must have recourse to metaphysics. And even those who scorn metaphysics admit its necessity involuntarily when they say, for example (as they often do): 'The best constitution is that in which the power rests with laws instead of with men.' For what can be more metaphysically sublime than this idea, although by the admission of those who express it, it also has a well-authenticated objective reality which can easily be demonstrated from particular instances as they arise. But no attempt should be made to put it into practice overnight by revolution, i.e. by forcibly overthrowing a defective constitution which has existed in the past; for there would then be an interval of time during which the condition of right would be nullified. If we try instead to give it reality by means of gradual reforms carried out in accordance with definite principles, we shall see that it is the only means of continually approaching the supreme political good—perpetual peace.

A brief appendix follows in which Kant, in a reply to an anonymous review,[21] comments mainly on the theory of private right, but also repeats his views on the sacredness and inviolability of civil constitutions and again denies absolutely any right to rebellion.

The Contest of Faculties[1]

In the introductory part of the work, Kant explains how the division into the three 'higher faculties' (Theology, Law and Medicine) on the one hand, and the 'lower faculty' (Philosophy) on the other, arose. He explains that governments must take an interest in the so-called 'higher faculties', because their work has an influence on the people, whereas the philosophical faculty is free to pursue scholarship and judge the teaching of the other faculties without interference from the government. Its only concern is to speak the truth freely, thus merely following the commands of man, who is free by nature.

Kant further points out that there must be statutes issued by the government regulating the teaching of the 'higher faculties'. The Bible, the law of the land and the medical regulations of the state form the basis of the teaching of the 'higher faculties', but if they violate these boundaries and seek to enter the field in which reason rules, they come into conflict with the philosophical faculty.

Kant subsequently points out that it is legitimate for the philosophical faculty to question the findings of the higher faculties. To do so does not imply criticism of the government; it involves merely a contest between the faculties (though not a war) about what is true. The government never protects the higher faculties because their public doctrines, opinions and statements are true. It protects them only because advantages may accrue to the government if it does so.

In the next section, Kant examines the contest between the philosophical and the theological faculties, which arises from the divergence between ecclesiastical doctrine and religious faith, between laws given by the arbitrary will of another person and the laws arrived at by inner reason. The next section (printed below) deals with the contest between the faculty of philosophy and the faculty of law. In the final section of the work, he discusses the contest between the faculties of philosophy and medicine. Kant writes rather amusingly, though somewhat bizarrely, about various kinds of psychological therapy, about the power of the mind to conquer sensations of disease merely by strength of will. He further discourses on diet, hypochondria, sleep, eating, drinking, and the alleviation and prevention of disease by correct breathing. This section concludes this interesting, though strange, work. It was the last large work to be published by Kant in his lifetime.

A RENEWED ATTEMPT TO ANSWER THE QUESTION: 'IS THE HUMAN RACE CONTINUALLY IMPROVING?'[2]

I

WHAT SORT OF KNOWLEDGE ARE WE LOOKING FOR?

What we are seeking to know is a portion of human history. It is not a history of the past, however, but a history of future times, i.e. a *predictive* history. But if it is not discoverable from known laws of nature (as with eclipses of the sun and moon, which can be foretold by natural means) and can only be learnt through additional insight into the future supplied by supernatural revelation, it must be termed *prognosticative* or *prophetic.**
Besides, we are here concerned not with the natural history of mankind (as we should be if we asked, for example, whether new races of man might emerge in future times), but with the *history of civilisation*. And we are not dealing with any *specific* conception of mankind (*singulorum*), but with the *whole* of humanity (*universorum*), united in earthly society and distributed in national groups. All this is implied if we ask whether the human *race* (as a whole) is continually improving.

2

HOW CAN WE ATTAIN SUCH KNOWLEDGE?

We can obtain a prophetic historical narrative of things to come by depicting those events whose *a priori* possibility suggests that they will in fact happen. But how is it possible to have history *a priori*? The answer is that it is possible if the prophet himself occasions and *produces* the events he predicts.

It was all very well for the Jewish prophets to foretell that the state to which they belonged would sooner or later suffer not only decline, but also complete dissolution; for they were themselves the architects of their fate. As leaders of the people, they had loaded their constitution with so many ecclesiastical (and thence also civil) burdens that their state became completely unfit to exist in its own right, particularly in its relations with neighbouring nations. Thus the jeremiads of the priests naturally went unheeded, because these same priests stubbornly stuck to their belief in the untenable constitution they had themselves created, so that they were themselves able to foresee the consequences with infallible certainty.

---

* Those, from pythonesses[3] to gypsies, who dabble in prophecy with neither knowledge nor honesty, are known as *false prophets*.

Our politicians, so far as their influence extends, behave in exactly the same way, and they are just as successful in their prophecies. One must take men as they are, they tell us, and not as the world's uninformed pedants or good-natured dreamers fancy that they ought to be. But 'as they are' ought to read 'as we have *made them* by unjust coercion, by treacherous designs which the government is in a good position to carry out'. For that is why they are intransigent and inclined to rebellion, and why regrettable consequences ensue if discipline is relaxed in the slightest. In this way, the prophecy of the supposedly clever statesmen is fulfilled.

Various divines also at times prophesy the complete decline of religion and the imminent appearance of the Antichrist, all the while doing the very things that are best calculated to create the state of affairs they describe. For they are not taking care to impress on the hearts of their congregation moral principles which would directly lead to an improvement. Instead, they see observances and historical beliefs as the essential duties, supposing that these will indirectly produce the same results; but although they may lead to mechanical conformity (as within a civil constitution), they cannot produce conformity in moral attitudes. Nevertheless, these divines complain at the irreligion which they have themselves created, and which they could accordingly have foretold without any special gift of prophecy.

3

SUBDIVISIONS WITHIN THE CONCEPT OF WHAT WE
WISH TO KNOW OF THE FUTURE

There are three possible forms which our prophecy might take. The human race is either continually *regressing* and deteriorating, continually *progressing* and improving, or at a permanent *standstill*, in relation to other created beings, at its present level of moral attainment (which is the same as continually revolving in a circle around a fixed point).

The first statement might be designated *moral terrorism*, the second *eudaemonism*[4] (which, if the goal of human progress were already visible from afar, might also be termed *chiliasm*),[5] while the third could be called *abderitism*.[6] For in the latter case, since a genuine standstill is impossible in moral affairs, rises and falls of equal magnitude constantly alternate, in endless fluctuation, and produce no more effect than if the subject of them had remained stationary in one place.

a

The terroristic conception of human history

A process of deterioration in the human race cannot go on indefinitely, for mankind would wear itself out after a certain point had been reached. Consequently, when enormities go on piling up and up and the evils they produce continue to increase, we say: 'It can't get much worse now.' It seems that the day of judgement is at hand, and the pious zealot already dreams of the rebirth of everything and of a world created anew after the present world has been destroyed by fire.

b

The eudaemonistic conception of human history

We may readily agree that the sum total of good and evil of which our nature is capable always remains unchanged, and can neither be augmented nor reduced within any one individual. And how could the quantity of good of which a person is capable possibly be increased? For it would have to be done by his own free agency as a subject, and before he could do it, he would in turn require a greater store of goodness than he already possessed int he first place. After all, no effects can exceed the capacity of their effective cause; and the quantity of goodness in man must therefore remain below a certain level in proportion to the amount of evil with which it is intermixed, so that man cannot work his way beyond a given limit and go on improving further. Thus eudaemonism, with its sanguine hopes, appears to be untenable. Its ideas of constant human progress and improvement would seem of little use to a prophetic history of mankind.

c

The hypothesis of abderitism in the human race as a definition of its future history

This point of view probably has the majority of subscribers on its side. To start off swiftly along the way of goodness without persevering on it, and instead, to reverse the plan of progress in order at all costs to avoid being tied to a single aim (even if only from a desire for variety); to construct in order to demolish; to take upon ourselves the hopeless task of rolling the stone of Sisyphus uphill, only to let it roll back down again: such is the industrious folly which characterises our race. In view of all this, it does not so much seem that the principle of evil within the natural character of mankind is amalgamated or fused with that of goodness, but rather that the one is neutralised by the other, with inactivity as the result (or a standstill, as in the case under discussion). This empty activity of backward and forward motion, with good and evil continually alternating, would mean that all the interplay of members of our species on earth ought merely to be regarded as a farce. And in the eyes of reason, this cannot give any higher a value to mankind than to the other animal species, whose interaction takes place at less cost and without any conscious understanding.

4

THE PROBLEM OF PROGRESS CANNOT BE SOLVED
DIRECTLY FROM EXPERIENCE

Even if it were found that the human race as a whole had been moving forward and progressing for an indefinitely long time, no-one could guarantee that its era of decline was not beginning at that very moment, by virtue of the physical character of our race. And conversely, if it is regressing and deteriorating at an accelerating pace, there are no grounds for giving up hope that we are just about to reach the turning point (*punctum flexus contrarii*) at which our affairs will take a turn for the better, by virtue of the moral character of our race. For we are dealing with freely acting beings to whom one can *dictate* in advance what they *ought* to do, but of whom one cannot *predict* what they actually *will* do, and who are capable, if things go really badly and they experience evils incurred through their own actions, of regarding these evils as a greater incentive to do better than they did in the past. But as the Abbé Coyer[7] says: 'Poor mortals! Nothing is constant among you but inconstancy.'

Perhaps it is because we have chosen the wrong point of view from which to contemplate the course of human affairs that the latter seems so absurd to us. The planets, as seen from the earth, sometimes move backward, sometimes forward, and at other times remain motionless. But seen from the sun—the point of view of reason—they continually follow their regular paths as in the Copernican hypothesis. Yet some thinkers, otherwise not deficient in wisdom, prefer to stick firmly to their own interpretation of phenomena and to the point of view they originally adopted, even at the price of involving themselves to an absurd degree in Tychonic[8] cycles and epicycles. It is our misfortune, however, that we are unable to adopt an absolute point of view when trying to predict free actions. For this, exalted above all human wisdom, would be the point of view of *providence*, which extends even to *free* human actions. And although man may *see* the latter, he cannot *foresee* them with certainty (a distinction which does not exist in the eyes of the divinity); for while he needs to perceive a connection governed by natural laws before he can foresee anything, he must do without such hints or guidance when dealing with *free* actions in the future.

If it were possible to credit human beings with even a limited will of innate and unvarying goodness, we could certainly predict a general improvement of mankind, for this would involve events which man could himself control. But if man's natural endowments consist of a mixture of evil and goodness in unknown proportions, no-one can tell what effects he should expect from his own actions.

5

A PROPHETIC HISTORY OF THE HUMAN RACE MUST NEVERTHELESS START FROM SOME SORT OF EXPERIENCE

In human affairs, there must be some experience or other which, as an event which has actually occurred, might suggest that man has the quality or power of being the *cause* and (since his actions are supposed to be those of a being endowed with freedom) the *author* of his own improvement. But an event can be predicted as the effect of a given cause only when the circumstances which help to shape it actually arise. And while it can well be predicted in general that these circumstances must arise at some time or another (as in calculating probabilities in games of chance), it is impossible to determine whether this will happen during my lifetime, and whether I shall myself experience it and thus be able to confirm the original prediction.

We must therefore search for an event which would indicate that such a cause exists and that it is causally active within the human race, irrespective of the time at which it might actually operate; and it would have to be a cause which allowed us to conclude, as an inevitable consequence of its operation, that mankind is improving. This inference could then be extended to cover the history of former times so as to show that mankind has always been progressing, yet in such a way that the event originally chosen as an example would not in itself be regarded as the cause of progress in the past, but only as a rough indication or *historical sign* (*signum rememorativum, demonstrativum, prognostikon*). It might then serve to prove the existence of a *tendency* within the human race as a *whole*, considered not as a series of individuals (for this would result in interminable enumerations and calculations) but as a body distributed over the earth in states and national groups.

6

AN OCCURRENCE IN OUR OWN TIMES WHICH PROVES
THIS MORAL TENDENCY OF THE HUMAN RACE

The occurrence in question does not involve any of those momentous deeds or misdeeds of men which make small in their eyes what was formerly great or make great what was formerly small, and which cause ancient and illustrious states to vanish as if by magic, and others to arise in their place as if from the bowels of the earth. No, it has nothing to do with all this. We are here concerned only with the attitude of the onlookers as it reveals itself *in public* while the drama of great political changes is taking place: for they openly express universal yet disinterested sympathy for one set of protagonists against their adversaries, even at the risk that their partiality could be of great disadvantage to themselves. Their reaction (because of its universality) proves that mankind as a whole shares a certain character in common, and it also proves (because of its disinterestedness) that man has a moral character, or at least the makings of one. And this does not merely allow us to hope for human improvement; it is already a form of improvement in itself, in so far as its influence is strong enough for the present.

The revolution which we have seen taking place in our own times in a nation of gifted people⁹ may succeed, or it may fail. It may be so filled with misery and atrocities that no right-thinking man would ever decide to make the same experiment again at such a price, even if he could hope to carry it out successfully at the second attempt. But I maintain that this revolution has aroused in the hearts and desires of all spectators who are not themselves caught up in it a *sympathy* which borders almost on enthusiasm, although the very utterance of this sympathy was fraught with danger. It cannot therefore have been caused by anything other than a moral disposition within the human race.

The moral cause which is at work here is composed of two elements. Firstly, there is the *right* of every people to give itself a civil constitution of the kind that it sees fit, without interference from other powers. And secondly, once it is accepted that the only intrinsically *rightful* and morally good constitution which a people can have is by its very nature disposed to avoid wars of aggression (i.e. that the only possible constitution is a republican one, at least in its conception),* there is the *aim*, which is also

---

* This does not mean, however, that a people which has a monarchic constitution can thereby claim the right to alter it, or even nurse a secret desire to do so. For a people which occupies extended territories in Europe may feel that monarchy is the only kind

a duty, of submitting to those conditions by which war, the source of all evils and moral corruption, can be prevented. If this aim is recognised, the human race, for all its frailty, has a negative guarantee that it will progressively improve or at least that it will not be disturbed in its progress.

All this, along with the *passion* or *enthusiasm* with which men embrace the cause of goodness (although the former cannot be entirely applauded, since all passion as such is blameworthy), gives historical support for the following assertion, which is of considerable anthropological significance: true enthusiasm is always directed exclusively towards the *ideal*, particularly towards that which is purely moral (such as the concept of right), and it cannot be coupled with selfish interests. No pecuniary rewards could inspire the opponents of the revolutionaries with that zeal and greatness of soul which the concept of right could alone produce in them, and even the old military aristocracy's concept of honour (which is analogous to enthusiasm) vanished before the arms[10] of those who had fixed their gaze on the *rights* of the people to which they belonged,* and who regarded themselves as its protectors. And then the external public of onlookers sympathised with their exaltation, without the slightest intention of actively participating in their affairs.

of constitution which can enable it to preserve its own existence between powerful neighbours. And if the subjects should complain, not because of their internal government but because of their government's behaviour towards the citizens of foreign states (for example, if it were to discourage republicanism abroad), this does not prove that the people are dissatisfied with their own constitution, but rather that they are profoundly attached to it; for it becomes progressively more secure from danger as more of the other nations become republics. Nevertheless, slanderous sycophants, bent on increasing their own importance, have tried to portray this innocuous political gossip as innovationism, Jacobinism and conspiracy, constituting a menace to the state. But there was never the slightest reason for such allegations, particularly in a country more than a hundred miles removed from the scene of the revolution.

* It may be said of such enthusiasm for asserting the rights of man: *postquam ad arma Vulcania ventum est,—mortalis mucro glacies ceu futilis ictu dissiluit.*[11]—Why has no ruler ever dared to say openly that he does not recognise any *rights* of the people against himself? Or that the people owe their happiness only to the *beneficence* of a government which confers it upon them, and that any pretensions on the part of the subject that he has rights against the government are absurd or even punishable, since they imply that resistance to authority is permissible? The reason is that any such public declaration would rouse up all the subjects against the ruler, even although they had been like docile sheep, well fed, powerfully protected and led by a kind and understanding master, and had no lack of welfare to complain of. For beings endowed with freedom cannot be content merely to enjoy the comforts of existence, which may well be provided by others (in this case, by the government); it all depends on the *principle* which governs the provision of such comforts. But welfare does not have any ruling principle, either for the recipient or for the one who provides it, for each individual will define it differently. It depends, in fact, upon the will's *material* aspect, which is empirical and thus incapable

7

THE PROPHETIC HISTORY OF MANKIND

In these principles, there must be something *moral* which reason recognises not only as pure, but also (because of its great and epoch-making influence) as something to which the human soul manifestly acknowledges a duty. Moreover, it concerns the human race as a complete association of men (*non singulorum, sed universorum*),[12] for they rejoice with universal and disinterested sympathy at its anticipated success and at all attempts to make it succeed.

The occurrence in question is not, however, a phenomenon of revolution, but (as Erhard[13] puts it) of the *evolution* of a constitution governed by *natural right*. Such a constitution cannot itself be achieved by furious struggles—for civil and foreign wars will destroy whatever *statutory* order has hitherto prevailed—but it does lead us to strive for a constitution which would be incapable of bellicosity, i.e. a republican one. The actual *form* of the desired state might be republican, or alternatively, it might only be republican in its *mode of government*, in that the state would be administered by a single ruler (the monarch) acting by analogy with the laws which a people would give itself in conformity with universal principles of right.

Even without the mind of a seer, I now maintain that I can predict from the aspects and signs of our times that the human race will achieve this end, and that it will henceforth progressively improve without any more total reversals. For a phenomenon of this kind which has taken place in human history *can never be forgotten*, since it has revealed in human nature an aptitude and power for improvement of a kind which no politician could have thought up by examining the course of events in the past. Only nature and freedom, combined within mankind in accordance

of becoming a universal rule. A being endowed with freedom, aware of the advantage he possesses over non-rational animals, can and must therefore follow the *formal* principle of his will and demand for the people to which he belongs nothing short of a government in which the people are co-legislators. In other words, the rights of men who are expected to obey must necessarily come before all considerations of their actual wellbeing, for they are a sacred institution, exalted above all utilitarian values; and no matter how benevolent a government is, it may not tamper with them. These rights, however, always remain an idea which can be fulfilled only on condition that the *means* employed to do so are compatible with morality. This limiting condition must not be overstepped by the people, who may not therefore pursue their rights by revolution, which is at all times unjust. The best way of making a nation content with its constitution is to *rule* autocratically and at the same time to *govern* in a republican manner, i.e. to govern in the spirit of republicanism and by analogy with it.

with principles of right, have enabled us to forecast it; but the precise time at which it will occur must remain indefinite and dependent upon chance.

But even if the intended object behind the occurrence we have described were not to be achieved for the present, or if a people's revolution or constitutional reform were ultimately to fail, or if, after the latter had lasted for a certain time, everything were to be brought back onto its original course (as politicians now claim to prophesy), our own philosophical prediction still loses none of its force. For the occurrence in question is too momentous, too intimately interwoven with the interests of humanity and too widespread in its influence upon all parts of the world for nations not to be reminded of it when favourable circumstances present themselves, and to rise up and make renewed attempts of the same kind as before. After all, since it is such an important concern of the human race, the intended constitution must at some time or another finally reach that degree of stability which the lessons of repeated experience will not fail to instil into the hearts of everyone.

Thus the proposition that the human race has always been progressively improving and will continue to develop in the same way is not just a well-meant saying to be recommended for practical purposes. Whatever unbelievers may say, it is tenable within the most strictly theoretical context. And if one considers not only the events which may happen within a particular nation, but also their repercussions upon all the nations of the earth which might gradually begin to participate in them, a view opens up into the unbounded future. This would not be true, of course, if the first epoch of natural convulsions, which (according to Camper[14] and Blumenbach[15]) engulfed the animal and vegetable kingdoms before the era of man, were to be followed by a second in which the human race were given the same treatment so that other creatures might take the stage instead, etc. For man in turn is a mere trifle in relation to the omnipotence of nature, or rather to its inaccessible highest cause. But if the rulers of man's own species regard him as such and treat him accordingly, either by burdening him like a beast and using him as a mere instrument of their ends, or by setting him up to fight in their disputes and slaughter his fellows, it is not just a trifle but a reversal of the *ultimate purpose* of creation.

8

THE DIFFICULTY OF MAXIMS DIRECTED TOWARDS THE
WORLD'S PROGRESSIVE IMPROVEMENT AS REGARDS
THEIR PUBLICITY

Popular enlightenment is the public instruction of the people upon their duties and rights towards the state to which they belong. Since this concerns only natural rights and rights which can be derived from ordinary common sense, their obvious exponents and interpreters among the people will not be officials appointed by the state, but free teachers of right, i.e. the philosophers. The latter, on account of the very freedom which they allow themselves, are a stumbling-block to the state, whose only wish is to rule; they are accordingly given the appellation of 'enlighteners', and decried as a menace to the state. And yet they do not address themselves in familiar tones to the *people* (who themselves take little or no notice of them and their writings), but in *respectful* tones to the state, which is thereby implored to take the rightful needs of the people to heart. And if a whole people wishes to present its grievance (*gravamen*), the only way in which this can be done is by publicity. A *ban* on publicity will therefore hinder a nation's progress, even with regard to the least of its claims, the claim for natural rights.

Another thing which is concealed (transparently enough) by legal measures from a certain people is the true nature of its constitution. It would be an affront to the majesty of the people of Great Britain to say that they lived under an *absolute monarchy*. Instead, it is said that their constitution is one which *limits* the will of the monarch through the two houses of parliament, acting as representatives of the people. Yet everyone knows very well that the influence of the monarch upon these representatives is so great and so infallible that the aforesaid houses make no decisions except those which His Majesty wishes and recommends through his minister. Now and again, the latter will certainly recommend decisions wherein he[16] knows and indeed *ensures* that he will meet with contradiction (as with the abolition of the slave trade), simply in order to furnish ostensible proof of parliamentary freedom. But this sort of approach has the insidious effect of discouraging people from looking for the true and rightfully established constitution, for they imagine they have discovered it in an instance which is already before them. Thus a mendacious form of publicity deceives the people with the illusion that the monarchy is *limited**

* A cause whose nature is not directly perceptible can be discovered through the effect which invariably accompanies it. What is an *absolute* monarch? He is one at whose com-

186

by a law which emanates from them, while their representatives, won over by bribery, secretly subject them to an *absolute monarch*.

All forms of state are based on the idea of a constitution which is compatible with the natural rights of man, so that those who obey the law should also act as a unified body of legislators. And if we accordingly think of the commonwealth in terms of concepts of pure reason, it may be called a Platonic *ideal (respublica noumenon)*, which is not an empty figment of the imagination, but the eternal norm for all civil constitutions whatsoever, and a means of ending all wars. A civil society organised in conformity with it and governed by laws of freedom is an example representing it in the world of experience *(respublica phaenomenon)*, and it can only be achieved by a laborious process, after innumerable wars and conflicts. But its constitution, once it has been attained as a whole, is the best qualified of all to keep out war, the destroyer of everything good. Thus it is our duty to enter into a constitution of this kind; and in the meantime, since it will be a considerable time before this takes place, it is the duty of monarchs to govern in a *republican* (not a democratic) manner, even although they may *rule autocratically*. In other words, they should treat the people in accordance with principles akin in spirit to the laws of freedom which a people of mature rational powers would prescribe for itself, even if the people is not literally asked for its consent.

9

WHAT PROFIT WILL THE HUMAN RACE DERIVE FROM PROGRESSIVE IMPROVEMENT?

The profit which will accrue to the human race as it works its way forward will not be an ever increasing quantity of *morality* in its attitudes. Instead, the *legality* of its attitudes will produce an increasing number of actions governed by duty, whatever the particular motive behind these actions

mand war at once begins when he says it shall do so. And conversely, what is a *limited* monarch? He is one who must first ask the people whether or not there is to be a war, and if the people say that there shall be no war, then there will be none. For war is a condition in which *all* the powers of the state must be at the head of state's disposal.

Now the monarch of Great Britain has waged numerous wars without asking the people's consent. This king is therefore an absolute monarch, although he should not be so according to the constitution. But he can always bypass the latter, since he can always be assured, by controlling the various powers of the state, that the people's representatives will agree with him; for he has the authority to award all offices and dignities. This corrupt system, however, must naturally be given no publicity if it is to succeed. It therefore remains under a very transparent veil of secrecy.

may be. In other words, the profit will result from man's good *deeds* as they grow ever more numerous and successful, i.e. from the external phenomena of man's moral nature. For we have only *empirical* data (our experiences) on which to base this prediction—that is, we base it on the physical cause of our actions in so far as they actually take place as phenomena, not on the moral cause which contains the concept of duty as applied to what ought to happen, and which can be determined by processes of pure *a priori* thinking.

Violence will gradually become less on the part of those in power, and obedience towards the laws will increase. There will no doubt be more charity, less quarrels in legal actions, more reliability in keeping one's word, and so on in the commonwealth, partly from a love of honour, and partly from a lively awareness of where one's own advantage lies; and this will ultimately extend to the external relations between the various peoples, until a cosmopolitan society is created. Such developments do not mean, however, that the basic moral capacity of mankind will increase in the slightest, for this would require a kind of new creation or super- natural influence. For we must not expect too much of human beings in their progressive improvements, or else we shall merit the scorn of those politicians who would gladly treat man's hopes of progress as the fantasies of an overheated mind.*

10

WHAT SEQUENCE CAN PROGRESS BE EXPECTED
TO FOLLOW?

The answer is: not the usual sequence *from the bottom upwards*, but *from the top downwards*.

To expect that the education of young people in intellectual and moral culture, reinforced by the doctrines of religion, firstly through domestic instruction and then through a series of schools from the lowest to the

---

* It is certainly *agreeable* to think up political constitutions which meet the requirements of reason (particularly in matters of right). But it is *foolhardy* to put them forward seri- ously, and *punishable* to incite the people to do away with the existing constitution.

Plato's *Atlantis*,[17] More's *Utopia*,[18] Harrington's *Oceana*[19] and Allais' *Severambia*[20] have successively made their appearance, but they have never (with the exception of Cromwell's abortive attempt to establish a despotic republic) been tried out in practice. It is the same with these political creations as with the creation of the world: no-one was present at it, nor could anyone have been present, or else he would have been his own creator. It is a pleasant dream to hope that a political product of the sort we here have in mind will one day be brought to perfection, at however remote a date. But it is not merely *conceivable* that we can continually approach such a state; so long as it can be reconciled with the moral law, it is also the *duty* of the head of state (not of the citizens) to do so.

highest grade, will eventually not only make them good citizens, but will also bring them up to practise a kind of goodness which can continually progress and maintain itself, is a plan which is scarcely likely to achieve the desired success. For on the one hand, the people believe that the expense of educating their children should be met not by them but by the state; and on the other, the state itself (as Büsching[21] laments) has no money left over to pay qualified teachers who will carry out their duties with enthusiasm, since it needs it all for war. But apart from this, the whole mechanism of education as described above will be completely disjointed unless it is designed on the considered plan and intention of the highest authority in the state, then set in motion and constantly maintained in uniform operation thereafter. And this will mean that the state too will reform itself from time to time, pursuing evolution instead of revolution, and will thus make continuous progress. But those responsible for the desired education are also *human beings* who will therefore have to have had a suitable education themselves. And in view of the frailty of human nature and the fortuitous circumstances which can intensify its effects, we can expect man's hopes of progress to be fulfilled only under the positive condition of a higher wisdom (which, if it is invisible to us, is known as providence); and in so far as *human beings* can themselves accomplish anything or anything can be expected of them, it can only be through their negative wisdom in furthering their own ends. In the latter event, they will find themselves compelled to ensure that *war*, the greatest obstacle to morality and the invariable enemy of progress, first becomes gradually more humane, then more infrequent, and finally disappears completely as a mode of aggression. They will thereby enter into a constitution based on genuine principles of right, which is by its very nature capable of constant progress and improvement without forfeiting its strength.

Conclusion

A doctor who used to console his patients from day to day with hopes of imminent recovery, telling one that his pulse was better, and others that their faeces or perspiration heralded an improvement, etc., received a visit from one of his friends. 'How are you, my friend, and how is your illness?' was the first question. 'How do you think,' was the reply. '*I am dying of sheer recovery!*'

I do not blame anyone if political evils make him begin to despair of the welfare and progress of mankind. But I have confidence in the heroic medicine to which Hume refers, for it ought to produce a speedy cure.

'When I now see the nations engaged in war', he says, 'it is as if I witnessed two drunken wretches bludgeoning each other in a china-shop. For it is not just that the injuries they inflict on each other will be long in healing; they will also have to pay for all the damage they have caused.'[22] *Sero sapiunt Phryges.*[23] But the after-pains of the present war[24] will force the political prophet to admit that the human race must soon take a turn for the better, and this turn is now already in sight.

Appendix from 'The Critique of Pure Reason'[1]

TRANSCENDENTAL LOGIC II, DIALECTIC, I, 1: OF IDEAS IN GENERAL

A constitution allowing the *greatest possible human freedom* in accordance with laws which ensure *that the freedom of each can co-exist with the freedom of all the others* (not one designed to provide the greatest possible happiness, as this will in any case follow automatically), is at all events a necessary idea which must be made the basis not only of the first outline of a political constitution but of all laws as well. It requires that we should abstract at the outset from present hindrances, which perhaps do not arise inevitably out of human nature, but are rather occasioned by neglect of genuine ideas in the process of legislation. For there is nothing more harmful, or more unworthy of a philosopher, than the vulgar appeal to an allegedly contrary experience, which would not have existed at all if the above measures had been taken at the right time in accordance with ideas, and if crude concepts, for the very reason that they were derived from experience, had not instead vitiated every good intention. The more closely the legislation and government were made to harmonise with this idea, the rarer punishments would become, and it is thus quite rational to maintain (as Plato does) that none would be necessary at all in a perfect state. Even if the latter should never come about, the idea which sets up this maximum as an archetype, in order to bring the legal constitution of mankind nearer and nearer to its greatest possible perfection, still remains correct. For no-one can or ought to decide what the highest degree may be at which mankind may have to stop progressing, and hence how wide a gap may still of necessity remain between the idea and its execution. For this will depend on freedom, which can transcend any limit we care to impose.

191

$\mathcal{N}$otes to the Text

IDEA FOR A UNIVERSAL HISTORY WITH A COSMOPOLITAN PURPOSE

1 p. 41. *Idee zu einer allgemeinen Geschichte in weltbürgerlicher Absicht*, *AA* VIII, 15–31. First published in *Berlinische Monatsschrift*, IV (11 November 1784), 385–411. The initial reference is, as Kant says, to a passage in the *Gothaische Gelehrte Zeitungen*, 1784 (12, 11 February, p. 95).

2 p. 47. Charles Irénée Castel, Abbé de St Pierre (1658–1743). The reference is to his *Projet pour rendre la paix perpétuelle en Europe* (1712–13).

3 p. 47. The reference is to Rousseau's *Extrait du projet de paix perpétuelle* (1761).

4 p. 48. This refers to Epicurus' view that the universe was the result of a random concourse of atoms.

5 p. 50. Cf. p. 37, n. 1.

6 p. 52. 'Unknown territory.'

7 p. 52. The Septuagint, so named from the legend of its composition by seventy translators (*septuaginta* being the Latin word for seventy), or more exactly seventy-two, sent from Jerusalem to Alexandria at the request of King Ptolemy II Philadelphus (288–247 B.C.) of Egypt.

8 p. 52. Kant slightly mistranslates Hume who wrote: 'The first page of THUCYDIDES is...the commencement of real history', *Of the Populousness of Ancient Nations* (1751), David Hume, *Essays. Moral, Political and Literary* (ed. by T. H. Green and T. H. Grose) (London, 1875), I, Essay XI, 414.

AN ANSWER TO THE QUESTION: 'WHAT IS ENLIGHTENMENT?'

1 p. 54. *Beantwortung der Frage: Was ist Aufklärung?*, *AA* VIII, 33–42. First published in *Berlinische Monatsschrift*, IV (12 December 1784), 481–94. There is a reference in the original edition of the *Berlinische Monatsschrift* to p. 516 of the number of that journal published on 5 December 1783. This reference is to an essay by the Rev. Zöllner, 'Is it advisable to sanction marriage through religion?'. The relevant passage reads (in translation): '*What is Enlightenment?* The question, which is almost as important as the question *What is truth?*, should be answered before one begins to enlighten others. And yet I have never found it answered anywhere.'

2 p. 54. Literal translation: 'Dare to be wise'. Horace, *Epodes* I, 2, 40. Cf. Elizabeth M. Wilkinson and L. A. Willoughby (eds. and trs.), Friedrich

Schiller, *On the Aesthetic Education of Man* (Oxford, 1967), LXXIV ff.; cf. also Franco Venturi, 'Was ist Aufklärung? Sapere Aude!', *Rivista Storica Italiana*, LXXI (1959), 119 ff. Venturi traces the use made of this quotation from Horace throughout the centuries. Cf. also p. 5.

3 p. 54. 'Those who have come of age by virtue of nature.'

4 p. 55. The allusion is to Frederick II (the Great), King of Prussia (1740–86).

5 p. 58. 'Caesar is not above the grammarians.'

6 p. 58. Kant here refers, of course, to Frederick the Great.

7 p. 60. This allusion amounts to a repudiation of Julien Offray de Lamettrie's (1709–51) materialism as expressed in *L'Homme Machine* (1748).

8 p. 60. Anton Friedrich Büsching (1724–93), professor in the University of Göttingen, theologian and leading geographer of the day, editor of *Wöchentliche Nachrichten von neuen Landkarten, geographischen, statistischen und historischen Büchern*. Kant's reference is to XII, 1784 (Berlin, 1785), 291.

9 p. 60. Moses Mendelssohn (1729–86), a leading philosopher of the German Enlightenment. The reference is to Mendelssohn's essay 'Über die Frage: was heisst Aufklärung?' ('On the question: what is Enlightenment?'), *Berlinische Monatsschrift*, IV (9 September 1784), 193–200.

ON THE COMMON SAYING: 'THIS MAY BE TRUE IN THEORY, BUT IT DOES NOT APPLY IN PRACTICE'

1 p. 61. *Über den Gemeinspruch : 'Das mag in der Theorie richtig sein, taugt aber nicht für die Praxis'*, *AA* VIII, 273–313. First published in *Berlinische Monatsschrift*, XXII (September 1793), 201–84. As we know from Kant's notes for the essay (*AA* XXIII, 125 ff.; cf. also Rudolf Reicke, *Lose Blätter aus Kants Nachlaß*, V (Königsberg, 1889), 148 f. and 179), he was attacking an essay by the eminent mathematician and writer Abraham Gotthelf Kästner (1719–1800), *Gedanken über das Unvermögen der Schriftsteller Empörungen zu bewirken* (*Thoughts on the inability of writers to produce rebellion*) (Göttingen, 1793), in which Kästner satirised the apparently useless activities of theorising writers (cf. Dieter Henrich, (ed.), *Kant. Gentz. Rehberg. Über Theorie und Praxis* (Frankfurt/Main, 1967), p. 12). Kant also wished to show that the validity of a theory did not depend on its revolutionary consequences, thus dispelling ambiguities in the writing of his disciples. Cf. Henrich, *op. cit.* p. 12, who also refers to Johann Christian Gottlieb Schaumann (1768–1821), *Versuch über Aufklärung, Freiheit und Gleichheit...* (*Essay on Enlightenment, Freedom and Equality...*) (Halle, 1793).

2 p. 62. *Anschauung* is the term Kant uses (Translator's note).

3 p. 63. Possibly a reference to Edmund Burke's *Reflections on the Revolution in France* (1790); cf. the Everyman's Library Edition (London, 1910), pp. 55–6. It had been translated into German by Friedrich Gentz, as *Betrachtungen über die französische Revolution* (Berlin, 1793). Burke attacks those who theorise on politics without regard for experience. He uses the same quotation which Kant includes in this passage; cf. Paul Wittichen, 'Kant und Burke', *Historische Zeitschrift*, XCIII (1904), 254.

4 p. 63. 'Let him lord it there in his own court.' Aeolus in Virgil, *Aeneid* I, 140.

5 p. 63. The terms *Staatsrecht* und *Völkerrecht* are two of the numerous compounds Kant forms out of the word *Recht*, which itself occurs again and again in his political writings. For the sake of consistency, it has been rendered throughout by the English 'right', although it can often signify something more nearly equivalent to 'law' or 'justice'. Kant himself twice supplies helpful definitions of the term in the works printed in this volume: cf. p. 73 and the section *Introduction to the Theory of Right*, pp. 132–5, for the relevant passages. For further remarks by Kant on the same topic cf. *AA* XXIII, 255–6. (Translator's note.)

6 p. 64. Christian Garve (1742–98), a well-known philosopher of the German Enlightenment, whose work Kant greatly esteemed on account of Garve's sincerity. In this essay, Kant is refuting Garve's views as expressed in *Versuche über verschiedene Gegenstände aus der Moral, der Literatur und dem gesellschaftlichen Leben*, I (Breslau, 1792), particularly III–16. The passage is reprinted in Dieter Henrich (ed.), *Kant. Gentz. Rehberg. Über Theorie und Praxis* (Frankfurt/Main, 1967), pp. 134–8.

7 p. 67. 'A matter of mere opportunity.'

8 p. 73. Kant seeks here to refute Hobbes' political theory, which found its classic expression in the *Leviathan* (1651). The actual argument is explicitly directed against Hobbes' *De cive* (1642).

9 p. 80. 'The public welfare is the supreme law of the state.'

10 p. 82. Gottfried Achenwall (1719–72), professor in Göttingen and the leading statistician of the age. His *Ius naturae in usum auditorum* was published in Göttingen, 1755–6 (7th ed. 1781). Kant used this work as a textbook for his lectures on Natural Law, held twelve times between 1767 and 1788. The use of textbooks for lectures was customary.

11 p. 82. Charter granted to Brabant by Duke John III in 1354 in which the Duke undertook to maintain the integrity of the duchy and not to wage war, make treaties or impose taxes without consulting his subjects represented by the municipalities.

12 p. 83. These remarks refer to the French Revolution.

13 p. 83. Georges Jacques Danton (1759–94), the French revolutionary leader.

14 p. 83. This remark refers to the accession of William III of Orange and Mary to the British throne in 1688 (the Glorious Revolution). After James II had been overthrown, Parliament legislated for William's and Mary's accession, restricting the monarchy to the Protestant successors of James I.

15 p. 86. 'The judgement is uncertain, and experiments are dangerous.'

16 p. 87. 'If they catch sight of a man respected for his virtue and services, they are silent and stand close with ears alert.' Virgil, *Aeneid* I, 151–2.

17 p. 87. Cf. above, p. 60, n. 9.

18 p. 87. *Jerusalem, oder über religiöse Macht und Judentum* (Berlin, 1783), one of Mendelssohn's principal works.

19 p. 87. Gotthold Ephraim Lessing (1729–81), the German writer and dramatist. These views are expressed in *Die Erziehung des Menschengeschlechts* (1780).

20 p. 88. Sisyphus, a legendary Greek King of Corinth, was punished by the Gods for his misdeeds. His punishment involved continuously carrying a heavy stone to a mountain-top in Hades always to find that as soon as he reached the top the stone rolled down again (cf. Homer, *Odyssey* XI, 593–600).

21 p. 89. 'Something certain.'

22 p. 89. 'Something uncertain.'

23 p. 92. I have been unable to trace this quotation.

24 p. 92. Cf. p. 47, n. 2.

25 p. 92. Kant's quotation is in incorrect word order. It should run: *Ducunt volentem fata, nolentem trahunt* ('The fates lead him who is willing, but drag him who is unwilling'); Seneca, *Epistle* 107, 11.

PERPETUAL PEACE: A PHILOSOPHICAL SKETCH

1 p. 93. *Zum ewigen Frieden. Ein philosophischer Entwurf, AA* VIII, 341–86. First published Königsberg (Friedrich Nicolovius), 1795; 2nd enlarged edition (*ibid.*), 1796. The treatise was presumably inspired by the conclusion of the Treaty of Basle on 5 April 1795. Kant offered the treatise to his publisher Nicolovius on 13 August 1795 (Letters, No. 672, *AA* XII, 35, letter to Nicolovius, 13 August 1795).

2 p. 95. This is a reference to Britain.

3 p. 98. Josef Niklas, Imperial Count of Windischgrätz (1744–1802). This nobleman invited scholars to compete in solving the problem of how it might be possible to formulate legal contracts which would be incapable of more than one interpretation and which would make all disputes over changes in ownership impossible.

4 p. 99. Αἰών, personification of eternal Time.

5 p. 101. Frederick the Great.

6 p. 102. Jacques Mallet du Pan (1749–1800), a Swiss writer born near Geneva who espoused a moderate Royalism in the period of the French Revolution. Kant here presumably refers to the *Considérations sur la révolution de France et sur les causes qui en prolongent la durée* (Brussels, 1793), by Mallet du Pan (translated into German by Friedrich Gentz as *Über die französische Revolution und die Ursachen ihrer Dauer*, Berlin, 1794). At the end of this treatise Mallet du Pan speaks of a maxim which has guided him for fifteen years and which an English poet has given us in a couplet, referring to the verse of Pope quoted by Kant in the above passage. Kant, however, translates the verses differently from Gentz.

7 p. 102. Alexander Pope, *Essay on Man*, III, 303–4.

8 p. 102. Kant alludes to the following passage, which he does not render accurately, from Swift's *Tale of a Tub* (*Prose Works of Jonathan Swift*, Bohn Library edition, I (London, 1900), 55): 'Wisdom is a hen, whose cackling we must value and consider, because it is attended with an egg; but then lastly, it is a nut, which, unless you choose with judgment, may cost you a tooth, and pay with nothing but a worm.'

9 p. 102. *Titus* Flavius Vespasianus (39–81), Roman Emperor (79–81).

10 p. 102. *Marcus Aurelius* Antoninus (121–80), Roman Emperor (161–80).

11 p. 102. Titus Flavius *Domitianus* (51–96), Roman Emperor (81–96).

12 p. 102. Lucius Aurelius *Commodus* (161–92), Roman Emperor (180–92). Titus and Marcus Aurelius are known for their beneficent government, Domitian and Commodus for their cruelty as rulers.

13 p. 103. Hugo Grotius (1583–1645), Dutch jurist and statesman. His main work is *De iure belli et pacis* (1625). He was a leading interpreter of Natural Law.

14 p. 103. Samuel Freiherr von Pufendorf (1632–94), an important theorist of Natural Law, professor in the university of Heidelberg (1661), in the university of Leyden (1670), subsequently historiographer in Berlin. His principal work is *De iure naturae et gentium* (1672).

15 p. 103. Emmerich von Vattel (1714–67), Swiss jurist and diplomat in Saxon service. His principal work is the *Droit des Gens* (1758).

16 p. 105. 'Wicked frenzy rages savagely with blood-stained mouth.' *Aeneid* I, 294–6.

17 p. 106. The full title is rather lengthy; in shortened form, it reads: *Alphabetum Tibetanum missionum apostolicarum commodo editum... Studio et labore Fr. Augustini Antonii Georgii eremitae Augustinui* (Romae, 1762). It is known as a ponderous compilation; the author was the Augustinian monk and missionary, Antonio Agostino Giorgi (1711–97).

18 p. 107. Johann Eberhard Fischer (1697–1771), historian, Professor of History and member of the Academy at St Petersburg, member of the second expedition to Kamchatka (1733–43). The reference is to his *Quaestiones Petropolitanae* (Göttingen and Gotha, 1770) (*De variis nominibus imperii Sinarum* §2, p. 81).

19 p. 107. Bukhara, city which is now in Usbek S.S.R., giving its name to the country around it.

20 p. 107. Hesychius, a Greek grammarian of Alexandria (probably fifth or sixth century A.D.), author of an important Greek dictionary.

21 p. 107. The hierophants were expounders of sacred mysteries, initiated men.

22 p. 107. This is probably an allusion to Johann Georg Hamann's ΚΟΓΖΟΜ-ΠΑΖ *Fragmente einer apokryphischen Sibylle über apokalyptische Mysterien* (Weimar, 1779) which was written in reply to the following two books: Johann August Starck, *Apologie des Ordens der Frey-Mäurer* (Berlin, 1778) and Christoph Meiners, *Über die Mysterien der Alten* (Leipzig, 1776). (Cf. J. G. Hamann, *Sämtliche Werke*, III [Vienna, 1951], 215–28; cf. also 452 ff.). Kant, according to a letter from Hamann to Herder, wrote a long letter to Hamann pointing out that this word Κογξ'Ομπαξ was derived from the Tibetan, as Kant had only very recently discovered. Hamann refused to accept this view and found it ridiculous (cf. Letter to J. G. Herder, 18 April 1783, J. G. Hamann, *Briefe*, V, Frankfurt/Main, ed. Arthur Henkel (1955), 36; Kant's letter to Hamann is not extant). The allusion would have been intelligible to those who followed the continuous battle of words between Kant and Hamann, only too frequently concealed in obscure footnotes, etc. The personal relations between Kant and Hamann, incidentally, were quite good. The word Κογξ'Ομπαξ occurs in Hesychius' dictionary. The meaning is still disputed.

23 p. 107. Fertility cult of Demeter and Persephone in Eleusis near Athens.

24 p. 107. (Abbé) Jean Jacques Barthélemy, *Voyage du jeune Anacharsis en Grèce, dans le milieu du quatrième siècle avant l'ère vulgaire*, 5 vols. (Paris, 1788). Translated into German by Johann Erich Biester, *Reise des jüngeren Anacharsis durch Griechenland* (Part v, Berlin, 1793).

25 p. 107. Mathurin Veyssière de La Croze (1661–1739), Benedictine monk, member of the Prussian Academy of Sciences.

26 p. 107. Pater Franciscus Horatius or Francisco Orazio della Penna, a missionary who lived in Lhasa (1735–47), known for his accurate description of Tibet.

27 p. 107. Epopt—one initiated into the Eleusinian mysteries.

28 p. 107. This unusual footnote indicates Kant's wide geographical and ethnological interests.

29 p. 108. 'Nature the contriver of things (i.e. of the world)', Lucretius, *De rerum naturae* v, 234.

30 p. 108. 'As soon as he has given the command, they obey without fail.'

31 p. 109. 'To harness griffins with horses.' Virgil, *Eclogues* viii, 27, *iungentur iam gryphes equis.*

32 p. 109. 'A single cause does not suffice.'

33 p. 112. Cf. p. 92, n. 25.

34 p. 113. Presumably Friedrich Bouterwek (1766–1828), professor in Göttingen, disciple of Kant.

35 p. 115. 'Woe to the vanquished.'

36 p. 116. 'No one is obliged to do anything he is incapable of doing.'

37 p. 116. Matt. x. 16.

38 p. 120. 'Act first and justify your actions later.'

39 p. 120. 'If you are the perpetrator, deny it.'

40 p. 120. 'Divide and rule.'

41 p. 120. 'The chief among his peers.'

42 p. 121. Possibly 'Qui s'excuse s'accuse.'

43 p. 123. Literally: 'Let justice prevail even if the world perish.'

44 p. 124. 'You for your part must not give way to troubles, but confront them the more boldly.' Virgil, *Aeneid* vi, 95.

45 p. 128. Or rather its ruler (Translator's note).

46 p. 129. Cf. p. 64, n. 6. The exact title of this treatise is *Abhandlung über die Verbindung der Moral mit der Politik oder einige Betrachtungen über die Frage, inwiefern es möglich sei, die Moral des Privatlebens bei der Regierung der Staaten zu beobachten* (*Treatise on the connection of morality with politics or some observations on the question to what extent it is possible to observe the morality of private life in the government of states*) (Breslau, 1788).

47 p. 129. The beginning (in translation) runs as follows: 'A satisfactory answer to that question is beyond my horizon.'

THE METAPHYSICS OF MORALS

1 p. 131. *Die Metaphysik der Sitten*, *AA* vi, 203–493. First published Königsberg (Friedrich Nicolovius), 1797. The many Latin legal terms in this treatise derive from Achenwall's *Ius naturae* (cf. p. 82, n. 10).

2 p. 132. *Einleitung in die Rechtslehre*, *AA* vi, 229–33.

3 p. 132. Writer of Latin fables who lived about A.D. 50.

4 p. 133. This is the first of several instances in the *Introduction to the Theory of Right* where Kant uses the German term *Willkür*. The term has various meanings, but in this particular extract, it signifies the will's power of choice or freedom of choice. Since neither of these expanded expressions can be used to render *Willkür* on every occasion without undue awkwardness, the more concise English 'will' has been adopted throughout, although it is more exactly equivalent to the German term *Wille* than to *Willkür*. (Translator's note.)

5 p. 135. This passage is somewhat difficult to translate, since Kant is exploiting the ambiguity not only of the word *recht* ('right'), but also of the words *krumm* and *schief*. *Krumm*, applied to a line, signifies 'curved', but in the present ethical context, it also has overtones of 'crooked' or 'illegal'. Similarly, *schief* means 'oblique' in geometry, but in other contexts it may indicate that which deviates from the straight paths of morality or is on the wrong side of the law. (Translator's note.)

6 p. 136. *Das öffentliche Recht, AA* VI, 309–55.

7 p. 139. 'No harm is done to a man by an act when he consents to it.'

8 p. 139. 'In either the natural or the political sense.'

9 p. 140. 'Together and individually.'

10 p. 142. 'From a badly trained ruler to a ruler who is better trained.'

11 p. 142. 'The welfare of the state is the supreme law.'

12 p. 144. These remarks are specifically directed against Achenwall, *Ius naturae in usum auditorum*, §§203–6.

13 p. 148. Cf. p. 142, n. 10.

14 p. 156. Arthur Balmerino, 6th Baron, a Scottish nobleman who was executed on 11 August 1746 after capture in the battle of Culloden (1746) for taking part in the Scottish Jacobite Rebellion (1745–6) under the Young Pretender (Prince Charles Edward).

15 p. 157. 'To prefer life to honour', Juvenal, *Satires* III, 8, 83.

16 p. 157. Cesare Beccaria, Marchese de Bonesana (1735–94), Italian jurist, who, in his main work, *Dei delitti e delle pene* (1764), is a passionate critic of the severe penal codes of his age and argues for change, appealing to the cause of the Enlightenment.

17 p. 164. This reference is of course to Louis XVI (1754–93), King of France (1774–93), who called the Estates-General together in Versailles in 1789, after they had not met for 175 years, so that they should solve the financial problems of France.

18 p. 168. 'The laws are silent in times of war.' Cicero, *Pro Milone* 4, 10.

19 p. 171. In the later seventeenth century and the first half of the eighteenth century, The Hague was the centre of European diplomacy. The numerous treaties and conventions signed there included the Treaty of the Triple Alliance (1688), the Concert of The Hague (1710), and the Treaty of Peace between Spain, Savoy and Austria (1717). The Netherlands Estates-General (1576–1795), in which the sovereignty of the seven United Provinces of the Netherlands did not reside but whose task it was to reach a consensus of opinion among the provinces, also met in The Hague. It is not clear to which of these events or bodies Kant is referring.

20 p. 173. Cf. p. 60, n. 8.

21 p. 175. The review appeared in the *Göttingische Anzeigen von gelehrten Sachen unter Aufsicht der Königlichen Gesellschaft der Wissenschaften*, Part 28 (18 February 1797) (reprinted in *AA* xx, 445–53). The reviewer, it is believed, was Friedrich Bouterwek, professor in the University of Göttingen; cf. p. 113, n. 34.

THE CONTEST OF FACULTIES

1 p. 176. *Der Streit der Facultäten*, *AA* vii, 1–116. First published Königsberg (Friedrich Nicolovius), 1798.

2 p. 177. *Erneuerte Frage: Ob das menschliche Geschlecht im beständigen Fortschreiten zum Besseren sei*, *AA* vii, 77–94.

3 p. 177. Prophetic priestesses of the Delphic oracle.

4 p. 178. Eudaemonism usually means the teaching that all human activity is determined by a striving for happiness. It is derived from the Greek word Εὐδαιμονία. Kant does not use it in that sense, however.

5 p. 178. Originally, the belief that the millennium will be established on earth before the Day of Judgement.

6 p. 178. After a novel by Christian Martin Wieland, the eighteenth-century German writer, called *Geschichte der Abderiten* (*The Story of the Abderites*) (1774–81), in which human follies are satirised. Abdera was a city in ancient Greece whose inhabitants were alleged to be particularly foolish.

7 p. 180. Gabriel François Coyer (1707–82), French Jesuit, author of a *Dissertation sur la différence des anciennes religions* (Paris, 1755).

8 p. 180. The reference is to Tycho Brahe (1546–1601), Danish astronomer who, in order to refute Copernicus, elaborated an astronomical system of his own, the Tychonic system. He put forward the theory that the sun and the moon rotate around the earth, but that the planets rotate round the sun. His theory was well thought of by many at the time.

9 p. 182. This is, of course, a reference to the French Revolution.

10 p. 183. The reference is to the Wars of the French Revolution.

11 p. 183. Kant misquotes the first words. It should read: *Postquam arma dei ad Vulcania ventum est...* 'Now that he was faced by Vulcan's arms, his mortal blade was shattered by the blow like brittle ice.' Virgil, *Aeneid* xii, 739–41.

12 p. 184. 'Not of individuals, but of mankind as a whole.'

13 p. 184. Johann Benjamin Erhard (1766–1827), a physician and friend of Kant's, who esteemed Erhard highly. Erhard published several political treatises including an essay *Über das Recht des Volkes zu einer Revolution* (*On the Right of the People to Revolution*) (Jena, 1794), to which Kant alludes here.

14 p. 185. Petrus Camper (1722–89), a Dutch anatomist. The allusion is to a work published in German translation, *Über den natürlichen Unterschied der Gesichtszüge im Menschen...* (ed. A. G. Camper) (Berlin, 1792), §3.

15 p. 185. Johann Friedrich Blumenbach, Professor of Medicine in the University of Göttingen from 1776. He greatly furthered the study of comparative anatomy. Cf. his *Handbuch der Naturgeschichte* (Göttingen, 1779), p. 44 and pp. 474 ff.

16 p. 186. This is a reference to George III (1738–1820), King of Great Britain and Ireland (1760–1820).

17 p. 188. Atlantis here refers to the myth of a city engulfed by the sea, mentioned by Plato in the *Timaeus*.

18 p. 188. *Utopia* (1516). The exact title of this work is *De optima rei publicae statu, deque nova insula Utopia*. It was written by Sir Thomas More (1478–1535), the eminent humanist who was Lord Chancellor of England (1529–32).

19 p. 188. *Oceana*, a treatise by James Harrington (1611–77), the English political philosopher who projected the ideal state for England.

20 p. 188. A reference to the *Histoire des Sévarambes* (first published in English, London, 1675; Paris, 1677 and 1679), a political novel by Denis Vairasse d'Allais, a French writer of the seventeenth century (translated into German by J. G. Müller as *Geschichte der Sevaramben*, Itzehoe, 1783).

21 p. 189. Cf. p. 60, n. 8.

22 p. 190. The likely source for this passage is: 'I must confess, when I see princes and states fighting and quarrelling, amidst their debts, funds, and public mortgages, it always brings to my mind a match of cudgel-playing fought in a *China* shop.' (Hume, *Of Public Credit, Essays Moral, Political and Literary*, ed.cit. I, 371. I owe this reference to Professor Lewis Beck White who drew my attention to the fact that he had identified this passage in his edition *Immanuel Kant: On History* (Indianapolis and New York, 1963), p.124.

23 p. 190. 'The Phrygians learn wisdom too late' (i.e. they are wise after the event).

24 p. 190. Presumably this remark refers to the war between France and Austria which was ended by the Treaty of Campo Formio (17 November 1797). It could also refer to the war between France and Prussia which was ended by the Treaty of Basle (5 April 1795). Kant probably wrote this section of the *Contest of Faculties* some considerable time before its publication (cf. *AA* VII, 338 ff. for a full discussion of the origin of the treatise by Karl Vorländer).

APPENDIX FROM 'THE CRITIQUE OF PURE REASON'

1 p. 191. *Kritik der Reinen Vernunft*: Transcendentale Logik II, Dialektik, I, 1: Von den Ideen überhaupt, *AA* IV, 201–2.

Bibliography

EDITIONS IN GERMAN

The standard edition is the one published by the *Preussische Akademie der Wissenschaften*, generally called the *Akademieausgabe* (abbreviated as *AA*, Berlin, 1902 ff.). Other useful editions are that by Ernst Cassirer and others, Berlin, 1912–22 and the *Insel-Ausgabe* (*Werke*, ed. Wilhelm Weischedel, Wiesbaden, later Frankfurt/Main, 1956–64). On this latter edition, the paperback edition of the Suhrkamp Verlag (*Theorie-Werkausgabe*, 12 vols., Frankfurt/Main, 1968) is based.

Gablentz, Otto H. von der (ed.). *Kants politische Schriften.* Cologne and Opladen, 1965.

Rossman, Kurt (ed.). *Der Streit der Fakultäten.* Heidelberg, 1947.

Schmidt, Raymund (ed.). *Die drei Kritiken.* Stuttgart, 5th ed., 1949.

Ein Reinschriftfragment zu Kants 'Streit der Fakultäten'. *Kant-Studien*, LI. 1959/60.

TRANSLATIONS

Beck, Lewis White (trs.). *Perpetual Peace* (Library of Liberal Arts, No. 54). New York, 1957. We were unable to consult this volume.

Butler, Nicholas Murray (prefaced by). *Perpetual Peace.* New York, 1939. (Follows the translation of 1796.)

Campbell Smith, M. (ed. and trs.). *Perpetual Peace.* London, 1903.

Friedrich, Carl J. *Inevitable Peace.* Cambridge, Mass., 1948.

(ed., with an introduction). *The Philosophy of Kant. Immanuel Kant's Moral and Political Writings.* New York, 1949.

This volume includes *inter alia*:
'Idea for a Universal History with Cosmopolitan Intent'
'What is Enlightenment?'
'Concerning the Common Saying: This May be True in Theory, But Does Not Apply in Practice'
'Eternal Peace'.

Hastie, W. (ed. and trs.). *The Philosophy of Law.* Edinburgh, 1887.

(ed. and trs.). *Kant's Principles of Politics.* Edinburgh, 1891.

Ladd, John (ed. and trs.). *The Metaphysical Elements of Justice.* Indianapolis, New York, Kansas City, 1965.

Morrell, J. D. (trs.). *Perpetual Peace.* London, n.d. [1884].

O'Brien, Helen (trs., with an introduction by Jessie H. Buckland). *Kant's Perpetual Peace* (Texts for Students of International Relations, No. 7). London, 1927.

Trueblood, Benjamin (trs.). *Perpetual Peace.* Boston, 1897.

BIBLIOGRAPHY

CRITICAL WRITINGS ON KANT

[Abbreviation: *Annales de Philosophie Politique* = *APP* (published by the Institut International de Philosophie Politique, volume IV, Paris, 1962; it is devoted to *La Philosophie Politique de Kant*).]

Armstrong, A. C. 'Kant's Philosophy of Peace and War'. *Journal of Philosophy*, XXVIII. 1931.

Beck, Lewis White. 'Les deux concepts Kantiens du vouloir dans leur contexte politique'. *APP*, IV. 1962 ('Kant's Two Conceptions of the Will in Their Political Context'. *Studies in the Philosophy of Kant*. New York, 1965).

Bobbio, Norberto. 'Deux notions de la liberté dans la pensée politique de Kant'. *APP*, IV. 1962.

Borries, Kurt. *Kant als Politiker. Zur Staats- und Gesellschaftslehre des Kritizismus*. Leipzig, 1928.

Bourke, John. 'Kant's Doctrine of "Perpetual Peace"'. *Philosophy*, XVII. 1942.

Brown, Stuart M., Jr. 'Has Kant a Philosophy of Law?'. *Philosophical Review*, LXXXI. 1961.

Caird, Edward. *The Critical Philosophy of Immanuel Kant* (2 vols., 2nd ed.). Glasgow, 1909.

Cassirer, Ernst. *Kants Leben und Lehre* (Werke, ed. E. Cassirer, XI, Berlin, 1918). *Rousseau, Kant, Goethe* (History of Ideas Series, No. 1). Princeton, N.J., 1945.

Cohen, Hermann. *Kants Begründung der Ethik nebst ihren Anwendungen auf Recht, Religion und Geschichte*. Berlin, 1877 (2nd ed. 1910).

Cohen, Morris R. 'A Critique of Kant's Philosophy of Law'. *The Heritage of Kant*, ed. by George Tapley Whitney and David F. Bowers. New York, 1962.

Engel, S. Morris. 'On the Composition of the *Critique*. A Brief Comment'. *Ratio*, VI. 1964.

Friedrich, Carl J. 'L'essai sur la paix. Sa position centrale dans la morale de Kant'. *APP*, IV. 1962.

Goldmann, Lucien. *La Communauté humaine et l'univers chez Kant*. Paris, 1948.

Gregor, Mary J. *Laws of Freedom. A Study of Kant's Method of Applying the Categorical Imperative in the Metaphysik der Sitten*. Oxford, 1963.

Haensel, Werner. *Kants Lehre vom Widerstandsrecht*. Kant-Studien, Ergänzungsheft 60. Berlin, 1926.

Hassner, Pierre. 'Situation de la philosophie politique chez Kant'. *APP*, IV. 1962.

Henrich, Dieter (ed.). *Kant. Gentz. Rehberg. Über Theorie und Praxis*. Frankfurt/Main, 1967.

Jaspers, Karl. 'Kant'. In *Die großen Philosophen*, I. Munich, 1957.

Körner, Stephan. *Kant*. Harmondsworth, Middlesex, 1955 (German trs. by Elisabeth Serelman-Küchler and Maria Nocken, Göttingen, 1967). 'Kant's Conception of Freedom'. Dawes Hicks Lecture. *Proceedings of the British Academy*, LIII. 1967.

Kretschmann, Philip M. 'An Exposition of Kant's Philosophy of Law'. *The Heritage of Kant*, ed. by George Tapley Whitney and David F. Bowers. New York, 1962.

Lisser, Kurt. *Der Begriff des Rechts bei Kant*. Kant-Studien, Ergänzungsheft 58. Berlin, 1922.

BIBLIOGRAPHY

Moog, Willy. *Kants Ansichten über Krieg und Frieden.* Darmstadt, 1917.
Paton, H. J. *Kant's Metaphysic of Experience—a commentary on the first half of the Kritik der reinen Vernunft* (2 vols.). London, 1936.
The Categorical Imperative. A Study in Kant's Moral Philosophy. London, 1947.
Polin, Raymond. 'Les relations du peuple aux ceux qui le gouvernent d'après Kant'. *APP*, IV. 1962.
Popper, Karl R. 'Kant's Critique and Cosmology'. *Conjectures and Refutations. The Growth of Scientific Knowledge* (2nd ed.). London, 1965.
Reiss, H[ans] S[iegbert]. 'Kant and the Right of Rebellion'. *Journal of the History of Ideas*, XVII. 1956.
Ruyssen, Théodore. 'La philosophie de l'histoire selon Kant'. *APP*, IV. 1962.
Saner, Hans. *Kants Weg vom Krieg zum Frieden, I: Widerstreit und Einheit, Wege zu Kants politischem Denken.* Munich, 1967.
Schulz, Uwe. *Kant in Selbstzeugnissen und Bilddokumenten* (Rowohlts Monographien). Hamburg, 1965.
Schwarz, Wolfgang. 'Kant's Philosophy of Law and International Peace'. *Philosophy and Phenomenological Research*, XXIII. 1962.
Villey, Michel. 'Kant dans l'histoire du droit'. *APP*, IV. 1962.
Vlachos, Georges. *La Pensée politique de Kant. Métaphysique de l'ordre et dialectique du progrès.* Paris, 1962.
Vorländer, Karl. 'Kants Stellung zur französischen Revolution'. *Philosophische Abhandlungen Hermann Cohen gewidmet.* Berlin, 1912.
Weil, E. 'Kant et le problème de la politique'. *APP*, IV. 1962.

OTHER WORKS

Aris, Reinhold. *A History of Political Thought in Germany, 1789–1815.* London, 1936.
Barnard, F. M. *Herder's Social and Political Thought: From Enlightenment to Nationalism.* Oxford, 1965.
Basch, Victor. *Les Doctrines politiques des philosophes classiques d'Allemagne.* Paris, 1927.
Bruford, W. H. *Germany in the Eighteenth Century.* Cambridge, 1935.
Culture and Society in Classical Weimar, 1775–1806. Cambridge, 1962.
Buchdahl, Gerd. *The Image of Newton and Locke in the Age of Reason* (Newman History and Philosophy of Science Series, 6). London and New York, 1961.
Cairns, Huntington. *Legal Philosophy from Plato to Hegel.* Baltimore, 1949.
Cassirer, Ernst. *Die Philosophie der Aufklärung.* Tübingen, 1932 (*The Philosophy of the Enlightenment*, trs. Fritz Koelln and James Pettegrove. Princeton, N.J., 1951).
Cobban, Alfred. *In Search of Humanity. The Role of the Enlightenment in Modern History.* New York, 1960.
A History of Modern France (new and revised edition, 2 vols.). London, 1962.
Rousseau and the Modern State (2nd ed.). London, 1964.
Collingwood, R. G. *The Idea of History.* Oxford, 1946.
Cranston, Maurice William. *John Locke. A Biography.* London and New York, 1957.

BIBLIOGRAPHY

D'Entrèves, A. P. *Natural Law.* London and New York, 1951.

Droz, Jacques. *L'Allemagne et la Révolution Française.* Paris, 1949.

Gierke, Otto Friedrich von. *Natural Law and the Theory of Society, 1500–1800* (ed. and trs. Ernest Barker, 2 vols.). Cambridge, 1934.

The Development of Political Theory (trs. by Barnard Freyd). New York, 1939.

Gooch, G. P. *Germany and the French Revolution.* London, 1920.

'German Views of the State.' *The German Mind and Outlook* (by G. P. Gooch *et al.*). London, 1945.

Frederick the Great. The Ruler, the Writer, the Man. London, 1947.

Gough, J. W. *The Social Contract. A Critical Study of its Development.* Oxford, 1936.

John Locke's Political Philosophy. Eight Studies. Oxford, 1950.

Grimsley, Ronald. *Jean-Jacques Rousseau. A Study in Self-awareness.* Cardiff, 1961.

Hazard, Paul. *La Crise de la conscience européenne (1680–1715).* Paris, 1935 (*The European Mind (1680–1715)*, trs. J. Lewis May. London, 1953).

La Pensée européenne au XVIII siècle. De Montesquieu à Lessing (3 vols.). Paris, 1946 (*European Thought in the Eighteenth Century*, trs. J. Lewis May. London, 1953).

Hendel, Charles William. *Jean-Jacques Rousseau. Moralist* (2 vols.). Oxford, 1934.

Kedourie, Eli, *Nationalism.* London, 1960.

Laslett, Peter (ed.). *Locke's Two Treatises of Government.* Cambridge, 1960.

Lively, Jack F. (ed.). *The Enlightenment.* London, 1966.

Metzger, Wilhelm. *Gesellschaft, Recht und Staat in der Ethik des deutschen Idealismus.* Heidelberg, 1917.

Oakeshott, Michael [Joseph] (ed.). *Hobbes' Leviathan.* Oxford, n.d. [1946].

Peters, Richard. *Hobbes.* Harmondsworth, Middlesex, 1956.

Popper, Karl Raimund. *The Open Society and its Enemies* (2 vols., 2nd ed.). London, 1952.

Reiss, H[ans] S[iegbert]. *The Political Thought of the German Romantics, 1793–1815.* Oxford, 1955.

'The Concept of the Aesthetic State in the Work of Schiller and Novalis'. *Publications of the English Goethe Society*, XXVI. 1957.

'Fichte als Politischer Denker'. *Archiv für Rechts- und Sozialphilosophie*, XLVIII. 1962.

Politisches Denken in der Deutschen Romantik. Berne and Munich, 1966.

'Justus Möser und Wilhelm von Humboldt. Konservative und liberale politische Ideen im Deutschland des 18. Jahrhunderts'. *Politische Vierteljahresschrift*, VIII. 1967.

Santayana, George. *Egotism in German Philosophy.* London and Toronto, 1916.

Schnabel, Franz. *Deutsche Geschichte im 19. Jahrhundert* (4 vols.). Freiburg, 1948–51.

Valjavec, Fritz. *Geschichte der abendländischen Aufklärung.* Vienna, 1961.

Vaughan, Charles Edwyn, *Studies in the History of Political Philosophy before and after Rousseau* (ed. A. G. Little, 2 vols.). Manchester, 1925.

Watkins, Frederick (ed.). *Hume: Theory of Politics.* Edinburgh and New York, 1951.

(ed.). *Rousseau: Political Writings.* Edinburgh and New York, 1953.

BIBLIOGRAPHY

Wilkinson, Elizabeth M. and Willoughby, L. A. (ed. and trs.). *Friedrich Schiller: On the Aesthetic Education of Man, in a Series of Letters*. Oxford, 1967.

Willoughby, L. A. 'Schiller on Man's Education to Freedom through Knowledge'. *Germanic Review*, XXIX. 1954.

Index

A NAMES

Achenwall, Gottfried (*Ius naturae*), x, 82, 194, 197
Alethophiles, 5
Allais, *see* D'Allais
Alphabetum Tibetanum, 106 f., 196
Altai Mountains, 111
Althusius, Johannes, 10
America, 111
American Revolution, 3 f., 14 f., 27
Arctic, 108, 110
Aristotle, 39
Athens, 169
Aufklärung, see Enlightenment
Augustine [St], 108

Balmerino, Arthur, 6th Baron, 156, 198
Barbary Coast, 106
Barthélemy [Abbé], Jean Jacques, 197
Beccaria, Cesare Marchese de Bonesana, 157, 198
Bedouins, 106
Berlinische Monatsschrift, 48, 60, 192
Bible, 52 n. (Genesis, Acts) 110 n. (St Matthew), 116, 197
Blumenbach, Johann Friedrich, 185, 199
Bouterwek, Friedrich, 113, 197, 199
Brahe, Tycho, *see* Tycho Brahe
Britain, 29, 82 ff., 169, 186 f.
Bukhara, 107, 196
Burke, Edmund, 193
Büsching, Anton Friedrich, 173, 189, 193

Camper, Petrus, 185, 199
Cape (of Good Hope), 106
Charles I, 31, 145
China, 106 f.
Christians, 110
Christianity, 173
Cicero, 69
Commodus, Lucius Aelius Aurelius, 102, 196

Copernicus, Nicolaus, 2, 17, 180
Coyer [Abbé], Gabriel François, 180, 199
Cromwell, Oliver, 188

D'Allais, Denis Vairasse, 188 n., 200
Danton, Georges, 83, 194
Descartes, René, 6
Domitianus, Titus Flavius, 102, 196
Dutch, 106

Egypt, 192
Eleusian Mysteries, 107 n.
England (see also Britain), 4, 6–9, 31
Enlightenment, 5–10, 13, 15, 54–60, 89
Epicurean concourse, 48
Epicurus, 192
Erhard, Johann Benjamin, 184, 199
Eskimos, 111
Europe, 94, 107, 110 f., 171, 182 n.

Fichte, Johann Gottlieb, 13, 34, 36
Finns, 111
Fischer, Johann Eberhard, 107, 196
Frederick II [the Great], 2, 7 ff., 10 f., 25, 58, 101
Frederick William II, 2
French Revolution, 3 f., 7, 14 f., 27, 30 f., 37, 182
Fries, Jakob Friedrich, 14

Garve, Christian, 64, 66 f., 129, 194
Genesis, *see* Bible
Gentz, Friedrich von, 12
George III, 200
Germany, 7–10, 173
Giorgi, Antonio Agostino, 107 n., 196
Goethe, Johann Wolfgang von, 7
Gothaische Gelehrte Anzeigen, 41, 192
Gothic, 111
Great Britain, *see* Britain

206

B SUBJECTS

INDEX

Mathematics, 62, 135
Methodism, see Index of Names
Miracles, 108 n.
Monarch, Monarchy (Sovereign, Head of State), 30, 58 f., 74 f., 77, 80–6, 90 f., 93 f., 100 f., 102 n., 103, 118, 120, 124–8, 138, 140, 142–7, 151 ff., 157, 159 f., 161–7, 183 n., 184–8
Money, 95, 114, 155, 160
Morality, 17 ff., 63, 65–72, 83, 88 f., 109, 114, 116, 118, 121 n., 123 ff., 127, 129 ff., 146 n., 150, 187, 189
Murder, 145 n., 146 n., 156–9

National Debt, 51, 95, 164
Nationalism, 13
Natural Law, see Index of Names
Nature, 36 ff., 41–8, 50–3, 59, 69, 72, 90, 108–12, 114, 116 f., 119, 122 ff., 145 n., 153, 172, 174, 177, 184
Nature, State of, 25, 27, 82, 96 ff., 102, 104, 113, 121, 127, 129, 136 ff., 157, 159, 164–8, 170 f., 174
Neutrality, 170
Nobility, 152 f., 163

Obrigkeitsstaat, see Index of Names
Oligarchy, 161 n.
Original sin, 38

Parliament, 146, 169, 186
Peace, 33 ff., 47, 90–100, 104 f., 108 f., 111–15, 117, 121–4, 127, 129 f., 144, 147, 151, 165, 168–71, 174 f.
Pietism, see Index of Names
Police, 149, 151
Poverty, 150
Power, 35, 39, 45, 50, 76, 81, 85, 94, 101, 104, 115, 117, 120, 127, 137, 143 ff., 163, 167 ff., 174
Practice (see also Theory), 39, 61–4, 68, 70, 72, 86, 92 f., 109, 112, 116 f., 119, 121, 123–5, 173
Progress, 36 f., 49, 57 f., 88–91, 130, 136, 138, 141, 147 f., 150, 153, 156, 160, 178 ff., 182 f., 186, 188 f., 191
Property, 22, 26, 75 f., 78, 83, 94, 136, 138, 141, 147 f., 150, 153, 156, 160, 164, 166, 168, 171, 174
Providence, 53, 88, 90 f., 108 f., 124, 180, 189
Punishment, 154–8, 160, 168

Quietism, see Index of Names

Reason, 5, 35–40, 42 ff., 47, 55, 57, 59, 63, 65, 67 f., 70, 72 f., 79, 83, 85 f., 90, 92, 98, 99 n., 103 ff., 109, 112 f., 115 f., 118 f., 122–5, 131 ff., 135, 138, 143, 145 n., 158, 161, 174, 176, 180, 184, 187, 188 n.
Rebellion (see also Revolution), 27, 30, 31, 32, 38, 81–4, 86, 119 f., 126 f., 144, 145 n., 147, 175, 178
Rechtsstaat, see Index of Names
Reform, 146, 151, 175, 185
Regicide, 31
Religion, 2, 6 ff., 56–9, 85, 88, 109, 114, 150 f., 176, 178, 188
Republic, Republicanism, 25, 29 f., 32–5, 37, 59, 100 ff., 104 f., 112, 118, 122, 163 f., 171, 174, 182, 183 n., 184, 187, 188 n.
Revolution (see also Rebellion), 3 f., 48, 51 f., 55, 101, 118, 145 n., 146 f., 162, 175, 182, 183 n., 184 f., 189
Right (Recht), 21 ff., 28 f., 32–8, 63, 73–7, 80–7, 90 f., 97 f., 100, 102–6, 108, 112 f., 116–139, 143 f., 145 n., 146 n., 147, 149–52, 158, 161–5, 168–75, 183 ff., 188 n., 189
Rights, 22, 25–8, 31–3, 47, 58, 74 f., 77, 79–87, 94–7, 99 n., 102, 104, 105 n., 106, 108, 112, 117, 123, 125 ff., 130, 136 f., 139 ff., 143 f., 147, 150 f., 153 f., 156 f., 160 f., 163, 166 ff., 170 f., 174, 182 f., 186 f.
Roman Law, see Index of Names

Science, 1, 6, 9, 17, 36
Secret Societies, 149
Slavery, 26, 169 f., 186
Sovereign, Sovereignty (see also Monarch, Monarchy), 10, 24–32, 34, 38
Spies, 168
State, 22, 24–8, 32 ff., 47–52, 58, 73–6, 78, 80 ff., 84 n., 90–9, 101–6, 112, 114 f., 117 f., 120, 121 n., 123–9, 136–44, 146 n., 147–54, 156 f., 159–71, 173 f., 177, 181 f., 183 n., 184, 186 f., 189, 191
Statistics, 41

Taxation, 149 f., 164
Teleology, 36, 42, 109 n.
Terrorism, 178 f.

210

Cambridge Studies in the History and Theory of Politics

STUDIES

1867: Disraeli, Gladstone and Revolution: the passing of the Second Reform Bill, by Maurice Cowling

The social and political thought of Karl Marx, by Shlomo Avineri

Men and citizens: a study of Rousseau's Social Theory, by Judith Shklar

Idealism, politics and history: sources of Hegelian thought, by George Armstrong Kelly

The impact of Labour 1920-1924: the beginning of modern British politics, by Maurice Cowling

Alienation: Marx's conception of man in capitalist society, by Bertell Ollman (second edition)

The politics of Reform 1884, by Andrew Jones

Hegel's theory of the modern state, by Shlomo Avineri

Jean Bodin and the rise of absolutist theory, by Julian H. Franklin

The social problem in the philosophy of Rousseau, by John Charvet

The impact of Hitler: British politics and British policy 1933-1940, by Maurice Cowling

Social science and the ignoble savage, by Ronald L. Meek

Freedom and independence: a study of the political ideas of Hegel's 'Phenomenology of mind', by Judith Shklar

In the Anglo-Arab labyrinth: the McMahon-Husayn correspondence and its interpretations, 1914-1939, by Elie Kedourie

The Liberal mind, 1914-1929, by Michael Bentley

TEXTS

Liberty, equality, fraternity, by James Fitzjames Stephen. Edited with an introduction and notes by R. J. White

Vladimir Akimov on the dilemmas of Russian Marxism 1895-1903. An English edition of 'A Short History of the Social Democratic Movement in Russia' and 'The Second Congress of the Russian Social Democratic Labour Party', with an introduction and notes by Jonathan Frankel

J. G. Herder on social and political culture. Translated, edited and with an introduction by F. M. Barnard

The limits of state action, by Wilhelm von Humboldt. Edited with an introduction and notes by J. W. Burrow

Kant's political writings. Edited with an introduction and notes by Hans Reiss; translated by H. B. Nisbet

Karl Marx's critique of Hegel's 'Philosophy of right'. Edited with an introduction and notes by Joseph O'Malley; translated by Annette Jolin and Joseph O'Malley

Lord Salisbury on politics. A selection from his articles in 'The Quarterly Review' 1860-1883. Edited by Paul Smith

Francogallia, by François Hotman. Latin text edited by Ralph E. Giesey, English translation by J. H. M. Salmon

The political writings of Leibniz. Edited and translated by Patrick Riley

Turgot on progress, sociology and economics: a philosophical review of the successive advances of the human mind on universal history. Reflections on the formation and distribution of wealth. Edited, translated and introduced by Ronald L. Meek

Texts concerning the revolt of the Netherlands Edited with an introduction by E. H. Kossman and A. F. Mellink

Regicide and revolution: speeches at the trial of Louis XVI. Edited with an introduction by Michael Walzer; translated by Marian Rothstein

Georg Wilhelm Friedrich Hegel: lectures on the philosophy of world history: reason in history. Translated from the German edition of Johannes Hoffmeister by H. B. Nisbet and with an introduction by Duncan Forbes

A Machiavellian treatise, by Stephen Gardiner. Edited and translated by Peter S. Donaldson

The political works of James Harrington edited by J. G. A. Pocock